Reconstructing Consensus
American Foreign Policy since the Vietnam War

Richard A. Melanson

Acting Director
International Relations Program
Brown University

Professor of Political Science
Kenyon College

St. Martin's Press
New York

Senior editor: Don Reisman
Project management: Caliber Design Planning, Inc.
Cover design: Darby Downey
Cover art: Salem Krieger

Manufactured in the United States of America.
54321
fedcba

For information, write:
St. Martin's Press, Inc.
175 Fifth Avenue
New York, NY 10010

ISBN: 0-312-05238-3 (cloth)
       0-312-04651-0 (paper)

Library of Congress Cataloging-in-Publication Data

Melanson, Richard A.
      Reconstructing consensus : American foreign policy since the
   Vietnam War / Richard A. Melanson.
          p.   cm.
      Includes bibliographical references.
      ISBN: 0-312-05238-3
      1. United States—Foreign relations—1945– I. Title.
   E840.M43   1990   90-39670
   327.73—dc20   CIP

Published and distributed outside North America by:

MACMILLAN EDUCATION LTD.

Houndsmills, Basingstoke, Hampshire RG21 2XS and London

Companies and representatives throughout the world.

ISBN: 0-333-55101-X

Preface

The Vietnam War shattered the domestic foreign policy consensus so painstakingly constructed by presidents Truman, Eisenhower, and Kennedy and seriously damaged America's cold war strategy of global containment. For these reasons this book—unlike most surveys of recent U.S. foreign policy—begins not in 1945 but with the Nixon administration, nor does it pretend to be encyclopedic in either scope or detail. It has, rather, two more specific aims: (1) to describe and evaluate the grand designs, strategies, and tactics of presidents since Richard Nixon, and (2) to examine the efforts of these presidents to sell their foreign policies to an often skeptical Congress and public. Indeed, because of the divisive impact and continuing legacy of Vietnam, presidents from Richard Nixon to Ronald Reagan (and perhaps even George Bush) have believed that the reconstruction of domestic consensus constituted their most fundamental foreign policy challenge.[1] This book, accordingly, pays a great deal of attention to the rhetoric used by these presidents to mobilize public and elite support for their foreign policy initiatives. And we will argue that this blizzard of presidential words has frequently made it difficult to distinguish between the rhetoric and reality of American foreign policy—a tendency that became especially noteworthy during the Reagan years.

To structure and focus the comparisons[2] of these administrations' foreign policies, I have posed the same six questions to all of them:

1. What were the domestic priorities of each president?
2. How did each perceive the problem of governance?
3. What were the relationships of (1) and (2) to each administration's foreign policy?
4. What were the grand designs, strategic objectives, and tactics of the Nixon (Ford), Carter, Reagan, and early Bush foreign policies?

5. How did these presidents attempt to legitimate their foreign policies to the bureaucracy and the public?
6. Did any of them reconstruct a domestic foreign policy consensus comparable to that of the pre-Vietnam era?

Chapter 1 discusses the elusive yet important concept of domestic foreign policy consensus and disaggregates it into policy, cultural, and procedural components. It then reviews the main axioms and conditions of the cold war consensus and shows how the Vietnam War rather dramatically altered them. Next this chapter argues that modern/rhetorical presidents[3] since World War II have tried to construct and sustain consensus by seeking to legitimate the grand designs, strategic objectives, and tactics of their foreign policies to the attentive public and political elites.[4] Finally, it reviews some of the legitimation—that is, sales—techniques used by cold war and post-Vietnam presidents.

Chapters 2 through 5 focus on the six questions posed above. There are, however, a few variations in the format of each. Chapter 2 supplements discussion of the grand design, strategy, and tactics of the Nixon foreign policy with an examination of his attempts to legitimate his Vietnam strategy. I do so because Nixon perceived a close link between the attainment of "peace with honor" and the development of superpower détente. Because of the dramatic shifts in Jimmy Carter's foreign policy between the first two and last two years of his presidency, Chapter 3 argues that there were, in effect, distinct grand designs, strategies, and tactics that separated the earlier period from the later. Thus I compare and contrast these "world order" and "neo-containment" approaches. Chapter 4 looks closely at two mini-case studies as well as the overall design, strategy, and tactics of the Reagan foreign policy. Here I investigate two specific legitimation efforts (one successful and one largely not)—the Grenada "rescue mission" and aid for the Nicaraguan "Democratic Resistance." Chapter 5 glances at the first eighteen months of the Bush foreign policy.

On the basis of the structured, focused comparisons undertaken in Chapters 2, 3, 4, and 5, Chapter 6 offers a summary of the major conclusions, and speculates about the likely character of U.S. foreign policy in the 1990s.

My research strategy has been to rely on unclassified documents, particularly presidential speeches. These have proved very useful to a study partly focused on presidential rhetoric. I have supplemented these materials with secondary sources, the memoirs of leading participants, and personal interviews conducted with Nixon, Carter, and Reagan officials over a period of about eight years beginning in 1981. I would like to thank these people, many of whom wish to remain anonymous, for their generous assistance. I would also like to acknowledge the financial support provided for my research by the Institute for the Study of World Politics and the following people who made a variety of contributions to this project: David Mayers, Charles Neu, Andrew Z. Katz, Robert W. Tucker, David Skidmore, Dan E. Caldwell, Richard Smoke, Whittle Johnston, Kenneth W. Thompson, Ralph Levering, John Lewis Gaddis, Pio Uliassi, and Steven Van Evera. I also want to thank the following reviewers for St. Martin's Press: Jules R. Benjamin, Daniel Franklin, Lloyd C. Gardner, Joyce K. Kallgren, Steven Livingston, John M. Rothgeb, Jr., and Roslyn Simowitz. Finally, I wish to thank Pat Bosch and Carol Singer of Kenyon College for their word processing and library expertise, respectively.

NOTES

1. Because Gerald Ford relied heavily on the advice of Henry Kissinger, pursued the grand design and strategic objectives (if not always the tactics) of Nixon's foreign policy, and was compelled to begin his fight for the 1976 Republican nomination barely a year after becoming president, this study does not give him a separate chapter. Rather it treats Ford's foreign policy as essentially an extension of Nixon's and thus discusses it in the course of Chapter 2.

2. Alexander M. George, "Case Studies and Theory Development: The Method of Structured, Focused Comparison," in Paul Gordon Lauren, ed., *Diplomacy: New Aproaches in History, Theory, and Policy* (New York: The Free Press, 1979), 43–68. Among the more noteworthy examples of works employing this method are John Lewis Gaddis, *Strategies of Containment: A Critical Appraisal of Postwar American National Security Policy* (New York: Oxford University Press, 1982); Alexander M. George and Richard Smoke, *Deterrence in American Foreign Policy: Theory and Practice* (New York: Columbia University Press, 1974); Richard Smoke, *War: Controlling Escalation* (Cambridge, MA: Harvard University Press, 1977); Barry R. Posen, *The Sources of Military Doctrine: France, Britain, and Germany between the World Wars* (Ithaca: Cornell University Press, 1984); and Stephen M. Walt, *The Origins of Alliances* (Ithaca: Cornell Univeristy Press, 1987).

3. See Theodore J. Lowi, *The Personal President: Power Invested, Promise Unfulfilled* (Ithaca: Cornell University Press, 1985) and Jeffrey K. Tulis, *The Rhetorical Presidency* (Princeton: Princeton University Press, 1987). These concepts are discussed in Chapter 1 of the present study.

4. Alexander M. George, "Domestic Constraints on Regime Change in U.S.

Foreign Policy: The Need for Policy Legitimacy," in Ole R. Holsti, Randolph M. Siverson, and Alexander M. George, eds., *Change in the International System* (Boulder, CO: Westview Press, 1980), 233–62. The literature dealing explicitly with the domestic legitimacy of American foreign policy remains meager. See, for example, two essays by B. Thomas Trout: "Rhetoric Revisited: Political Legitimation and the Cold War," *International Studies Quarterly* 19 (1975): 251–74 and "Legitimating Containment and Détente: A Comparative Analysis." Paper prepared for delivery at the annual meeting of the Midwest Political Science Association, Chicago, IL, April 1979; and Dan Caldwell, *American-Soviet Relations: From 1947 to the Nixon-Kissinger Grand Design* (Westport, CT: Greenwood Press, 1981).

Contents

CHAPTER 1

In Search of Consensus

Consensus, like *balance of power*, *national interest*, and *bipartisanship* is a frequently used and much abused term. More than twenty years ago the sociologist Edward Shils offered a now classic definition:

> Consensus is a particular state of the belief system of a society. It exists when a large proportion of the adult members of a society, more particularly a large proportion of those concerned with decisions regarding the allocations of authority, status, rights, wealth and income, and other important and scarce values about which conflict might occur, are in approximate agreement in their beliefs about what decisions should be made and have some feeling of unity with each other and with the society as a whole.[1]

To claim that consensus exists whenever interested adults are in approximate agreement about what decisions should be made implies that consensus describes social agreement along a wide spectrum ranging from the general to the specific and from the lofty to the mundane. Even the more narrow notion of *political consensus* embraces a near-universe of activity. In short, because the word *consensus* has been used to describe agreement about almost anything, its utility has been frequently questioned.

Yet investigating the domestic dimensions of American foreign policy virtually compels discussion of *consensus*, if only because presidents, their advisers, and members of Congress and the media routinely do. The term must be taken seriously because of its central role in contemporary American political discourse. And, indeed, if carefully defined and applied, it can provide useful insights into this crucial aspect of American foreign policy.

A brief review of U.S. foreign policy in this century should illustrate this point. For example, serious foreign policy disagreements abounded in the decades before World War II. The bitter debates over overseas annexations, entry into the Great War, the Treaty of Versailles, and interwar neutrality represent important episodes in the internal politics of American foreign policy. Moreover, some of these struggles involved vital constitutional issues about executive and legislative powers in foreign affairs. Thus Henry Cabot Lodge opposed the Treaty of Versailles not as an isolationist but as a senator convinced that the League Covenant would enable presidents to make commitments and wage wars without congressional approval. The Neutrality Acts of the 1930s, Lend Lease, and Roosevelt's undeclared naval war against Germany in 1941 provoked similar constitutional questions about presidential-congressional procedures. But on another level these serious policy and procedural disputes masked profound confusion about the requirements of American security. What kinds of international conditions promote or weaken United States security? Should the United States seek merely to protect its physical security or must it also act to preserve or export its political and economic institutions? How best could either of these goals be achieved? Such questions yielded a variety of frequently discordant answers in these years.

From the late 1940s to the mid-1960s presidents offered foreign policies that apparently enjoyed substantial public and elite support.[2] The alleged requirements of the cold war largely overcame the often paralyzing divisiveness of the interwar period and lent a certain coherence, purpose, and predictability to American foreign policy. Some contemporary and retrospective critics, however, plausibly argued that cold war presidents, by baldly and simplistically inflating the Communist "threat," had manufactured an artificial consensus that stifled domestic dissent, rigidified U.S. foreign policy, and ultimately trapped them in their own rhetoric.[3] In short, the search for consensus had encouraged cold war presidents to present platitudinous, highly symbolic foreign policies embodying rather vague national, but supposedly universal, values.

But to ask if presidents *should* try to create domestic foreign policy consensus is a somewhat irrelevant question inasmuch as most presidents—Nixon was a partial exception—have acted on the premise that consensus is both possible and desirable, have worked hard to achieve it, and have done so despite the fact that there exists no generally accepted definition of consensus! Rather than offer advice to presidents about this issue I will make the following argument.

First, cold war presidents from Harry S Truman to Lyndon Johnson shared the conviction that public and elite support for foreign policy could be most effectively built on a framework of global, anti-Communist containment. Second, from the late 1960s to the late 1980s, U.S. presidents—haunted and constrained by the legacy of Vietnam—tried to sustain America's international "relevance" in the face of widespread domestic fears about the costs of military intervention. Third, these post-Vietnam presidents confronted a public increasingly preoccupied with domestic economic interests but simultaneously demanding that the United States remain a global leader. Fourth, Presidents Richard Nixon, Jimmy Carter, and Ronald Reagan attempted to grapple with this post-Vietnam world by unveiling grand designs and foreign policy strategies in conflict with those of their immediate predecessors. These, in turn, provoked vigorous reactions from divided domestic elites now arrayed along ideologically adversarial lines. Finally, these presidents, in reaction to such difficult and often contradictory domestic realities, relied heavily on rhetoric, theater, and public relations to mobilize support for their foreign policies, with Ronald Reagan and his "handlers" transforming this disturbing tendency into an art form. The result was that by the late 1980s "rhetorical" presidents had further widened the always prominent gap between words and deeds in American foreign policy.

In sum, the quest for foreign policy consensus has been both an understandable presidential response to a fragmented, potentially stalemated, domestic political system, and a dangerous opportunity for them to simplify and rigidify their foreign policies. The absence of consensus risks turning every foreign policy issue into a highly politicized domestic dispute, yet the search for consensus has often entailed the articulation of doctrinal, moralistic foreign policies ill-suited to serve the interests of the United States.

THE ELEMENTS OF CONSENSUS

To help clarify the inevitably slippery yet important concept of domestic foreign policy consensus I will disaggregate it into three components: policy, cultural, and procedural. Policy consensus involves substantial public and elite agreement about the grand design, strategy, and tactics of foreign policy. Cultural consensus entails broad, grass-roots agreement about an appropriate set of private and public values linked to America's international role. Procedural consensus refers to presidential-congressional understandings about the respective tasks to be performed by each governmental branch. The meaning of each will be made clearer as concrete examples are given. Here I will suggest that for about twenty years beginning shortly after World War II, American foreign policy was characterized by a relatively stable policy, cultural, and procedural domestic consensus.

Policy Consensus

During these two decades political elites, most notably the so-called foreign policy establishment, and the wider public, especially the better informed or attentive part of it, subscribed to a set of fundamental propositions about the nature of the international system, the requirements of American security, and the nation's proper orientation to the world. Chief among them were:

(1) *Alone among the nations of the Free World the United States has both the material power and the moral responsibility to create a just and stable international order.* While isolationism lingered for a time, after 1945 most prominently within parts of the Republican party, Senator Arthur Vandenberg's well-known conversion to internationalism and Dwight Eisenhower's victory over Robert Taft at the 1952 national convention signified important triumphs for the emerging activist consensus. To be sure, there remained a residue of "Asialationist" sentiment among some Republicans, while Democratic leaders inclined toward a Eurocentric orientation, but these divergent tendencies largely subsided after the termination of the Korean War. Public opinion data on this issue of global involvement repeatedly revealed wide support for the proposition that it was better for the United States "to take an active role in," rather than "stay out of," world affairs. Typically, support hovered around 70 percent, dipping a bit in 1946 and 1947 and again immediately after the Korean cease-fire and soaring to 79 percent in June 1965.[4] No comparable surveys were done on elite attitudes until 1974, but most analysts believe that until at least the early 1960s, political leaders led the public into accepting a greater U.S. role in the world.

(2) *In light of the interdependent nature of the world, U.S. security interests must be necessarily global.* As John L. Gaddis and others have shown, George F. Kennan and other Truman administration officials initially wished to limit America's interests to Western Europe, Japan, and the Western hemisphere because of both the perceived nature of the Soviet threat and the finite resources available to the United States. But the psychological difficulties of drawing and sustaining distinctions between vital and peripheral interests, the reluctance of Congress to provide aid to

Greece and Turkey, the frightening events of 1949, and the outbreak of the Korean War all conspired to compel the Truman administration, first rhetorically and then in actuality, to embrace a dramatically more expansive definition of the nature of the Soviet threat and the requirements of American security.[5] The operative metaphors became Dean Acheson's infectious rotten apple and Eisenhower's row of falling dominoes, for they expressed the widely held conviction that the United States could not afford to "pick and choose" the objects of its attention. Nevertheless, opinion surveys from these years indicated that the public retained a certain sense of priorities. For example, whereas opinion supported the Marshall Plan 57 percent to 21 percent in July 1947 and 65 percent to 13 percent in November 1948, the public was considerably more divided in July 1950 about sending military supplies to Chiang Kai-shek, with 48 percent in favor and 35 percent opposed. And while 74 percent approved of NATO in May 1950, only 55 percent wished to back this commitment with U.S. ground forces in January 1951. Support for sending American troops to Indochina ranged from 8 percent in August 1953 to 20 percent in May 1954, though approval increased rapidly—to 59 percent in March 1966—once the action was taken. And on the issue of dispatching U.S. armed forces to the Middle East to stop a hypothetical Russian invasion, opinion was divided in January 1957 with 50 percent in favor and 34 percent opposed. On the other hand, a March 1959 poll showed that fully 81 percent favored retention of United States troops in West Berlin even if it risked war.[6] We should be wary of reading too much into these results, but in general it appears that the commitment to Western Europe received a somewhat higher priority among the public, and that support inevitably grew in the immediate aftermath of all actual commitments.

(3) *Soviet and Soviet-inspired aggression and subversion constitutes the primary threat to world peace.* Here again Gallup poll results help to illuminate the public's attitude. As late as January 1947, 43 percent thought that Russia would cooperate with the United States in world affairs, but by June 1949 only 20 percent continued to believe so.[7] The opinion that "Russia is trying to build herself up to be the ruling power of the world" reached 76 percent in October 1947 and remained at comparably high levels for most of the next two decades. This apparently pervasive consensus, however, largely masked two complicating elements. First, even among the elites there remained disagreement about the sources of Soviet expansion with some analysts stressing Marxist-Leninist ideology, others emphasizing the long-standing aims of Russian nationalism, and still others focusing on the peculiarities of Stalin's personality. While these

divergent perceptions implied *policy* differences over whether or not Soviet-American cooperation would *ever* be possible, they remained dormant, for the most part, until at least the 1960s. The Soviet threat appeared so serious and immediate that speculation about its roots seemed abstract and irrelevant to most political leaders and almost all of the public. Second, U.S. policy makers, especially after the outbreak of the Korean War, repeatedly warned of an international Communist conspiracy, a monolithic threat to the Free World, an alien way of life dedicated to the extinction of American values, an unholy alliance cemented by an evil ideology. The American public shared this view, yet it was not one actually held by most Truman and Eisenhower officials. Recent scholarship has shown that foreign policy specialists as otherwise different as George F. Kennan and John Foster Dulles believed that real opportunities existed for fragmenting the Soviet bloc, though they disagreed about the appropriate tactics to pursue.[8] For them the Soviet empire was surprisingly fragile, probably overextended, and vulnerable to fissures. The anti-Communist public consensus of these years, in fact, resulted, in part, from the rhetorical exaggerations of presidents and their advisers, exaggerations that involved a wide range of foreign policy issues.[9]

(4) *The policy of containment represents the best way to stop further Soviet and Soviet-sponsored expansion.* Containment, though originally designed to deny Western Europe and Japan to the Soviet Union, was gradually universalized, first, rhetorically, in the Truman Doctrine, and later, in deed, during the Korean War. Yet even in its most exuberant form, containment remained a bounded crusade, more tolerated than loved by a public and elite consensus that preferred it to the alternatives of isolationism, rollback strategy, and preventive war. Some commentators, like Kennan and Walter Lippmann, worried about the cohesiveness of far-flung "collective security" pacts, and many more people (particularly within the Eisenhower administration) doubted America's ability to pay for global containment without incurring severe domestic costs, but, on balance, this policy seemed a responsible mixture of idealism and pragmatism. While some prominent Republicans in the early 1950s paid rhetorical homage to a liberation theology that preached against Yalta and the China sell-out, its hollowness became evident as early as June 1953 during worker unrest in East Berlin and was fully discredited by the Hungarian Revolution. What little opinion data exists suggests a public unwilling to risk war in order to recapture lost territory but equally opposed to accepting additional Communist triumphs. For example, in September 1962, at a time of severe U.S.-Cuban tension, only 24 percent of those polled by Gallup counte-

nanced the use of American troops to overthrow Castro, while 63 percent were opposed.[10] In sum, despite the noted frustrations and expense of containment most Americans saw it as a prudent alternative that promised to keep the peace by demonstrating strength, resolve, and restraint to adversaries.

(5) *The United States must possess nuclear weapons in order to help deter a Soviet attack on it and its allies.* Much of the public certainly worried about the risks of nuclear war during these years, and this nervousness dramatically increased during episodes like the Berlin and Cuban Missile crises, but most Americans believed that nuclear weapons enhanced U.S. security and wished to preserve nuclear superiority. Interestingly, a 1955 Gallup Poll indicated that only 27 percent thought that humankind would be destroyed in a full-scale Soviet-American nuclear war,[11] though large majorities opposed a United States preemptive nuclear attack. Indeed, this "deterrence through superiority" tenet so thoroughly dominated discourse that policy alternatives—for example, equivalence, freeze build-down, mutual elimination—were not even posed to the public by polling organizations until the issue of atmospheric testing emerged in the late 1950s.

(6) *A stable, open world economy required American leadership.* While the public typically focused attention more on personal, pocketbook issues like unemployment, recession, and inflation, political leaders shared the conviction that adherence to the Bretton Woods arrangements would lessen the likelihood of a new world depression. Some protectionist sentiment lingered and occasionally proved politically potent as, for example, when the International Trade Organization treaty failed to win Senate approval; but on balance the presumed lessons of the 1930s convinced most in Congress and almost everyone in the executive that the trade wars, competitive devaluations, and currency blocs of that decade had directly contributed to the outbreak of World War II. A powerful U.S. economy tied to multilateral institutions like the General Agreement on Tariffs and Trade (GATT), the World Bank, and the International Monetary Fund (IMF) would encourage growth and inoculate the Free World against instability that could be exploited by Communists.

(7) *The United States must assume leadership in organizations like the United Nations.* Public support for the United Nations remained remarkably high during these decades despite misgivings about how well the organization performed. In a 1947 Gallup survey 85 percent favored the UN, and 77 percent did a decade later. In 1947, when asked if the U.S. should stay in the organization even if Russia continued to block the will of the

majority of members, 73 percent said yes. Four years later, 75 percent approved of United States membership, and in 1962, 90 percent favored membership. At the same time, far fewer Americans expressed satisfaction with the work performance of the UN. Thus in 1947 only 39 percent were pleased with the progress made by the United Nations, and in 1951, 24 percent rated its performance as good, 30 percent fair, and 36 percent poor, in large part, no doubt, because of the frustrations brought on by the Korean War.[12] This high and sustained level of support for U.S. membership (and leadership) brings us back, in fact, to the first tenet of the cold war consensus—that the U.S. must play an active role in world affairs. During the early postwar decades large majorities of the public and the political elites believed that this active role could best be served as the leader of a Free World military and economic alliance. Taken together these fundamental propositions formed a foreign policy ethos for twenty-odd years that lay at the heart of the policy consensus.

Cultural Consensus

Particularly in the 1950s, social analysts like David Riesman, Vance Packard, William H. Whyte, and Paul Goodman ridiculed the conformity, materialism, and banality of American life and warned that large organizations, suburbia, the educational system, and other contemporary atrocities threatened to transform the population into herds of exceptionally well-behaved sheep. Others noted the growing intolerance of cold war America and pointed to McCarthyism, loyalty oaths, security checks, the intrusiveness of the House Un-American Activities Committee, and a renewed focus on the symbols of civil religion (e.g., "under God" in the Pledge of Allegiance and "In God We Trust" on the currency) as trends that would eventuate in the imposition of a repressive "garrison state."[13] Eisenhower himself worried that the economic and political costs of the cold war, expressed most vividly in the military-industrial complex, would destroy fundamental individual liberties.

Yet if some commentators emphasized the stultifying conformity of American society, others celebrated the American way of life. Much of the popular media, from *Life* magazine to "Father Knows Best," projected widely shared symbols of normalcy and respectability: a stable family life, home ownership, rising prosperity, and community status.[14] In the academic community Talcott Parsons and Walt Rostow disseminated strongly positive views of "Americanism." Parsons contended that American society retained a "moral mission" rooted in family life and religious values wherein the individual sacrificed for the good of community and nation.[15] And Rostow discovered a unique "American style" whose enduring strength had withstood the insecurities produced by the cold war. For him, too, family, religion, and social stability demonstrated strong evidence of the fundamental health and character of the American identity.[16] Nothing better captured the cultural core of this era than the Nixon-Khrushchev kitchen debate of the opening of the American National Exhibition in Moscow during the summer of 1959. The vice president's performance received an extraordinarily enthusiastic reception at home, all the more remarkable because instead of discussing weapons, geopolitics, or ideology the two leaders carried on a lengthy, often heated, exchange about the relative merits of American and Soviet appliances. For Nixon the essence of the good life lay within the walls of the suburban house, and he "proclaimed that the 'model home,' with a male breadwinner and a full-time female homemaker, and adorned with a wide array of consumer goods, represented the essence of American freedom."[17] Under the shadow of the bomb and the Communist threat the nuclear family had emerged as a dramatically private statement of stability.

All of these analysts, whether critical or admiring, saw an America during these decades that evinced a strong measure of cultural consensus. Moreover, there appeared to be a solid symbiotic relationship between this consensus and those broadly shared propositions about U.S. foreign policy. Indeed, more than one policy maker welcomed the "Communist challenge" as a catalyst that could reinvigorate Americans' sense of duty and mission. Eisenhower and John Foster Dulles repeatedly sounded this theme, and even Kennan seemed momentarily captured by its allure, for he concluded "the Sources of Soviet Conduct" by asking his Americans to be grateful to a Providence which, by "providing this . . . implacable challenge, has made their entire security as a nation dependent on their pulling themselves together and accepting the responsibilities of moral and political leadership that history plainly intended them to bear."[18] And, indeed, this cultural consensus was characterized by an ethic of national sacrifice. No doubt the oft-bemoaned rampant consumerism of this period seemed to clash with the exigencies of the "struggle against Communism," but these consumers nevertheless tolerated a peacetime draft and a defense spending burden that represented nine percent of the gross national product and almost half of the federal budget.[19]

Procedural Consensus

Central to the procedural cold war consensus was a series of votes in the Congress from 1945 to 1964 highly supportive of major presidential initiatives. United States membership in the United Nations, NATO, the Organization of American States (OAS), and the South East Asian Treaty Organization (SEATO); aid to Greece and Turkey; the Marshall Plan; ratification of the Japan Peace Treaty, the Korea Defense Pact, the Formosa Security Pact and the Nuclear Test Ban Treaty; and regional resolutions covering Formosa, the Middle East, Berlin, Cuba, and Indochina all received at least 70 percent of the vote with several claiming virtual unanimous support. Yet these overwhelming majorities pointed as well to a procedural consensus in executive-congressional relations which had been fostered by Roosevelt, partly threatened by Truman, revived by Eisenhower, and sustained by Kennedy. At the same time, however, the strength of this consensus can easily be exaggerated. For example, Congress prevented the State Department from administering Marshall Plan aid despite Truman's vehement protests; the Nuclear Test Ban Treaty was ratified only after many false starts and a great deal of compromise; and the Eisenhower Doctrine (Middle East Resolution) was delayed by several months by a Congress that ultimately diluted its contents.

The experience of the interwar period played a major role in defining the nature of this procedural consensus. After the bitterness produced by the League of Nations debate and sharp divisions evident in the 1930s on the neutrality issue, Roosevelt began a serious effort in 1942 to make planning more coherent and unified for postwar international organizations. It involved, in essence, a three-step process, which would be utilized in regard to a broad range of foreign policy themes during the next quarter century. First, FDR included key members of Congress—senators in particular—and leaders of prominent public organizations in the postwar planning process. This direct involvement helped to win their approval for the outline of an internationalist foreign policy that featured U.S. leadership in a host of multilateral institutions. Second, FDR, in concert with these members of Congress and private citizens, launched a public relations campaign to win the support of the broader public and the remainder of Congress. The final step involved obtaining congressional approval for a joint resolution endorsing the proposed course of action.[20]

But this procedure did not always work. Roosevelt himself seriously compromised it by his refusal to involve members of Congress or the leaders of influential private associations in another aspect of postwar planning—the Yalta agreements. Some would later call these accords treasonous, for others they were merely unconstitutional, but their legacy would haunt the Democratic party for the next twenty years. Truman's decision not to ask Congress for a declaration of war or some other legislative action during the Korean conflict did not directly violate the procedural consensus, for senior congressional Democrats had warned that such authorization was both constitutionally unnecessary and politically risky. Nevertheless, as the costs of the war mounted, many in Congress (some of them Democrats) criticized Truman's decision and, after the president announced the dispatch of troops for NATO in early 1951, the Senate passed a nonbinding resolution directing the executive to seek congressional approval for additional deployments.

The process functioned most smoothly during the Eisenhower years, but even Ike was compelled to fend off the Bricker amendment in its various manifestations. This amendment, which received surprisingly strong (though primarily Republican) Senate support in an era of supposed unchallenged presidential supremacy in foreign affairs, would have made executive agreements more difficult to conclude and treaties harder to ratify. Some proponents did view it as a means to prevent future Yaltas and Koreas, but Senator Bricker and his chief ally, the American Bar Association, proposed these amendments primarily because of their belief that treaties like the UN Charter and the proposed international agreements on human rights violated the U.S. Constitution. And many southerners who backed these amendments specifically hoped that they would prevent courts from ruling that the UN Charter invalidated state segregation laws. President Eisenhower and his advisers, in order to try and defeat the Bricker amendment, portrayed it as a dangerous threat to executive prerogatives in foreign affairs, but, in fact, its primary appeal was to states' rights and racial politics.[21]

Notwithstanding this rather peculiar episode, it was during the Eisenhower administration that the procedural cold war consensus flourished. The congressional joint resolution became an effective policy device, an element in the containment strategy, whereby presidents sought to win public and congressional support for proposed actions in order to deter would-be adversaries from doubting the genuineness of U.S. commitments. Some members of Congress objected to these predated declarations of war on the grounds that they constituted presidential blank checks to deploy troops and spend money without restriction, but most felt that they strengthened U.S. foreign policy and deterred war.[22] Interestingly, even these constitutional reservations largely vanished during the Kennedy and

Johnson administrations as the Cuba, Berlin (concurrent rather than joint), and Gulf of Tonkin resolutions swept through Congress with enormous majorities.

In sum, the procedural consensus rested on the widely shared assumption that the executive was the ultimate authority in making foreign policy commitments and in deciding if threats to them required the use of force.

The Foreign Policy Establishment

The so-called foreign policy establishment constituted the most important para-institutional expression of the cold war consensus. Indeed, so invisible did the establishment seem that few observers even noted its existence until it had begun to disintegrate in the late 1960s. Not until 1973 did it receive serious analytical attention, and, then quite tellingly, it fell to a left-leaning British journalist, Godfrey Hodgson, to write its obituary.[23] In part, this obtuseness stemmed from the reluctance to accept the reality of a foreign policy establishment functioning at the very center of a democratic polity. Moreover, the concept itself suffers from ambiguity. While it may have played a role in U.S. foreign policy comparable to that of the permanent government at Whitehall or the Quai d'Orsay, its lack of a clear institutional base made it more difficult to identify its members. Yet surely this relatively small group of foreign policy "amateurs" who frequently went down to Washington in these years—men like John McCloy, Robert Lovett, Averill Harriman, John McCone, Robert Bowie, Dean Acheson, C. Douglas Dillon, Paul Nitze, and George F. Kennan—formed an identifiable elite sharing some fairly obvious characteristics. Although a disproportionate number of its members (particularly among the older generation) came from privileged northeastern backgrounds featuring prep school and Ivy League educations, it depended less on sociology and genealogy than on a common history, a shared approach, a preferred policy, an aspiration, an instinct, and a technique.[24] Though this foreign policy elite did not emerge as a powerful force until after World War II, its origins can be traced back to the small group of advisers which gathered around Colonel House at Versailles to help lay plans for a democratic postwar world under American leadership. When the treaty was defeated in 1920, these businessmen and academics, now joined by a handful of international bankers and corporate lawyers, continued to press for a liberal internationalist foreign policy. Through meetings and seminars at the Council on Foreign Relations and articles published in *Foreign Affairs* this group was able to survive the "normalcy" of the 1920s and the economic nationalism of the 1930s even if it was unable to convert many to its cause. World War II provided the opportunity to implement its vision, and many of its members gained valuable governmental experience, particularly in the OSS (Office of Strategic Services). The war imparted a sense of power, accomplishment, destiny, and political involvement that gave them the confidence and stature to eagerly seek key roles in postwar American foreign policy.

Seeing themselves as bipartisan counterweights to the anticipated isolationist resurgence (especially in Congress), members of this influential group were convinced that America's reluctance to exert its power during the interwar years had helped to trigger World War II, and so were determined to employ the presidency to build an internationalist consensus at home. Certain that the United States possessed the material resources to achieve world leadership, the establishment believed that it had to supply the missing moral and spiritual ingredients necessary to transform crude power into international authority. Though they themselves rarely stood for election, these men had an instinct for the political center—an instinct which buttressed their aspiration to serve as educators to an America whose traditional tendency had been to vacillate dangerously between self-righteous isolation and evangelical exhortation. And while members of the establishment feared international Communism as a mortal threat to western values and institutions, they were unsympathetic to those who wished to ferret out subversives at home. They were, moreover, animated by a passionate devotion to public service, seeing it not as a career opportunity or a chance to make contacts for a lucrative, post-government life, but as a calling, a moral obligation to serve the president.

In short, the establishment both embodied and helped to construct the cold war consensus. Substantively its members embraced that widely shared set of cold war propositions about the nature of the international system and America's role in it. Procedurally they desired a strong presidency willing to enlist congressional support for its foreign policy initiatives but determined to assert its broad constitutional prerogatives. And culturally these unusual Americans, while far from typical in their backgrounds and positions, nevertheless thought they reflected those spiritual and civic values optimistically identified by Parsons and Rostow as central to the American way of life.

The cold war consensus has frequently been idealized in the years since Vietnam, especially by those who wished to restore global anti-Communist containment to its formerly exalted position in American foreign policy. This nostalgia overlooks the fact that U.S. policy successes during the cold war largely resulted from its enjoyment of a unique—and temporary—hegemony produced by the outcome of World War II. It also forgets that the old consensus supported a foreign policy often characterized by ideological rigidity and geopolitical imprudence. On the other hand, contemporary observers and participants tended simultaneously to underrate the solidity of the domestic consensus and exaggerate the permanence and inevitability of America's extraordinary global position.

Embroiled as they were in the demands and frustrations of daily duties, cold war policy makers understandably focused on immediate problems, and these issues often did seem to pulsate with those "partisan, utterly consensus-free foreign policy debates" noted by Neustadt and May.[25] Easily overlooked was the widespread adherence to fundamental tenets about the proper U.S. approach to the world, the generalized deference to a wise and powerful presidency, and the broadly held conviction that sacrifice was necessary to preserve the superiority of the American way of life. Yet these elements did contribute significantly to a relatively stable and orderly policy-making environment.

At the same time, both the public and the political elites tended to assume that America's extraordinary international position was natural and permanent, providential evidence of moral superiority. The highly unusual circumstances that had produced this happy situation were largely ignored, though now see it seems clear that U.S. global dominance facilitated the creation of the domestic foreign policy consensus. America could afford the luxury of the essentially superficial squabbles that passed for foreign policy debates in these years, for it enjoyed a significant margin of power. This margin proved less sustainable than many at the time believed, and with its demise the largely unappreciated domestic consensus would emerge, in retrospect, as a central feature of the early postwar era.

SINCE THE COLD WAR CONSENSUS

Changes in Public Opinion

Since the 1960s public and elite beliefs about the nature of the international system and America's role in it have changed; however, the content and significance of that change are hard to specify. If a "followership model" once described the structure of public opinion during the cold war, surely it has grown less relevant during the last two decades. In essence it included a layer of leadership that in large measure agreed on the ends and means of U.S. foreign policy, an attentive public that followed this leadership, and a noninternationalist, mostly inert, mass public generally uninterested and uninvolved in foreign affairs. The prevalent foreign policy values of the cold war—"conservative internationalism"—reflected those fundamental propositions that were enumerated earlier in this chapter and were shared by leaders and the attentive public alike. The mass public—less educated and largely ignorant of world affairs—was suspicious of an active U.S. global role and inclined to oppose lengthy, costly military involvements not directly related to U.S. security but simultaneously wished America to remain strong.[26]

The simple elegance of the followership model, however, has been replaced by a more complex and volatile structure of opinion that bears only a slight resemblance to its cold war predecessor.[27]

First, foreign policy issues had dominated public opinion polls from the late 1940s through 1960s. The public consistently named issues like the containment of Communism or the danger of war as being of primary importance to the nation. By the time of the 1964, 1968, and 1972 elections, surveys indicated a fairly even split between domestic and international concerns. But since 1976 the economy—usually concerns about inflation and unemployment—has been perceived by the public as its most urgent priority, and in the late 1980s drugs emerged as the chief national concern. In 1976, for example, 78 percent mentioned economic problems and only six percent cited international issues as important; and even in 1980, in the wake of Afghanistan and with U.S. hostages still in Iran, 77 percent listed economic problems as of primary importance and only 15 percent mentioned foreign policy.[28] In 1988 the budget deficit and drug trafficking topped the list. Compared with their cold war counterparts post-Vietnam presidents have faced a public more concerned with the quality of domestic life than with more traditional national security issues.

Second, after Vietnam, political elites and the attentive public lost their previous cohesiveness and divided into ideologically distinct camps. By the 1970s internationalists now came in at least two varieties: cold war conservative, or militant, and post–cold war liberal, or cooperative.[29] The first group essentially favored the restoration of the foreign policies followed by presidents from Truman to Kennedy. Its adherents supported the containment of the Soviet Union through a combination of confrontational and cooperative strategies, overt and covert aid to antileftists in the Third World, and a well-funded defense establishment.[30] They saw considerable validity in the domino theory, believed the Soviet Union to be expansionist, and were convinced that the United States must be willing and able to employ its military power in pursuit of its interests.[31] Moreover, this group portrayed the international system in East-West terms: totalitarianism versus democracy, Communism versus capitalism, repression versus freedom.[32] Liberal internationalists argued that for a variety of reasons—for example, the Sino-Soviet split, Vietnam, the diffusion of military and economic power, Third World nationalism, the emergence of complex, transnational interdependence—the world of the 1970s had fundamentally changed from that of the 1940s and 1950s. They rejected the domino theory as a dangerous, self-fulfilling prophecy, viewed the Soviet Union as primarily defensive in its goals, and were deeply skeptical about the utility (and morality) of U.S. military force in peripheral areas. And they viewed the international system more as a global unity beset by common problems than as the arena of superpower competition. Thus the arms race, natural resource depletion, environmental degradation, and international economic inequality were perceived as the most pressing problems. Yet despite the apparent gulf separating conservative and liberal internationalists, both bestowed on the United States primary responsibility for implementing their respective agendas and both approached foreign policy in highly moralistic terms.[33]

Third, in the post-Vietnam era, the mass public continued to support policies that embodied the values of peace and strength, but with some important changes. Largely noninternationalist in outlook, this large group maintained an instinctive aversion to foreign involvement unless U.S. security seemed obviously at stake. And then it favored quick, conclusive action, not prolonged stalemate. Because the noninternationalist public did not possess ideological attitudes, it had supported U.S. foreign policy during the early postwar decades as long as that policy seemed to preserve peace and protect national security. Except for Korea, where a limited, inconclusive war was fought, and the missile gap of the late 1950s, when the United States appeared to be seriously threatened, the mass public remained inert. But after the Vietnam War this group allied itself at different times with liberal internationalists, who promised peace through détente and arms control, and conservative internationalists, who offered strength with arms increases.[34] Thus the ideological fragmentation of the elites and attentive public created distinct foreign policy poles that periodically attracted and repelled the noninternationalist mass. These working coalitions, however, have proved to be short lived because the groups that comprised them had few common attitudes, linked only by the current fears and concerns of the mass public.

William Schneider has persuasively argued that this unstable coalition pattern has been made even more volatile by the growing impact of television news on foreign policy attitudes. By exposing the mass public to information about foreign affairs that could be easily ignored in newspapers and magazines, television news has created a "vast *inadvertent* audience" for foreign policy issues.[35] The impact of this information, frequently conveyed through vividly dramatic images, has been significant in helping to form new, though shallow, opinions. Moreover, this relentless bombardment of information "offends the noninternationalist sensibilities" of the audience and lowers its patience toward foreign policies that do not deliver quick results.[36] Television, in short, has intensified the mass public's continuing concerns about peace and strength by creating more negative and volatile moods and has made U.S. foreign policy makers more vulnerable to repudiation by a public scurrying from one coalition to another.

In sum, a "fragmentation/swing" model has replaced that of cold war followership as the most accurate depiction of foreign policy attitudes in post-Vietnam America, and its emergence has surely complicated the efforts of presidents to win and keep public support for their foreign policies.

Institutional Changes

Several institutional changes further added to the increased complexity of the foreign policy–making environment and altered the conditions which had formerly helped facilitate the executive-congressional procedural consensus. In part, these changes resulted from the emergence of those distinct foreign policy orientations among the elites and attentive public noted earlier, and, in part, they made it more difficult to heal these ideological splits.

While Congress was not quite so docile and deferential in the earlier postwar decades as critics of the imperial presidency later claimed, executive-legislative relations in that era did embody more order and harmony than those of the last twenty years. First, important structural reforms in Congress made it much more difficult for presidents to strike and enforce deals by working with a handful of senior legislative leaders. Stripped of many of their old privileges and prerogatives by the reform movement of the early 1970s, these leaders no longer found it easy to deliver votes on presidential foreign policy initiatives. Moreover, the proliferation of committees and subcommittees dealing with various aspects of foreign policy vastly increased the number of legislators whose support needed to be curried.[37] Congress as a body, largely because of Vietnam and Watergate, no longer automatically trusted presidents and their advisers to provide accurate information, one major result being a dramatic increase in the size of Capitol Hill staffs. From 1947 to 1976 the number of personal staffers rose from 2,030 to 10,190, and whereas it was a rare senator who had a foreign policy specialist, now almost all do, as do a growing number of House members. By 1979 the 539 senators, representatives, and nonvoting delegates employed approximately twenty-four thousand people working in fifteen different buildings around Washington. The size of committee staffs similarly grew. For example, the Senate Foreign Relations staff went from twenty-five in 1960, to thirty-one in 1970, to sixty-two in 1975, and the House Foreign Affairs Committee staff jumped from fourteen to twenty-one then to fifty-four over the same period.[38] Far from simply providing foreign policy information to legislators who in earlier days had been wholly dependent on executive sources, these staffers frequently functioned as powerful advocates of positions opposed by the White House. Staff experts like Richard Perle, Paula Stern, Jan Kalicki, Brian Atwood, John Carbaugh, and Larry K. Smith played crucial roles in contentious issues ranging from the Jackson-Vanik amendment and SALT II to the Turkish arms embargo and the Panama Canal treaties. And, again in contrast to the cold war era when many members of Congress seemingly relished their ignorance of foreign policy as a reflection of their trust in presidential judgment, during the last two decades many became avid consumers of congressional foreign policy expertise. One result was the emergence of a new type of legislator—the *bona fide* foreign policy expert—who, by total immersion in a necessarily narrow range of issues (or subissues), could often mount damaging challenges to executive positions or, occasionally, provide useful support.

Second, the preferred cold war era device of the joint congressional resolution was replaced by an extended, yet fitful, series of efforts by Congress to limit the foreign affairs prerogatives of the president. Beginning with senatorial attempts in the early 1970s to restrict Nixon's ability to wage war in Southeast Asia, they soon came to involve both houses of Congress in issues that included human rights, arms sales, covert operations, and the deployment of U.S. armed forces abroad. The legislative veto, at least until the *Chadha* decision by the Supreme Court in 1983, functioned as a favored instrument of congressional assertiveness in foreign affairs. In short, the procedural consensus of the early postwar decades largely evaporated and in its place emerged a protracted, inconcusive struggle between presidents who resented this legislative "micromanagement," and a Congress that frequently found it easier to limit exec-utive freedom than to take responsibility for its own actions. The results often bordered on chaos.

Third, the explosion of television news coupled with advances in tele-communications technology made it much easier for members of Congress to gain wide audiences for their views. The proliferation of television shows like ABC's *This Week with David Brinkley*, CNN's *Crossfire*, and the *MacNeil-Lehrer News Hour* on PBS, which purport to examine cur-rent issues in depth, almost guaranteed access to senators and congress people who opposed the foreign policy initiatives of the president. The resulting "point-counterpoint" format provided legislators with enormous incentives to dissent from executive positions and thus made policy con-sensus ever more elusive. Moreover, developments in satellite technology allowed members of Congress to appear daily on local television shows in their districts through video feeds using equipment provided by the Repub-lican and Democratic parties. If local outlets were willing to accept these feeds it became a simple matter for members to explain the independence of their foreign policy positions directly to the folks back home.[39]

Finally, lobbying, while hardly a new phenomenon in American poli-tics, became an integral part of the foreign policy process as domestic pressure groups, foreign governments, and the executive found the post-Vietnam environment particularly conducive to these activities. The lack of a domestic foreign policy consensus, the decline of party discipline on Capitol Hill, the emergence of single-issue politics, the growing impor-tance of so-called intermestic issues (e.g., foreign trade), and the dramatic diffusion of power in Congress all contributed to this environment.[40] By 1987 there were 23,011 lobbyists registered with the secretary of the Sen-ate—compared with 365 in 1961—or 43 for every member of Congress.[41] The president became but one lobbyist—though an exceptionally influen-tial one—in a continual bidding war for congressional support. Obviously such an atmosphere drastically diminishes the chances of establishing and sustaining a workable executive-legislative foreign policy procedural con-sensus.

Institutional changes within the presidency since Vietnam were much less significant than those in Congress. Since the early 1950s the locus of foreign policy–making power shifted back and forth between the national security assistant and the secretary of state, and this pattern continued in the post-Vietnam era. On balance, the result was a relative increase in the power of the National Security Council (and the White House staff) at the expense of the State Department, yet these perturbations, while inevitably well publicized, remained quite superficial, for they occurred within the context of a much more fundamental institutional reality: the modern presidency. Franklin Roosevelt's creation of the "plebiscitory presidency" vastly increased centralized political power and stimulated ultimately unreasonable demands by the public on whomever occupied the White House. These "personal presidents," though apparently invested with enormous power, inevitably failed to fulfill popular expectations.[42] By slavishly following the dictum, "He who can mobilize the masses may also mobilize the elite," modern presidents, at least until Reagan, have frequently ended by alienating almost everybody.[43] Theodore Roosevelt began and Woodrow Wilson completed the institutionalization of a "rhetorical presidency" which, in its quest for effective, popular leadership spawned several serious dilemmas of governance.[44] Oratorical skill became a *sine qua non* of presidential leadership, and presidents are now expected to make direct appeals to the people for support. Presidents once reserved this tool for genuine crises—world war or severe economic depression—but more recently they have routinely relied on popular, rhetorical leadership to *create* crises, real and spurious.[45] Consequently demagoguery has repeatedly stalked the presidency:

> This surfeit of speech by politicians constitutes a decay of political discourse. It replaces discussion structured by the contestability of opinion inherent to issues with a competition to please or manipulate the public. It is increasingly the case that presidential speeches themselves have become the issues and events of modern politics rather than the medium through which issues and events are discussed and assessed.[46]

Post-Vietnam presidents did not reverse this trend. They relied increasingly on television to communicate directly with the electorate, and the use of this medium provided strong incentives to make ever more urgent rhetorical appeals. The growing inclination to "go public" institutionalized a "full time, rhetorical manufacturing plant" in the White House[47] frequently dominated by zealous speechwriters "eager to mount crusades of words against ideological enemies." At the same time, post-Vietnam presidents—for mostly personal reasons—became less involved in crafting speeches and statements, even as they made more public appearances.[48] This sort of writing process did not encourage efforts to reconcile conflicting views within administrations. Instead this process either sought to paper over significant policy differences, as with Ford and Carter, or else became exaggerated attempts to convey a presidency's dominant ideology, as with Reagan.

After Vietnam, presidents delivered their foreign policy messages in a domestic environment of relative dissensus. They often tried to restore direction and determination to American foreign policy "by subsuming all policy discourse within any one of several incommensurable set of beliefs."[49] Some of these presidents also headed "political factions committed to distinct, even ideological, policy positions," which they sought to implement once they were in office.[50] As a result rhetorical, personal appeals by presidents frequently proved divisive and, in turn, stimulated rhetorical, personal appeals by political opponents. Furthermore, in contrast to cold war presidents, who could ground their foreign policy initiatives in the set of core axioms that enjoyed broad public support, their post-Vietnam successors, largely lacking that ready-made base, were compelled to construct working coalitions on an issue-by-issue basis, often at a considerable price. The difficult task of building these alliances, in turn, intensified the pressure on presidents to engage in direct, rhetorical, and frequently inflated appeals to the public.

Para-Institutional Changes

Not only did post-Vietnam presidents confront a Congress that bore scant resemblance to its cold war counterpart, but the old foreign policy establishment had been similarly fragmented. In place of the remarkable group of gifted, privileged, foreign policy amateurs that shared a common outlook, the unifying experience of World War II, and a passion for public service, there arose ambitious, professional counterelites vying for influence over American foreign policy. Several factors account for this rather dramatic change. In part it resulted from an inevitable generational turnover. Members of the old establishment, while noted for their unusual longevity, nevertheless tended to die, and several factors conspired to make the successor generation different from its cold war elders. The diffusion of political power away from the Northeast, the growing democratization of American culture, the emergence of strong, professional graduate training in international relations at several universities, the divisive experience of Vietnam, and the increased importance of intermestic issues all undermined the authority of the old establishment. Foreign policy advice in the post-Vietnam decades has been dominated by full-time foreign policy professionals—prolific, seemingly ubiquitous experts who waged ink wars and partisan battles in the hope of catching the attention of powerful politicians.[51] Frequently housed in highly ideological think tanks and writing for openly partisan journals, many of these experts eschewed the proper decorum of disagreement that characterized the old establishment in favor of shibboleths and caricature:

> Professional politicians might have been able to shrug off such things as just business, but not intellectuals. Thus, personal animosities added a bitter edge to everything else! Motives were always being questioned, and no one in the opposing camps was to be given the benefit of the doubt. For those out of power, it meant getting back in. It meant not giving the President an inch.[52]

Whatever its flaws the old establishment did function as a reasonably reliable anchor for cold war presidents—a reservoir of steady, relatively nonpartisan advice. Post-Vietnam presidents lacked this important resource, for warring counterelites replaced the cohesive old establishment. In this atmosphere the achievement of elite consensus for foreign policy initiatives became an exceedingly elusive goal.

The Erosion of the Cultural Consensus

The stable, white, middle-class, nuclear family composed of working father and housewife mother and cemented by such values as patriotism, anti-Communism, and civic-mindedness provided the cold war consensus with cultural stability, if only as a unifying myth. No doubt it remained so for millions of Americans in the post-Vietnam era. But it should be obvious that the old cultural consensus largely disintegrated in the face of successive challenges. Racial conflict, the civil rights movement, and the youthful counterculture of the 1960s; the sexual revolution and women's movement; large-scale immigration from Asia, Central America, and the Caribbean; the emergence of a drug culture; and the aging of the American population constituted but a few of the phenomena that in many ways transformed cold war America. At the very least they muddied the notion of a single, preferred American way of life by forging alternative life-styles and emergent social structures.

The foreign policy consequences of this cultural fragmentation were less clear. No doubt African-Americans played a major role in elevating the importance of South Africa in the public consciousness. Likewise Latin and Asian immigrants attached less importance to Soviet and European issues. And by the 1980s stemming the flow of illegal drugs had surfaced as a major *national security* concern of the American people. On balance, these social changes probably made foreign policy issues less dominant

and increased the importance of newer concerns like day care, the homeless, education, and the environment.

FOREIGN POLICY LEGITIMATION

At the very least, domestic consensus describes the condition produced by broad agreement among members of the executive and congress, political elites, the attentive public, and the mass public about the basic purposes of American foreign policy. Exactly *how much* agreement must exist before a consensus results remains debatable. We have argued that major foreign policy initiatives in the first two postwar decades received more overall support than those undertaken since the Vietnam War. Moreover, we have suggested that for a basically pluralistic polity like the United States to sustain a coherent, consistent, and reasonably effective long-term foreign policy, a relatively broad and stable domestic consensus is essential, though it hardly guarantees success and can, in fact, prove dangerous. A democratic consensus can impart authority to foreign policy by sharing and supporting its premises, purposes, and values. While consensus can hardly assure steady diplomacy, an effective foreign policy may be impossible without it. Furthermore, in a political system like that of the United States consensus usually implies *legitimacy*. Regimes can draw legitimacy from a variety of sources—God, tradition, the soil, lineage, revolution, laws, and so on—but in the United States foreign policy legitimacy primarily depends on whether that policy is generally construed to be valued and proper within the overall domestic political context.[53]

As in the cold war era, at those times when a consensus did exist, it did not "just happen." Presidents worked diligently to achieve domestic legitimacy for their foreign policies. We have reviewed the role that historical, political, institutional, para-institutional, and cultural factors have played in encouraging or discouraging the achievement of consensus. Equally significant, however, have been the self-conscious efforts of presidents to *legitimate*—or "sell"—their foreign policies. Indeed, this process of policy legitimation constitutes the primary means presidents employ to construct consensus. Presidents and their foreign policy advisers try to provide interpretive images of the international situation that are compatible with domestic experience to justify the necessity, urgency, and character of their actions. Legitimation establishes the broad purposes of policy by translating its objectives into an understandable and compelling reflection of the domestic society's dominant norms. As such it represents a political act within the context of national politics and characteristically relies on politically potent symbols to link foreign policy and these internal norms.[54]

Presidents cannot expect to achieve and maintain foreign policy legitimacy merely by adhering scrupulously to constitutional requirements, by duly consulting with Congress, by avoiding unreasonable secrecy and deception, or by brokering the demands of domestic interest groups.[55] On the other hand, those who oppose the substance of a foreign policy frequently disguise their opposition by claims that the president violated accepted *procedures* in making that policy. For example, early congressional opponents of the Vietnam War usually did not charge that American interests were not at stake in Vietnam, but that Lyndon Johnson and Richard Nixon had exceeded their constitutional authority or had deceived Congress and the public about the nature and cost of their military strategies. Later, as antiwar dissent mushroomed, direct assaults on the *content* of America's Vietnam policy became common in Congress, but the collapse of the procedural consensus antedated and anticipated the decline of the substantive consensus. Policy legitimation, then, involves more than following legitimate procedures, although a president who flagrantly ignores or grossly violates them risks opposition, especially if the substance of his foreign policy proves controversial.

A president can achieve foreign policy legitimacy only if he can convince enough members of the executive, the Congress, and the electorate that his policy objectives are desirable and feasible. The desirability of foreign policy legitimacy depends on the degree to which the policy appears to embody and enhance basic national values, while its feasibility reflects the president's success in convincing people that he knows how to achieve these appealing long-range goals.[56] Alexander M. George separates these two components of policy legitimacy into what he calls the normative and cognitive, though the distinction may be, in practice, somewhat artificial. He suggests that foreign policies aiming to establish a new international system or regime—such as the grand departures of Wilson, Franklin Roosevelt, Truman, and Nixon—possessed an internal architecture comprising (1) the design-objective of the policy; (2) the strategy used to achieve it; and (3) the tactics employed to implement that strategy; and that presidents, to be successful, must obtain cognitive legitimacy for all three components. That is, "a president must be able to plausibly claim that he and his advisers possess the relevant knowledge and competence needed to choose correct policies and carry them out effectively."[57] We would add that the foreign policies of *all* postwar presidents—whether or not advertised as "grand departures"—have featured the sort of internal architecture that George describes, and that presidents must not only be able to obtain "cognitive legitimacy" for the contents of that architecture but "normative legitimacy" as well. In other words, foreign policy must also be seen as proper and desirable insofar as it reflects—in design-objectives, strategy, and tactics—core national values and purposes.

The legitimacy of foreign policy must encompass a variety of individuals and groups ranging from the president and his senior advisers to the level of the mass public. Consequently, as one moves from the highest level of policy making, through the bureaucracy, the political elites, the attentive public, to the mass public one will encounter a considerable simplification of the beliefs and assertions offered in support of the foreign policy's legitimacy.[58]

Legitimation can be divided into three analytical phases. During the *developmental* phase policy makers identify the structure and symbols of legitimation. In the case of cold war containment this phase emphasized the ideological gulf emerging between the Free World and the Communist camp. The second, or *assertive*, phase occurs when these potentially legitimate symbols are introduced into political discourse by senior policy makers in order to describe the international environment. Thus in 1947 the Truman Doctrine asserted that the dichotomous world situation required the United States to support free peoples who were resisting subjugation by armed minorities or outside pressures. During the *operational* phase policy actions are advanced within the general framework previously developed and asserted. The policy and instruments of global, anti-Communist containment followed logically from Truman's earlier rhetoric.[59] Such a sequential understanding of policy legitimation can help to illuminate this process by distinguishing an initial phase in which policy makers develop a compelling international image, a second phase where they tentatively test the waters of public opinion, and a third stage in which the new policy, appropriately adjusted, is unveiled. At the same time, however, foreign policy making and legitimation, especially in a pluralistic polity like the United States can often be remarkably improvisational. For example, even that most dramatic of postwar foreign policy departures—containment—only gradually and haltingly emerged as a coherent policy over a period of some years, and during that time, senior American officials were quite able to simultaneously accommodate remarkably inconsistent images of the international system and Soviet intentions.[60] Nevertheless, the perceived requirements of domestic politics have repeatedly encouraged presidents to explain their foreign policies to the public through heavy rhetorical reliance on emotional symbols and metaphors that misleadingly suggest simple truths about the nature of world politics and the Soviet Union. To that extent Nixon's "generation of peace" and Reagan's "era of democratic revolutions" followed in the tradition of Truman's "Free World" crusade as well as Wilson's "war to end all wars."

Cold war presidents typically employed four primary legitimation techniques: (1) reducing policies to comprehensive doctrines that articulated generally accepted principles; (2) offering simple, declaratory explanations of policies that appeared to be required by these doctrines; (3) relying upon symbols—historical and otherwise—to connect foreign policies to widely shared public values; and (4) overstating threats to national security while exaggerating the potential possessed by the recommended policy solution. Post-Vietnam presidents, as we will see, altered, but hardly abandoned these older devices.

Because the success or failure of legitimation affects the relative levels of domestic foreign policy support, the legitimation requirement creates a significant political constraint on foreign policy. This inevitable thrusting of foreign policy into the public arena can lead to distortion and oversimplification.[61] Harry Truman, for example, in his well-known determination to "scare hell out of the American people," relied on advertising executives to craft the Truman Doctrine. Some contemporary early cold war observers understood the dilemmas that presidents faced in "selling" their foreign policies domestically. For Hans J. Morgenthau,

> the conditions under which popular support can be obtained for foreign policy are not necessarily identical with the conditions under which a foreign policy can be successfully pursued. A tragic choice often confronts those responsible for the conduct of foreign affairs. They must either sacrifice what they consider good policy on the altar of public opinion, or by devious means gain popular support for policies whose true nature they conceal from the public.[62]

Moreover, the need to legitimate foreign policy frequently has encouraged presidents to unveil comprehensive frameworks that purported to explain the entire universe of international political behavior. Thus George F. Kennan recognized that

> [Americans] . . . seek universal formulae or doctrines in which to clothe or justify particular actions. We obviously dislike to discriminate. We like to find some general governing norm to which, in each instance, appeal can be taken, so that individual decision may be made not on their political merits but auto-

matically, depending on whether the circumstances do or do not fit the norm
we like, by the same token, to attribute a universal significance to decisions
we have already found it necessary, for limited and paradoxical reasons, to
take.[63]

The Vietnam War, with its consensus-shattering consequences, vastly
complicated the tasks of presidents Nixon, Ford, Carter, and Reagan to
publicly and bureaucratically legitimate their foreign policies, and they responded with sales strategies that frequently emphasized the personal and
the rhetorical, even more than had their cold war counterparts.

Curiously, students of American foreign policy have often overlooked
the key but subtle role played by "declaratory history" in the legitimation
efforts of all postwar presidents. Sharing the conviction that current policies require historical justification as well as contemporary rationales, they
have laced their public utterances with a variety of historical references,
including background contexts, trends, anecdotes, analogies, parallels, and
lessons. Together these pronouncements constitute an official or "declaratory" history of American foreign relations and international politics designed to legitimate their policies. Cold war presidents relied heavily on
the presumed "lessons" of the 1930s and the early postwar era to lend
additional credence to the policy of global containment. In defending his
actions in Korea Truman told a nationwide audience:

> If they had followed the right policies in the 1930s—if the free countries had
> acted together, to rush the aggression of the dictators, and if they had acted in
> the beginning, when the aggression was small—there probably would have
> been no World War II.[64]

And, in explaining the reasons for U.S. opposition to Soviet missiles in
Cuba, John F. Kennedy recalled:

> The 1930s taught us a clear lesson: Aggressive conduct, if allowed to grow
> unchecked and unchallenged eventually leads to war. This nation is opposed to
> war. We are also true to our word. Our unswerving objective, therefore, must
> be to . . . secure the withdrawal or elimination of these missiles from the
> Western Hemisphere.[65]

Or, to cite an example drawn from the 1940s, Lyndon Johnson evoked
similar memories in justifying the growing presence of United States
troops in Vietnam by asserting:

The central lesson of our time is that the appetite for aggression is never satisfied. To withdraw from one battlefield means only to prepare for the next. We must say in Southeast Asia—as we did in Europe—in the words of the Bible: 'Hitherto shalt thou come, but no further.'[66]

Sometimes presidential candidates used the 1930s to belittle the accomplishments of incumbent administrations. Thus, John Kennedy could compare the Eisenhower presidency to the cabinet of Neville Chamberlain:

Twenty-three years ago, in a bitter debate in the House of Commons, Winston Churchill charged the British Government with acute blindness to the menace of Nazi Germany, with gross negligence in the maintenance of the island's defenses, and with indifferent, indecisive leadership of British foreign policy and British public opinion. The preceding years of drift and impotency, he said, were 'the years the locusts have eaten.'
Since January 1953 this nation has passed through a similar period.[67]

In sum, cold war presidents attempted to create and sustain a historical consensus to buttress their foreign policy actions. In so doing they offered a publicly persuasive declaratory history that, in contrast to its academic counterpart, did not aspire to comprehensiveness, complexity, or controversy.

Post-Vietnam presidents did not abandon this legitimation technique, but because fewer and fewer people could remember the 1930s and 1940s, and because in an environment of domestic dissensus virtually all historical references could prove divisive, declaratory history lost a good deal of its former effectiveness. These presidents tended to emphasize the many ways in which the world had changed since these earlier decades. But when in the late 1970s and early 1980s the Soviet Union appeared bent on a new program of global expansion, Jimmy Carter, and especially Ronald Reagan, rediscovered the relevance of the "lessons" of the 1930s. The result was a declaratory history appropriate to wage a new cold war.[68] And when, by the late 1980s Soviet-American relations became more cordial, these "lessons" were once again returned to the shelf.

NOTES

1. Edward Shils, "The Concept of Consensus," in David L. Sills, ed., *International Encyclopedia of the Social Sciences* (New York: Crowell, Collier, and Macmillan, 1968), 260.

2. But not everyone would agree with this argument. Ernest R. May and Richard E. Neustadt, for instance, discovered "bitter, partisan, and utterly consensus-free debate about the loss of China, the long-term stationing of troops in Europe, the limiting of warfare in Korea, and whether a new war ought to be risked for Dien Bien Phu, Quemoy, or the Matsus" (*Thinking in Time: The Uses of History for Decision Makers* [New York: Free Press, 1986], 258–59). Thomas R. Hughes identified a "working dissent" composed of two distinct policy cultures— "security" and "equity"—that "disguised a real division in the American body politic over what constituted the American national interest" ("The Crack Up," *Foreign Policy* 40 [1980]: 52, 53). Jerel A. Rosati and John Creed found six important "schools of thought" among elites about United States foreign policy always present in the postwar decades ("Clarifying Concepts of Consensus and Dissensus: Evolution of Public Beliefs in United States Foreign Policy." Paper presented at the annual meeting of the International Studies Association, St. Louis, March 29–April 2, 1988). And after trying to determine if there had ever been a bipartisan foreign policy consensus in Congress during the cold war, Eugene R. Wittkopf and James M. McCormick admitted that their data and analyses could not provide a clear answer ("Was There Ever a Foreign Policy Consensus?" Paper presented at the annual meeting of the American Political Science Association, Washington, DC, September 1–4, 1988: 20). And I. M. Destler, Leslie Gelb, and Anthony Lake, while subscribing to the idea of a cold war, anti-Communist consensus, nevertheless disparaged the view that all politics had stopped at the water's edge:

> These were said to be the halcyon days of bipartisanship or nonpartisanship, of Democrat and Republican putting national interest above party interests. [But] Conservatives and liberals were at one another's throat constantly. There was never a time when Truman was not besieged. (*Our Own Worst Enemy: The Unmaking of American Foreign Policy* [New York: Simon & Schuster, 1984], 17.)

Indeed, presidential candidates made foreign policy a primary issue in the 1952, 1956, and 1960 campaigns.

3. See, for example, Michael Leigh, *Mobilizing Consent: Public Opinion and American Foreign Policy* (Westport, CT: Greenwood Press, 1976) and Richard A. Falk, "Lifting the Curse of Bipartisanship," *World Policy Journal* 1.1 (1983): 127–57.

4. Ole R. Holsti and James N. Rosenau, *American Leadership in World Affairs: Vietnam and the Breakdown of Consensus* (Boston: Allen & Unwin, 1984), 218.

5. Ole R. Holsti, "Public Opinion and Containment," in Terry L. Deibel and John Lewis Gaddis, eds., *Containment: Concept and Policy* (Washington, DC: National Defense University Press, 1986), 73.

6. John Lewis Gaddis, *Strategies of Containment: A Critical Appraisal of Postwar American National Security Policy* (New York: Oxford University Press, 1982), chapter 3.

7. Holsti, 76–78.

8. See, for example, John Lewis Gaddis, "Dividing Adversaries," in *The Long Peace: Inquiries into the History of the Cold War* (New York: Oxford University Press, 1987) and David A. Mayers, *Cracking the Monolith: United States Policy against the Sino-Soviet Alliance, 1949–1955* (Baton Rouge: Louisiana State University Press, 1986).

9. Ernest R. May, "The Cold War," in Joseph S. Nye, Jr., ed., *The Making of America's Soviet Policy* (New Haven: Yale University Press, 1984), 224–25.

10. Holsti, 78.

11. Daniel Yankelovich and Sidney Harmon, *Starting with the People* (Boston: Houghton Mifflin, 1988), 23–24.

12. George H. Gallup, *The Gallup Poll, Public Opinion 1935–1971* (New York: Random House, 1972), Vol. 1, 1935–1948: 617, 672, 681; Vol. 2, 1949–1958: 1028, 1519; Vol. 3, 1959–1971: 1754.

13. Allan C. Carlson, "Foreign Policy and 'the American Way': The Rise and Fall of the Post–World War II Consensus," *This World* 5 (1983): 25.

14. Carlson.

15. Carlson, 27.

16. Carlson, 29–30.

17. Elaine Tyler May, "Cold War–Warm Hearth: Politics and the Family in Postwar America," in Steve Fraser and Gary Berstle, eds., *The Rise and Fall of the New Deal Order, 1930–1980* (Princeton: Princeton University Press, 1989), 158.

18. George F. Kennan, "The Sources of Soviet Conduct," in Walter Lippmann, *The Cold War* (New York: Harper & Row, 1972), 76.

19. Gaddis, *Strategies of Containment*, 359.

20. William C. Gibbons, "Vietnam and the Breakdown of Consensus," in Richard A. Melanson and Kenneth W. Thompson, eds., *Foreign Policy and Domestic Consensus* (Lanham, MD: University Press of America, 1985), 97–98.

21. Duane L. Tannanbaum, "The Bricker Amendment Controversy: Its Origins and Eisenhower's Role," *Diplomatic History* 9.1 (1985): 79.

22. Gibbons, 101, 102.

23. Godfrey Hodgson, "The Establishment," *Foreign Policy* 10 (1973): 3–40.

24. Hodgson, 8.

25. Eisenhower advisors, personal interviews, 1983.

26. William Schneider, "Public Opinion" in Nye, Jr., ed., *The Making of America's Soviet Policy*: 12, 11.

27. William Schneider, Ralph Levering, Ole Holsti and James Rosenau, Charles Kegley and Eugene Wittkopf, Terry Deibel, and other analysts have helped to develop ways of understanding some of the differences between public opinion before and after Vietnam.

28. Ralph B. Levering, "Public Opinion, Foreign Policy, and American Politics Since the 1960s." Paper presented at the annual Baker Peace Conference, Ohio University, Athens, Ohio, April 1988: 12.

29. See, for example, Holsti and Rosenau.

30. Levering, "Public Opinion," 4.

31. Holsti and Rosenau, 115.

32. Schneider, "Public Opinion," 16.

33. Holsti and Rosenau identified another "belief system" within the United States leadership stratum—the third head of their metaphoric eagle—the semi-isolationists, and these attitudes described part of the attentive public as well. For these people America's conception of its international role had to be reduced, and domestic priorities reasserted. The U.S. military presence abroad, because it had led to unnecessary wars, needed to be scaled back, and, more generally, American foreign policy had to be less informed by military advice. Furthermore, this group believed that Presidents had accumulated excessive power in determining the national interest (Holsti and Rosenau, 128). Other analysts have questioned the degree to which semi-isolationism has constituted a discreet opinion outlook and have suggested that it be seen as a variant of liberal internationism. But regardless of how one slices up the elite and attentive public attitudes, and it can be done in different ways, the overall conclusion seemed clear: "consensus remains an inappropriate description of the [contemporary] domestic context in which American foreign policy is formulated and sustained" (Wittkopf, 445).

34. Schneider, "Public Opinion," 18.

35. Schneider, "Public Opinion," 19.

36. Schneider, "Public Opinion," 19, 20.

37. See, for example, Cecil V. Crabb, Jr., and Pat M. Holt, *Invitation to Struggle: Congress, the President, and Foreign Policy*, 2nd ed. (Washington, DC: Congressional Quarterly Press, 1984), 39.

38. Destler, Gelb, and Lake, 137.

39. Hedrick Smith, *The Power Game: How Washington Works* (New York: Random House, 1988), 131–35.

40. Crabb and Holt, 224.

41. Smith, 29.

42. Lowi, *The Personal President: Power Invested, Promise Unfulfilled.*

43. Lowi, 153.

44. Jeffrey K. Tulis, *The Rhetorical Presidency* (Princeton: Princeton University Press, 1987).

45. Tulis, 181.

46. Tulis, 178–79.

47. Roderick P. Hart, *The Sound of Leadership: Presidential Communication in the Modern Age* (Chicago: University of Chicago Press, 1987), 14.

48. Karen M. Hult and Charles Walcott, "Writing for the President: Evolution of an Organizational Function." Paper presented at the annual meeting of the American Political Science Association, Washington, DC, September 1–4, 1988: 1.

49. "Of Rifts and Drifts: A Symposium on Beliefs, Opinions, and American Foreign Policy," *International Studies Quarterly* 30 (1986): 373.

50. Destler, Gelb, and Lake, 237.

51. Destler, Gelb, and Lake, 124, 125.

52. Destler, Gelb, and Lake, 125.

53. Trout, B. Thomas, "Legitimating Containment and Détente." Paper presented to the annual meeting of the Midwest Political Science Association, Chicago, IL, April 1979: 2.

54. Trout, "Legitimating Containment and Detente," 3, 2, 4.

55. George, "Domestic Constraints," 234.

56. Trout, "Legitimating Containment and Détente," 4.

57. George, "Domestic Constraints," 236.

58. George, "Domestic Constraints," 236.

59. Trout, "Legitimating Containment and Détente," 5.

60. Deborah Welch Larson, *Origins of Containment: A Psychological Explanation* (Princeton: Princeton University Press, 1985).

61. Trout, "Legitimating Containment and Détente," 5–6.

62. Hans J. Morgenthau, *In Defense of the National Interest* (New York: Knopf, 1951), 224.

63. George F. Kennan, *Memoirs, 1925–1950* (Boston: Little, Brown, 1967), 322.

64. "Truman Defends American Policy, 1951" in Thomas G. Paterson, ed., *Major Problems in American Foreign Policy, Volume II: Since 1914*, 3rd ed. (Lexington, MA: D.C. Heath, 1989), 408.

65. "John F. Kennedy's Television Address, October 22, 1962" in Paterson, 521.

66. "Lyndon B. Johnson Explains Why Americans Fight in Vietnam," in Paterson, 573.

67. Quoted in Michael Roskin, "From Pearl Harbor to Vietnam: Shifting Generational Paradigms and Foreign Policy," *Political Science Quarterly* 89 (1974): 572.

68. For a fuller discussion of this concept see Richard A. Melanson, "Action History, Declaratory History, and the Reagan Years," *SAIS Review* 9.2 (1989), 225–46.

CHAPTER 2

The Nixon Administration

On January 20, 1969, Richard Nixon became only the second Republican to serve as president since 1933. He had been elected with 43 percent of the popular vote—the barest of pluralities—and was the first new President since Zachary Taylor to face opposition party control in both houses of Congress. Moreover, the country seemed to be coming apart, with urban riots and campus unrest dramatically symbolizing the apparent failure of Lyndon Johnson's simultaneous pursuit of war on poverty and war in Vietnam. The twin pillars of post–world War II America—the elaboration of the New Deal at home and the pursuit of global anti-Communism abroad—appeared, at the very least, to be tottering. For Henry Kissinger,

> The new Nixon Administration was the first of the postwar generation that had to conduct foreign policy without the national consensus that had sustained its predecessors largely since 1947. And our task was if anything more complex. We faced not only the dislocations of a war but the need to articulate a new foreign policy for a new era.[1]

Nixon, like Eisenhower, had inherited a stalemated, unpopular, Asian land war from the Democrats and, like Ike, had pledged to end it. Moreover, the Nixon Doctrine bore some resemblance to the New Look (Eisenhower's defense strategy), for both intended to prevent future military interventions in peripheral areas. But Nixon's inheritance was infinitely more troublesome than Eisenhower's and the resources available to him were much more limited. The nation in 1969 seemed more divided than at any time since the Civil War. The prestige of public institutions, including the presidency, had plummeted. According to Kissinger, "the internationalist establishment . . . collapsed before the onslaught of its children who questioned all its values."[2] Eisenhower had been able to reknit the foreign policy consensus in large measure because of his unusual national stature: a war hero who appeared to be above party, a unifier who could afford to be above politics. Yet in 1969, in much more difficult circumstances, Richard Nixon became president—a man whose background, behavior, and temperament hardly seemed equipped to reconstruct consensus.

Unlike Eisenhower, who before 1952 had trouble deciding if he was a Republican or a Democrat, Nixon had built his career on party and partisanship. With the instincts of a street fighter he had demolished Jerry Voorhis, Helen Gahagan Douglas, and Alger Hiss, and had been skillfully used by Eisenhower to do the sort of political dirty work that would have tarnished the general's image. After his decisive defeat by Pat Brown in the 1962 California gubernatorial race, Nixon remained active in Republican party affairs, loyally supporting Barry Goldwater in 1964, and traveling widely to speak on behalf of Republican candidates. The remarkable Republican comeback in 1966 added to his reputation as an effective, gritty campaigner and strengthened his position for the presidential nomination two years later.

He brought to the White House impressive foreign policy experience. Although as a rule Eisenhower excluded his vice president from the most sensitive national security decisions, he frequently sent Nixon on fact-finding and good will trips abroad, and Nixon took full advantage of these opportunities to curry personal relationships with foreign leaders as well as to learn a good deal about world political issues. These travels brought Nixon much publicity as, for example, the stoning incident in Caracas and the kitchen debate with Khrushchev. Later, as a private citizen, he continued to travel widely, sustaining relationships with foreign leaders, and writing about international issues, most notably a 1967 article in *Foreign Affairs* entitled "Asia after Vietnam."

Notwithstanding these calculated efforts to depict himself as a mature, worldly wise, and realistic statesman, many Democrats and journalists could not forgive his earlier excesses, including an apparently comfortable relationship with Joseph McCarthy and his vilification of Dean Acheson as the dean of the college of cowardly Communist containment. Nevertheless, Nixon's foreign policy views seemed to fit easily within the prevailing consensus, and he supported every major U.S. international initiative from the Marshall Plan to Vietnam. Indeed, if he had received a few more votes and defeated John Kennedy in 1960 there is every reason to believe that Nixon would have continued to pursue the main outline of Eisenhower's foreign policy. Consolidation and continuity would doubtless have been the guiding concepts of such a presidency. But, as it turned out, Nixon, who viewed life as a series of crises to be surmounted through personal discipline and will, found himself president at a time of genuine national crisis. Moreover, Nixon was by temperament a riverboat gambler and, given the simultaneous breakdown of the domestic and foreign policy consensus by 1968, Nixon had a great opportunity to take risks both at home and abroad.[3] Unlike Eisenhower, whose natural proclivity had been to chart a safe "middle way" designed to protect "the American way of life," Nixon was instinctively a "chance taker" who perceived reality in terms of the "big picture" and who was "not necessarily a respecter of the status quo."[4] Then, too, until January 1973 Nixon served, in effect, as a wartime president, and this unusual circumstance, which temporarily expanded the executive's extralegal powers, further tempted Nixon to achieve dramatic policy changes through presidential decree.[5]

THE NEW MAJORITY

Richard Nixon knew that the cold war consensus had been shattered. A number of academic commentators in the late 1960s argued that its passing was inevitable, the result of inexorable impersonal forces that had eroded the bases of public support for containment. Nixon did not deny that significant international changes had occurred, but he believed that the breakdown of the foreign policy consensus had been precipitated by the cowardly behavior of America's "leader class." This class, a concept fundamental to Nixon's political outlook, was an amalgam of the eastern establishment, the national press, senior federal bureaucrats, educational leaders, and other opinion makers that had provided political and moral leadership for the United States since World War II. During the Korean War, for example, when the military stalemate had soured many Americans on the conflict, Nixon remembered that the leader class had largely remained supportive of Truman's foreign policy and this loyalty had helped Eisenhower end the war in an honorable way.

But Nixon had grown contemptuous of the leader class particularly for its alleged pusillanimity over Vietnam. Instead of rallying to President Johnson's support many of its members had been converted by the simpleminded slogans of the antiwar protesters. Despite his opposition to many Great Society programs Nixon was genuinely distressed by the destruction of the Johnson presidency, hastened by the cowardly abandonment of its erstwhile supporters.[6]

Although middle America had grown weary and disillusioned because of the endlessness of the Vietnam War, Nixon did not believe that the newfound "isolationism" of the leader class accurately reflected the American heartland's values. Nor did Nixon, the poor boy and self-made man from Whittier, believe that its interests were being served by a centralized bureaucracy dispensing social welfare liberalism from Washington. In short, Nixon detected among lower- and middle-class whites a growing anger and resentment toward federal social engineers preaching the virtues of school busing, racial quotas, abortion, gun control, and school prayer bans. Reflecting on the 1968 election, Theodore H. White told journalist David Broder that America's leading cultural media, university thinkers, and influence makers, in their unprecedented fascination with experiment and change, had completely separated themselves from the "mute masses." "Mr. Nixon's problem," for Broder, was "to interpret what the silent people think and govern the country against the grain of what its more important thinkers think."[7]

For Nixon, then, the simultaneous breakdown of the domestic New Deal consensus and the cold war foreign policy consensus shared a common root: the failure of the leader class to stay in touch with middle America. In the first instance it had transformed the federal government from an economic friend of the "little man" into an intrusive social enemy. And in the second case the leader class's loss of will in the midst of the Vietnam War had led it to retreat into a sentimental isolationism at odds with the real majority's inclination. In response Nixon attempted to fashion a new majority which, besides breaking the back of the old Democratic economic coalition, would provide crucial support for his Vietnam policy and, later, his policy of détente.

It took some time for Nixon to articulate fully his new majority strategy. He had only rather hazy notions about it at first, though his so-called southern strategy of 1968 had aimed to take advantage of regional dissatisfactions with Johnson's racial and economic policies. Moreover, as he made clear in his memoirs, Nixon recognized that he and George Wallace together had polled more than 58 percent of the popular vote. Nevertheless, Nixon's early presidential speeches emphasized unity. In the first Inaugural Address he suggested that "we are torn by division wanting unity" and that "we cannot learn from one another until we stop shouting at one another."[8] On May 14, 1969, he made his first nationwide speech on Vietnam conciliatory in tone, and he planned to announce the first troop withdrawal in early June.

But, according to speech writer William Safire, Nixon did not want this initial withdrawal announcement to be misinterpreted as weakness:

He felt he needed to show that Richard Nixon was not going soft. Troop withdrawal, a part of orderly Vietnamization, must not be taken as "cut and run. . . ." And he was convinced that only tough-minded men with the power to command would achieve . . . a peace in Vietnam that guaranteed self-determination. He sensed that this was the time for a tough speech, for a reassertion of pride and confidence that would appall many liberals.[9]

Thus on June 4, 1969, before the graduating class at the Air Force Academy, Nixon abandoned the rhetoric of unity in favor of a much more provocative approach. Targeting domestic critics of a strong national defense for attack he claimed that "in some of the so-called best circles in America . . . [p]atriotism is considered by some to be a backward fetish of the uneducated and unsophisticated. Nationalism is hailed and applauded as a panacea for the ills of every nation—except the United States of America." "These isolationists," the president asserted, argue that "the United States is blocking the road to peace by maintaining its military strength at home and its defenses abroad" and offer simple and powerful slogans that touch "a responsive chord with many an overburdened taxpayer." Nixon admitted that he could easily "buy some popularity by going along with the new isolationists" but added that such a course would result in national and global disaster. He held "a totally different view of the world" and was convinced that "if America were to become a dropout in assuming the responsibility for defending peace and freedom in the world," "the rest of the world would live in terror" and would experience "the kind of peace that suffocated freedom in Czechoslovakia." "The skeptics and isolationists," Nixon claimed, had "lost the vision indispensable to great leadership. They observe the problems that confront us; they measure our resources and then they despair." Their timidity stood in direct contrast to the courageous astronauts who "inspire us," and who will allow "every American" to "stand taller" when they land on the moon. "When a nation believes in itself," the president concluded, "that nation can perform miracles," and "that is why I believe a resurgence of American idealism can bring a modern miracle, and that modern miracle is a world of peace and justice."[10]

By insinuating that anti-Vietnam critics were, in essence, hypocritical elitists, who, like countercultural dropouts, had allowed despair and selfishness to replace courage and vision, Nixon implied that there was another, better America comprised of decent, proud patriots who felt a moral responsibility for building a better world. This sort of "us versus them" rhetoric, so characteristic of the old Nixon, was harshly attacked in editorials in major newspapers across the country, but, according to Safire, the president believed that he had succeeded in putting his war critics on the defensive by making them vulnerable to the charge of isolationism.[11] In addition, he also laid the groundwork for an even more memorable address—the so-called silent majority speech of November 3, 1969.

Nixon scheduled this speech between two massive antiwar demonstrations in Washington and plainly intended to rob these protests of their anticipated impact. Even more than in the Air Force address he wanted to draw the battle lines clearly between the "folks" and the "elitists," the "mute masses" and the "noisy minority," and to underscore the importance he attached to the speech, Nixon wrote it himself.[12] After reporting that negotiations with North Vietnam remained stalemated, Nixon reiterated his commitment to Vietnamization and a phased U.S. withdrawal, but reserved the right to take "strong and effective measures" if Hanoi jeopardized "our remaining forces." He then focused on those who urged "an immediate precipitate withdrawal . . . without regard to the effects of that action." Branding this course "easy but wrong" the president predicted that, if followed, "our allies would lose confidence in America" and "far more dangerous, we would lose confidence in ourselves" as "inevitable remorse and devisive recrimination would scar our spirit as a people." Thus Nixon refused to allow "the policy of this Nation to be dictated by the minority who hold that point of view and who try to impose it on the nation by mounting demonstrations in the streets." To follow this "vocal minority," he warned, would bring an end to America as a "free society" and would ultimately lead to the suffocation of millions around the world by the "forces of totalitarianism" as America turned inward. Nixon then asked for support from "the great silent majority of my fellow Americans" to enable him to more quickly achieve a "just and lasting peace" in Vietnam. A divided America, he argued, would only prolong the war and provide encouragement to the enemy.[13]

Public response to the address was strongly favorable. Polls indicated that the public's approval of Nixon's Vietnam policy increased.[14] Supportive telephone calls and telegrams poured into the White House. The television networks, which was their custom in 1969, immediately scrutinized the speech but were thrown on the defensive a few days later when Vice President Spiro T. Agnew excoriated them for indulging in "instant analysis." More than three hundred members of the House of Representatives sponsored a resolution supportive of Nixon's Vietnam policy and more than sixty Senators expressed their approval in letters to Ambassador Henry Cabot Lodge.[15] In response President Nixon, on November 13, 1969, in separate speeches to the House and Senate, thanked those members for their loyalty. Nixon and Kissinger believed that the silent majority address had given them an additional six months of time to settle the war. The speech was tactically brilliant, because it allowed President Nixon to isolate and temporarily delegitimate a noisy minority allegedly clamoring for a precipitate withdrawal from Vietnam regardless of the consequences, while providing the silent majority with a concrete plan for an orderly pullout designed to protect national credibility and self-respect. He would juxtapose these so-called options again and again. And the public response to the speech further convinced Nixon that the silent majority was real and could be mobilized into a new majority.

According to Charles W. Colson, Special Assistant to the President from 1969 to 1973, as the "buckets of telegrams" supporting Nixon's November speech arrived at the White House, it began to strike the staff that they were hitting a responsive chord in Main Street, USA, about "standing firm in Vietnam." Colson and others also detected a growing frustration with the "big government excesses of the Great Society." Then in the spring of 1970, after the Cambodian incursion and the Kent State killings, a large group of "hard-hats" led a counterdemonstration of over 100,000 people to New York's Gracie Mansion. Nixon telephoned the leaders that evening and invited them to the White House to offer thanks. Ostentatiously piling their hats in the Roosevelt Room, these labor leaders' public support of Nixon constituted for Colson "a seminal event" and an "important symbol of an emerging political coalition."[16] Yet in stumping for Republican candidates in the 1970 elections Nixon hardly mentioned the social and cultural issues of such apparent concern to middle America. He did, to be sure, bemoan the breakdown of "law and order," particularly on certain "elitist" college campuses, but more importantly, he claimed that he needed a Republican majority in Congress to help achieve his goal of a "generation of peace."

The election results disappointed the White House, though staff members took satisfaction in James Buckley's success in defeating—though barely—two more liberal opponents in the New York senatorial race by appealing to white, traditionally Democratic, ethnic voters. Soon thereafter Nixon, Robert Haldeman, John Ehrlichman, John Mitchell, Colson, and other senior officials met at Key Biscayne to discuss the formation of a new Republican majority in 1972 by incorporating the increasingly conservative Catholic, ethnic, labor vote into the party's more traditional constituencies. This goal seemed within reach. These men had been impressed with the analyses recently offered by Kevin Phillips's *The Emerging Republican Majority*[17] and particularly, *The Real Majority* of Richard Scammon and Ben Wattenberg.[18] Noting that most Americans were not poor, young, or black, *The Real Majority* argued that the "Economic Issue," which had provided grist for the Democratic party since the depression, was being overtaken by the "Social Issue," a revolt by the middle and lower middle classes against the programs and permissiveness of 1960s style liberalism. Ironically, the authors of *The Real Majority*, who were Democrats, found a very receptive audience in the Nixon White House. Colson and other staff strategists frequently held discussions with them. The president, himself, was "profoundly impressed" when Scammon suggested to him that busing was an elitist program that would disrupt traditional neighborhoods without achieving its educational goals.[19]

Intrigued by the electoral implications of these arguments the Nixon administration made a determined effort to reach out to these traditional Democratic voters. Michael P. Balzano, himself a Democrat, played a central role in this strategy. Brought to the White House from the Office of Economic Opportunity by Colson, Balzano's constituency was blue-collar middle America. He met continually with ethnic organizations like the Sons of Italy, the Polish-American League, and the Latvian League, community groups built around specific issues like gun ownership and neighborhood preservation, a variety of Catholic organizations, and labor union representatives. Time and again Balzano heard the same message: These people perceived themselves to be the targets of social policies dictated by federal government bureaucrats, of changing rules in the Democratic party, and of the antiwar protest movement. They seemed especially annoyed by what they saw as Washington's assault on the "achievement ethic" in the form of waived entrance exams, racial quotas, and forced busing. But they also felt increasingly alienated from a social climate that encouraged abortion, free love, and permissiveness, and they interpreted many Health, Education, and Welfare (HEW) guidelines as attempts to destroy the family. Yet when they complained to Washington about these policies, "they were mocked as 'Archie Bunkers' by the liberal establishment."[20] These groups also felt abandoned by a Democratic party that appeared contemptuous of their concerns. Finally, they expressed to Balzano their outrage about the anti-Vietnam protest movement. He believed that many of them had come to oppose the war in large measure because the United States appeared unwilling to win it, but that they opposed a unilateral withdrawal, particularly if U.S. prisoners of war (POWs) remained in captivity. They were horrified by the tactics of some of the demonstrators. Indeed, according to Donald F. Rodgers, a Nixon labor advisor, the labor march in New York had been precipitated by construction workers who were angered when protesters burned the American flag, raised the North Vietnamese banner, and urinated on a statue of George Washington.[21] Balzano and Safire agreed that the protest movement's "stridency and violence did more than anything [else] to help Nixon crystallize his new majority."[22]

George McGovern's nomination in 1972 delighted the Nixon White House, for he proved the perfect foil for the new majority strategy. McGovern, a college professor claiming to embody the New Politics, could easily be portrayed as an isolationist elitist hopelessly insensitive to the needs of middle America. George Wallace had been removed as a rival to Nixon for these votes, and the economy in 1972 appeared prosperous and sound. According to Alonzo L. Hamby, "No American political leader was better equipped by temperament and outlook than was Nixon to engage in a politics of cultural confrontation designed to build a new majority of the resentful."[23]

Interestingly, however, Nixon increasingly saw this new coalition less as a Republican majority and more as *his* majority. In order to bring about a national political realignment he believed that liberal Republicans had to be purged and conservative and disillusioned Democrats welcomed. Nixon's new majority required a new minority to pummel and provoke. He rejected the consensual texture of Eisenhower's "middle way" or Johnson's "President of all the people" in favor of a confrontational "two-ideology system"[24] grounded in apparently irreconcilable social and cultural divisions.

Nixon quite characteristically felt that his own intentions were noble, and that his New Class opponents—intellectuals, the national media, bureaucrats, ultraliberal Hollywood celebrities, nonbusiness professionals—wished to destroy him and the values of his heartland supporters. No doubt these suspicions were far from unfounded, but Nixon exacerbated the situation by depicting himself as a stern, righteous moralist who steadfastly chose the right way over the easy way of his critics. The most extreme kinds of hard ball politics could be rationalized by the ultimate goals they promoted: a generation of peace in the world and the recreation of a spirit of self-reliance in the American character.[25]

In essence, Richard Nixon attempted to co-opt many of the old New Deal constituencies by binding them together with the glue of social and cultural politics. But in so doing he accepted the bulk of the New Deal's economic legacy. Professing to be a Keynesian, Nixon imposed wage and price controls to fight inflation, embraced the goal of the full employment economy, favored a guaranteed annual income, and wished to federalize the welfare system. His New Federalism did not intend to cut federal spending programs but tried to distinguish between "activities requiring large cash transactions and those primarily involving services."[26] Thus Nixon wanted to restore to the states some control over such functions as education, job training, and public health, while reserving to the federal government such issues as welfare, energy, and the environment. According to Otis L. Graham, Nixon presided "over a more rapid evolution toward planning than any other President since F.D.R."[27]

What distinguished Nixon's new majority was its social and cultural attributes rather than its economic character. Unlike the New Deal coalition its membership depended primarily on shared values. Unless all Americans could be converted to its outlook, it would be inevitably more ideological and more divisive than its predecessor. Nixon responded, then, to the breakdown of the domestic policy consensus in the 1960s, not with a new consensus but with a new majority whose health depended on the existence of a domestic enemy—the new minority.

Nixon neatly captured these themes in an important but oddly ignored radio address delivered shortly before the 1972 election. He began with an acknowledgment that "in the past generation there were cases in which power concentrated in Washington did much to help our people live in greater fairness and security and to enable our Nation to speak and act strongly in world affairs." But in the 1960s, he recalled, people had grown resentful and alienated because they felt frustrated "in dealing with a faceless machine called the Federal bureaucracy." Those who operated this bureaucracy frequently forgot that "government derives its power from 'the consent of the governed' and instead dismissed 'the will of the people' as 'the prejudice of the masses.'" Indeed, "a great many people in politics and elsewhere," in order to achieve "what they consider social justice," want to change America "by attacking [its] basic values." But, Nixon assured,

> There is no reason to feel guilty about wanting to enjoy what you get and what you earn, in wanting your children in good schools close to home, or about wanting to be judged fairly on your ability. Those are not values to be ashamed of; those are values to be proud of. Those are values that I shall always stand up for when they come under attack.[28]

On the other hand, he reminded his audience, a democratic leader "must be willing to take unpopular stands when they are necessary," but in those cases, "he has an obligation to explain it to the people, solicit their support, and win their approval." Nixon remembered that "one of those moments came" in late 1969 after his declaration that "we were going to end our involvement in the war in Vietnam with honor." He "understood the difference between settlement and surrender," yet "the organized wrath of thousands of vocal demonstrators who opposed that policy descended on Washington," and "commentators and columnists" speculated about "'the breaking of the president.'" In response Nixon, on November 3, delivered a nationwide address "to summon up the strength of our national character," and "the great silent majority of Americans—good people with good judgment who stand ready to do what they believe to be right—immediately responded." Their support "made it possible for the Government to govern successfully."[29]

Having thus "seen the will of the majority in action, responding to a call to responsibility, to honor, and to sacrifice," Nixon noted, "That is also why I speak with pride of the 'new majority' that is forming not around a man or a party, but around a set of principles that is deep in the American spirit":

> These are not the beliefs of selfish people. On the contrary, they are the beliefs of a generous and self-reliant people, a people of intellect and character whose values deserve respect in every segment of our population.

So, he concluded, "On matters affecting basic human values—on the way Americans live their lives and bring up their children—I am going to respect and reflect the opinion of the people themselves. That is what democracy is all about."[30]

By rhetorically transforming what some commentators were terming "the politics of resentment" into a set of solid values, President Nixon also, as we will see, attempted to enlist the new majority in his two major foreign policy goals: "peace with honor" in Vietnam and a "generation of peace" in the world.

PEACE WITH HONOR

There can be little doubt that if Richard Nixon had been elected President in 1960 he would have deepened America's commitment to South Vietnam. Certainly Nixon had shared the conviction held by almost every American leader of his generation that in order to preserve American security and global stability the right of the South Vietnamese people to national self-determination had to be guaranteed by the United States. But would Nixon have pursued the war strategy of Kennedy and Johnson? Probably not. As a private citizen Nixon had criticized the Laotian neutralization agreement of 1962, Washington's inconsistent treatment of President Diem, the gradual pace of the American military buildup, and U.S. reluctance to attack enemy sanctuaries. But these were tactical disputes; Nixon agreed that America's credibility as a superpower and alliance leader rested on its willingness to defend South Vietnam.

But by 1969 the United States "had been riven by protest and anguish," some of it "violent and ugly."[31] The psychological defeat of the Tet offensive, the assassinations of Martin Luther King and Robert Kennedy, urban riots, the tumult of the 1968 Democratic Convention, and serious campus unrest had confused and demoralized "the leadership groups that had sustained the great American postwar initiatives in foreign policy."[32] Public opinion had begun to swing toward withdrawal from Vietnam, though a substantial plurality continued to favor military victory. Yet the Johnson administration had seemed utterly paralyzed: a bombing halt of the North had resulted in stalemated peace talks, while U.S. ground forces were still being increased. As Kissinger put it,

> Richard Nixon inherited this cauldron. Of all choices he was probably the least suited for the act of grace that might have achieved reconciliation with the responsible members of the [domestic] opposition. Seeing himself in any case the target of a liberal conspiracy to destroy him, he could never bring himself to regard the upheaval caused by the Vietnam war as anything other than a continuation of the long-lived assault on his political existence. . . . He accepted [the protesters'] premises that we faced a mortal domestic struggle; in the process he accelerated and compounded its bitterness.[33]

As was true of his efforts to build a post–New Deal new majority, Nixon's attempts to extricate the United States from Vietnam required the existence of domestic enemies that he could flay in order to mobilize support for peace with honor.

Nixon never renounced his conviction that American credibility could only be maintained if the United States provided South Vietnam with a reasonable chance to determine its future, but he faced an American public whose weariness and frustration with the war severely narrowed his options. Nevertheless, Nixon set for himself an excruciatingly difficult task: to accomplish through the withdrawal of U.S. ground forces what had not been achieved with their presence.

On May 14, 1969, President Nixon delivered his first speech on Vietnam. In it he explicitly rejected what he described as two unacceptable alternatives: the imposition of a "purely military solution on the battlefield" and "a one-sided withdrawal from Vietnam or the acceptance in Paris of terms that would amount to a disguised American defeat."[34] He dismissed the latter course for several reasons. First, millions of South Vietnamese had placed their trust in America's commitment to help them, and "to abandon them now would risk a massacre that would shock and dismay everyone in the world who values human life." Second, a failure to meet these obligations would lower America's prestige by damaging the confidence that other nations had in its reliability. Third, a unilateral withdrawal would reward those in the Communist world "who scorn negotiation, who advocate aggression, who minimize the risks of confrontations with the United States." Thus "to move successfully from an era of confrontation to an era of negotiation . . . we have to demonstrate . . . that confrontation with the United States is costly and unrewarding." And fourth, the security of the non-Communist nations of Asia would be threatened by a unilateral American withdrawal from Vietnam.

With the partial exception of the third reason, which implied that the Communist world was no longer monolithic and that some elements might favor negotiations with the United States, Nixon's arguments against a precipitous withdrawal had already been made by both Kennedy and Johnson. Moreover, Nixon's basic goal sounded thoroughly familiar: "What we want is very little, but very fundamental. We seek the opportunity for the South Vietnamese people to determine their own future without outside interference."[35]

In contrast to the detailed arguments that he advanced against a "one-sided withdrawal" or a "disguised defeat" at the Paris talks, Nixon said little about why the United States would not seek "to impose a purely military solution on the battlefield." But Nixon knew that American public opinion would not tolerate the actions necessary to pursue such a course. In his memoirs Nixon recounted that during the presidential transition meetings at the Hotel Pierre he had weighed the costs of employing tactical nuclear weapons or bombing the Red River irrigation dikes and concluded that "the domestic and international uproar that would have accompanied the use of either of these knockout blows would have got my administration off to the worst start possible." And because it would take at least six months of dramatic conventional escalation to achieve victory, "there was no way I could hold the country together for that period of time in view of the number of casualties we would be suffering."[36] Publicly, however, Nixon merely reported that he and his advisers had "made a systematic, serious examination of all the alternatives open to us."[37]

Yet Nixon did not claim that it had been wise to intervene in Vietnam in the first place. In this speech he suggested that "repeating the old formulas and the tired rhetoric of the past is not enough."[38] Whatever may have been the situation a decade ago "we no longer have the choice of not intervening. We have crossed that bridge." And while we can honestly debate the advisability of our entry into the war and its subsequent conduct, "the urgent question today is what to do now that we are there."[39] Nixon then, even in this initial attempt to explain his Vietnam policy, argued that the issue was not whether the United States should have intervened but how the United States would withdraw. The *nature* of the withdrawal, Nixon would repeatedly contend during the next four years, would determine the character of post-Vietnam America and the post-Vietnam world. Thus, although public pressure had narrowed Nixon's real policy options to but one—withdrawal—Nixon's task was to convince the public that his pace of withdrawal was superior to those of his critics.

In Chapter 1 we suggested that in order to help legitimate current policy, presidents frequently offer a "declaratory history" of past policy. Richard Nixon used the opening section of his crucial silent majority speech to unfold a declaratory history of the U.S. involvement in the Vietnam War. According to this account "fifteen years ago North Vietnam, with the logistical support of Communist China and the Soviet Union, launched a campaign to impose a Communist government on South Vietnam by instigating and supporting a revolution."[40] The government of South Vietnam requested help from the United States, and President Eisenhower "sent economic aid and military equipment to assist the people of South Vietnam in their effort to prevent a Communist takeover." In 1962 President Kennedy sent sixteen thousand military personnel to Vietnam as combat advisers. Three years later President Johnson sent American combat forces to South Vietnam. Nixon recalled that Eisenhower, Kennedy, and Johnson all claimed that a U.S. withdrawal would "mean a collapse not only of South Vietnam, but Southeast Asia." Nixon agreed by arguing that "for the future of peace, precipitate withdrawal would be a disaster of immense magnitude." He vividly described how the North Vietnamese had massacred more than fifty thousand people in 1954 and had unleashed a "bloody reign of terror" in the city of Hué in 1968. In sum, Nixon embraced the essence of the official Kennedy-Johnson account of the U.S. entry into Vietnam—an account that was, at the very least, simplistic.

But Nixon broke with Johnson on the conduct of the war by reminding his audience that when he took office the war had been going on for four years; 31,000 Americans had been killed in action; the training program for South Vietnam was behind schedule; 540,000 Americans were in Vietnam with no plans to reduce the number; the United States had not put forth a comprehensive peace proposal at the Paris talks; and the conflict had caused domestic division and international criticism. Since becoming president, however, Nixon had begun to undertake "long overdue change" in American policy.[41] A series of diplomatic initiatives had been launched in Paris and elsewhere which, unfortunately, because of Hanoi's absolute intransigence, had not borne fruit. But Nixon's new policy of Vietnamization had allegedly strengthened the South Vietnamese to the point where over 60,000 American combat troops would soon be home, and United States casualties had "declined to the lowest point in three years."[42]

Nixon concluded, as we have seen, with a plea to the silent majority to support his policy of diplomacy, Vietnamization, and gradual, orderly withdrawal. If that majority rallied, then Nixon's plan would "end this war in a way that will bring us closer to that great goal to which Woodrow Wilson and every American President in our history has been dedicated— the goal of a just and lasting peace."[43]

This speech clearly revealed that President Nixon's perception of the stakes involved in Vietnam mirrored those of his immediate predecessors: American global credibility and South Vietnamese self-determination. Yet by 1969 a majority of Americans was demanding a U.S. withdrawal from Vietnam. Nixon responded by arguing that his kind of withdrawal would satisfy the public's yearning for peace while simultaneously preserving U.S. credibility and providing South Vietnam with a reasonable chance for survival.

Nixon realized that in order to maintain public support for his Vietnam policy, troop withdrawals, once begun, had to continue. The pace of the pull-out could be geared to public toleration, but it could not stop or be reversed. That recognition led Nixon, particularly in the early years of his administration, to look for ways to achieve a battlefield resolution of the war without alienating public opinion. For example, in September 1969 Kissinger established a special National Security Council (NSC) task force to explore new military options, including a "savage blow" approach, designed to defeat North Vietnam. Secretary of Defense Melvin Laird, the chief champion of Vietnamization, learned of the project and argued against it and against Nixon's position.[44] Consequently, no savage blows were unleashed, but the secret bombing of Cambodia and an expanded bombing campaign in South Vietnam were designed and clearly aimed at putting additional military pressure on Hanoi. Nixon and Kissinger also repeatedly tried to enlist Moscow's good offices in obtaining a North Vietnamese reciprocal withdrawal, which was one of the president's initial conditions for an American pull-out. That demand, along with the attempt to achieve a military victory, were subsequently dropped by Nixon, though available evidence does not indicate when these decisions were made. A. James Reichley, who conducted extensive interviews of administration officials in the late 1970s, believed that the widespread uproar following the Cambodian incursion in the spring of 1970 convinced Nixon that a mutual withdrawal had become impossible.[45]

But while quietly searching for ways to end the war on favorable military terms, publicly Nixon responded to the widespread demand for "no more Vietnams" with his Guam Doctrine of July 1969. Floated as a trial balloon in an off-the-cuff session with journalists during his around-the-world trip, the Guam—soon thereafter, Nixon—Doctrine rapidly emerged as a key element in both the administration's Vietnam policy and its developing détente strategy. In his rather rambling remarks Nixon predicted that just as the Pacific had brought war to the United States in World War II, Korea, and Vietnam, so the region would continue to constitute "the greatest threat" to world peace. But how can the United States "avoid becoming involved in another war in Asia?" Nixon asked. Not by withdrawal, "because whether we like it or not, geography makes us a Pacific power," but by continuing to play a "significant role."[46] Nixon then noted that in framing a post-Vietnam Asian policy the United States had to take account of "two great, new factors"—national and regional pride. The second factor, Nixon added, will have "a major impact on the future of Asia," and "Asians will say in every country that we visit [on the current trip] that they do not want to be dictated to from the outside. Asia for the Asians."[47] And, said Nixon, "that is the role we want. . . . We should assist, but we should not dictate. . . . We will give assistance to those [political and economic] plans. We will, of course, keep the treaty commitments we have. But . . . we must avoid that kind of policy that will make countries in Asia so dependent upon us that we are dragged into conflicts such as . . . Vietnam."[48]

From these inelegant sentences sprung a Nixon Doctrine that would subsequently be intoned in formulaic fashion in more than twenty presidential speeches. Thus in the silent majority address of November 1969 Nixon's Guam remarks had been codified as "principles" guiding future American policy toward Asia. According to Nixon they consisted of three elements:

- First, the United States will keep all of its treaty commitments.
- Second, America shall provide a shield if a nuclear power threatens the freedom of a nation allied with us or of a nation whose survival we consider vital to our security.
- Third, in cases involving other types of aggression, the United States will furnish military and economic assistance when requested in accordance with our treaty commitments. But it will look to the nation directly threatened to assume the primary responsibility of providing the manpower for its defense.[49]

In an important sense, the Nixon Doctrine could trace its lineage to Eisenhower's New Look. The New Look had attempted to find instruments that would credibly enable the United States to protect its global interests without risking additional, costly, direct military interventions on the "periphery" such as Korea. Eisenhower's answer had been to threaten the Soviet Union and China—the "center"—with nuclear weapons. The Nixon Doctrine also constituted an *instrumental* policy adjustment in the wake of an even more repugnant Asian war. Existing treaty commitments would be kept—though the doctrine failed to specify the reasons for doing so—but the United States would reduce the risks of future Vietnams by serving as a supply source, not a labor pool, for threatened allies. The New Look had been criticized as reckless and lacking in credibility, particularly after the Soviets enlarged their nuclear arsenal and developed strategic delivery systems. The response to the Nixon Doctrine was more confused. Some commentators saw in it reassuring evidence that the old "test case" mentality that had led to indiscriminate U.S. involvement was to be replaced by a new flexibility of selective engagement. Others feared that the doctrine tied the United States to a defense of the Asian status quo in an age that Nixon himself described as one of change and flux. Still others claimed that the doctrine provided no criteria for future interventions, for it failed to specify the nature of American interests or to define the character of the threat to them. Moreover, what would the United States do if its assistance proved inadequate to save a threatened ally? In regard to this last criticism Nixon and Kissinger apparently "hoped that the rhetoric of commitment . . . could continue, because the reality of détente would allow the commitments to remain unimplemented."[50] Indeed, after Soviet-American relations had begun to worsen again in the mid-1970s President Gerald Ford and Henry Kissinger used the doctrine to justify military aid to the Angolan rebels. Ironically, and as a measure of the confusion surrounding the Nixon doctrine, some senators maintained that Ford's policy toward Angola violated the Doctrine, just as some had earlier argued that the 1970 Cambodian incursion had done so.

But most of the public did not care if the Nixon Doctrine reflected an instrumental adjustment or a fundamental policy shift. It saw the doctrine as a promise that there would be "no more Vietnams." The public supported Nixon on Vietnam so long as regular troop withdrawals continued and American casualties kept decreasing, and it was those incessant demands that consistently narrowed Nixon's options.

Nixon himself did not at first fully grasp this reality. His tough rhetoric of the silent majority speech had apparently enabled him to mobilize public opinion behind his "just and lasting peace" strategy. Six months later Nixon gave another speech on Vietnam, laced with even harsher rhetoric, but this time the tactic backfired as public divisiveness and anger exploded. Opinion polls did not fully capture this contrast. Before the November 1969 speech 58 percent supported Nixon's handling of the war and afterward 64 percent did. Similarly, his April 30, 1970, address increased his Vietnam support seven points, from 46 percent to 53 percent.[51] But whereas a majority in Congress had lined up behind Nixon's announced policy in November, the Kent State and Jackson State killings in May stole the headlines, and Congress moved to halt funding for the Cambodian operation.

As an effort in foreign policy legitimation the April 30 speech was a disaster. Ten days earlier President Nixon had announced a decision to withdraw an additional 150,000 Americans from Vietnam during the next year. That announcement had been something of a bow to public opinion, because the size of the withdrawal was unprecedentedly large and involved a longer time period. It seemed to respond partly to those critics who had been urging a definite timetable for complete withdrawal on the president, but it had also been tempered by Nixon's warning that increased enemy activity in South Vietnam, Cambodia, and Laos that endangered the remaining U.S. troops would require "strong and effective measures."[52] Nixon began his April 30 address by claiming that North Vietnam had ignored his warning by increasing its "military aggression" throughout Southeast Asia. Hence, "to protect our men who are in Vietnam and to guarantee our withdrawal and Vietnamization programs," he announced that U.S.-South Vietnam "attacks are being launched this week to clean out major enemy sanctuaries on the Cambodian-Vietnam border."[53] Nixon quickly added that "this is not an invasion of Cambodia" and promised to withdraw as soon as North Vietnamese forces had been driven out of two areas along the border. In short, he sought to portray the operation as necessary to continue withdrawal and to protect remaining troops.

Nixon, it will be recalled, had concluded his November speech with some pointed references to noisy demonstrators and short-sighted isolationists. In April he ended with remarkably incendiary language that made the Cambodian incursion take on the appearance of a major military escalation. He described an age of international and domestic anarchy in which "great institutions which have been created by free civilizations in the last 500 years" are being "mindlessly attacked." At home "great universities are being systematically destroyed," while abroad "small nations all over the world find themselves under attack from within and from without." "If," Nixon predicted, "when the chips are down, the world's most powerful nation . . . acts like a pitiful, helpless giant, the forces of totalitarianism and anarchy will threaten free nations and free institutions throughout the world."[54] Claiming that "it is not our power but our will that is being tested," he mentioned great decisions made by previous presidents and noted that "in those decisions, the American people were not assailed by counsels of doubt and defeat from some of the most widely known opinion leaders of the Nation." Rejecting the advice of those who had allegedly urged him to "take the easy path," "blame this war on previous administrations . . . and . . . bring all of our men home immediately," Nixon contended that he "would rather be a one-term president and do what I believe is right than to be a two-term president at the cost of seeing America become a second-rate power and to see this Nation accept the first defeat in its proud 190-year history."[55] Five hundred years of Western Civilization as well as its future now apparently depended on whether U.S. armed forces were allowed to move a few miles inside the Cambodian border!

No doubt President Nixon had calculatedly employed this burning rhetoric to quell the anticipated screams from the antiwar movement and to remobilize the silent majority. But in his zeal to practice again the politics of cultural confrontation, Nixon had parodied the technique that had worked so well in the Air Force Academy and silent majority speeches. A bare majority continued to back his handling of the war, but domestic divisions deepened, and Nixon, who normally relished the combat of cultural politics, pointedly softened his words at his first news conference after the April 30 address. In response to a question about student demonstrators, he suggested that he agreed "with everything they are trying to accomplish" and characterized the Cambodian decision as "terribly difficult." Later he expressed regret that his "use of the word 'bums' was interpreted to apply to those who dissent" and even appeared willing to receive some of the protesters in the White House.[56]

Nixon wrote in his memoirs that the success of the Cambodian incursion had enabled him to drop one of his key negotiating conditions: that all North Vietnamese troops must be withdrawn from the south before a cease-fire could occur. To the contrary, the domestic repercussions following the April 30 speech convinced Nixon that he could no longer afford to press that condition even though it reduced the chances for South Vietnamese self-determination.[57] During the Cambodian episode and during operations such as Saigon's invasion of southern Laos in February 1971, the American mining of Haiphong harbor on the eve of the Moscow summit, and the Christmas 1972 bombing of Hanoi, public opinion proved somewhat more supportive of increased airpower than the expansion of the ground war. The latter seemed to set back the schedule for U.S. withdrawal from South Vietnam, while the former evidently entailed fewer risks of heavy American casualties.

After Nixon, in effect, abandoned the principle of mutual withdrawal in October 1970, only one major obstacle to peace with honor remained: the issue of President Thieu's resignation, which Nixon adamantly opposed. On this point he never yielded, though Hanoi refused to concede it for more than two years. But by allowing the continued presence of almost 150,000 North Vietnamese troops south of the demilitarized zone, Nixon, if he remained committed to the goal of a non-Communist South Vietnam, had also seemingly committed the United States to a policy of reintervention.

Nevertheless, by clinging to his objective of gradual, orderly withdrawal Nixon eventually led America out of Vietnam. The draft was terminated, the POWs came home, and the poisonous atmosphere that had dominated American politics for almost a decade began to dissipate. But as Alonzo L. Hamby has noted, "A policy initiated to heal the divisions in American life was presented in a confrontational style that perpetuated them."[58] In large measure, of course, this pugnaciousness symbolized the divisive cultural politics that Nixon had exploited to help build his "new majority." It permeated virtually all of his public—and privately taped—remarks. At his first news conference after the conclusion of the Paris Accords, Nixon's vindictiveness soured what should have been a gratifying moment. When asked what he might do to help heal the internal wounds caused by the war, Nixon replied,

Well, it takes two to heal wounds, and I must say that when I see that the most vigorous criticism, or shall we say, the least pleasure out of the peace agreement comes from those that were the most outspoken advocates of peace at any price, it makes one realize [sic] whether some want the wounds healed. We do.[59]

After claiming that his administration, against very great obstacles, had finally achieved a peace with honor, Nixon added that "I know it gags some of you to write that phrase, but it is true, and most Americans realize it is true, because it would be peace with dishonor had we . . . 'bugged out'!"[60] And in rejecting amnesty calls for draft evaders and war deserters, the elite/majority theme surfaced yet again. Those who served in Vietnam, he said, realized they

had very little support among the so-called better people, in the media and the intellectual circles and the rest, . . . certainly among some elements of the Congress—particularly the United States Senate—but which did have support among the majority of the American people . . . despite the fact that they were hammered night after night and day after day with the fact that this was an immoral war, that America should not be there, that they should not serve their country, that . . . they should . . . desert their country.[61]

"Peace with honor," Nixon inferred, the goal of the silent majority, had been accomplished despite the best efforts of a noisy minority, and he was not prepared to forgive and forget.

What, then, had President Nixon legitimated through his Vietnam policy? At the very least he had convinced a slender domestic majority that his way out of Vietnam promised an honorable and durable peace and that the so-called other way—"bugging out"—amounted to surrender and would inevitably necessitate future American interventions. In making this argument Nixon repeatedly suggested that the Vietnam War could be America's last war, but only if peace with honor was achieved. Moreover, as we will soon discover, he also claimed that improved relations with the Soviet Union and China depended on American perseverance in Vietnam. Needless to say, these represented bold, even extravagant, promises, yet they appealed to a war-weary public, eager for a relaxation of world tensions but reluctant to surrender in Vietnam.

Neither the policy of phased withdrawal from Vietnam nor the Nixon Doctrine, however, laid the basis for a new national consensus about U.S. military interventions on the periphery. This fact became obvious when first Nixon, and then Ford, asked Congress for the funds allegedly required to prevent the fall of South Vietnam in the wake of the Paris Accords. Nixon himself contended afterward that Watergate played a decisive role in emboldening Congress to lose the peace that he had won. No doubt it did constitute a very important factor in Congress' reluctance to authorize funds for Saigon from 1973 to 1975. But even a politically robust president would have been hard-pressed to persuade Congress to provide massive assistance to the Thieu government after the peace settlement. A Gallup Poll conducted on January 25, 1973, showed that an enormous majority— 80 percent—favored the terms of the Paris Accords and that 58 percent considered it peace with honor. Moreover, 57 percent thought that the Christmas bombing had helped persuade Hanoi to sign the agreement. At the same time, however, only 35 percent thought that the settlement would prove durable, 54 percent doubted that South Vietnam could withstand Communist pressures after the U.S. withdrawal, and fully 70 percent believed that North Vietnam would try in the next few years to conquer the south. Nevertheless, only 38 percent supported U.S. military assistance to Saigon—as presumably required by the Nixon Doctrine. Even more astonishing was the fact that a mere 17 percent favored renewed bombing of the North in case of an invasion, and only 13 percent counseled the sending of U.S. troops to prevent a Communist victory.[62] There was, in short, clear and overwhelming public opposition to reintervention of any sort well before Watergate began to damage Nixon.

Perhaps an untarnished Nixon could have roused the silent majority to again support large-scale military aid to South Vietnam. He had already proven an exceedingly adept player of cultural politics. On the other hand, Nixon staffers like Michael Balzano, who worked closely with many grassroots organizations that represented elements of the so-called new majority, believed that these groups desired essentially three things: an "honorable" withdrawal, the unconditional return of all POWs, and no amnesty for evaders and deserters.[63] Nixon had already delivered on all of these demands. Similarly, in Congress, even among conservative Republicans like Senator Norris Cotton of New Hampshire, there was little sentiment for continued U.S. involvement. In opposing the bombing of Cambodia in the spring of 1973 Cotton said, "As far as I am concerned, I want to get the hell out of there just as quick as possible, and I don't want to fool around to the point that they might take more prisoners."[64] On the other hand, perhaps a Nixon without Watergate could have persuaded Congress to provide "assistance from a distance," thus precluding the possibility of a direct U.S. reintervention. And it is possible, though by no means certain, that such aid would have saved the Thieu government.

Notwithstanding such speculative ruminations, however, we can suggest with some confidence that when Nixon and then Ford left office there existed deep dissensus among the public and the elites about the issue of U.S. military intervention abroad. We shall, of course, return to this theme again, because it has enormously complicated the conduct of American foreign policy for the last two decades.

A FULL GENERATION OF PEACE

Richard Nixon in 1969 had not only inherited a stalemated war in Vietnam from an administration apparently imprisoned in a "more of the same" mentality, but he also felt himself burdened by a foreign policy that had seriously ossified during the previous decade. In part, this paralysis stemmed from the obsessive attention that President Johnson had paid to Vietnam, while critical issues like Soviet-American relations and the Arab-Israeli conflict were largely submerged. But there remained a deeper problem. Both Nixon and Kissinger believed that the structure of international relations had changed significantly since the political bulwarks of American foreign policy had been established in the late 1940s. Because of the outcome of World War II the United States had briefly exerted inordinate international influence. That historical moment had inevitably given way to an emerging situation characterized by the growth of Soviet military power to parity, the remarkable economic recovery of Western Europe and Japan, and the fragmentation of monolithic Communism. The United States, however, had failed to devise a strategy to deal effectively with this new environment. A crude anti-Communism remained the wellspring of an American foreign policy that had become lost in an obsession with crisis management.[65] The results had been drift and incoherence in place of strategy and design.

Neither Nixon nor Kissinger celebrated the relative decline of American power. Had they been in office at an earlier time both surely would have eagerly pursued global containment. As it was, however, systemic circumstances they thought required the United States to adapt to change. Complicating this difficult task was the evaporation of the domestic consensus that had sustained U.S. international commitments and achievements. According to Kissinger, many Americans, demoralized by Vietnam, yearned for a return to isolationism.[66] The Nixon administration, then, faced a dual challenge: to devise a foreign policy not only appropriate to altered external circumstances but also able to command domestic support.

The Nixon-Kissinger grand design entailed the creation of a stable, ultimately multipolar international structure cemented by a shared sense of Great Power legitimacy.[67] Most essentially this structure would maintain and stabilize the nuclear peace by making the status quo palatable to the major powers. Soviet-American rivalry would be muted, though not eliminated, by regulating the nuclear arms race and by preventing regional disputes from escalating into dangerous direct confrontations. The Soviet Union, which, according to the old cold war paradigm, constituted an implacable, world-revolutionary foe, would now be viewed more traditionally as an ambitious, opportunistic rival that shared certain interests with the United States. Their conservative, largely nonideological design additionally insisted that the United States refrain from imposing its domestic order on the international framework. That is, the United States had to construct an unbreachable barrier between the universal claims of its internal political values and the sense of limits required by the new international equilibrium. Ideology would no longer constitute the litmus test of foreign policy. The United States, according to this vision, could continue to assert its global primacy by adroitly manipulating the balance. At the same time, Nixon and Kissinger at least partly realized that there was little in either the American domestic experience or its diplomatic record that had prepared it for such an eminently "European" role.

The Nixon-Kissinger strategy for realizing their grand design involved four main components. First, they recognized that little could be done so long as the Vietnam War sapped American power and poisoned the domestic political atmosphere. The war had to be terminated, but if not done correctly, a U.S. withdrawal could actually inhibit the emergence of a stable international equilibrium by raising serious questions about American resolve and credibility. Domestically, a precipitous pull-out, besides rewarding the hated better circles, would trigger bitter recriminations, ugly insinuations about who lost Vietnam, and a public unwillingness to support further American global activism.

Second, it was imperative to establish more normal relations with the People's Republic of China and to begin to integrate it into the international system. Normalization possessed several potential benefits. Closer Sino-American ties would at the very least obligate Moscow to devote greater military resources to its extremely lengthy border with China, thus reducing somewhat the Soviet threat to NATO. They would also heighten the diplomatic isolation of North Vietnam and encourage it to accept a compromise settlement of the war. In addition, a Sino-American rapprochement might encourage China to play a more constructive international role by replacing its rhetoric of world revolution with more traditional diplomatic behavior. Finally, both Nixon and Kissinger saw substantial domestic political benefits in normalization. Historically the American public had evinced an almost irrational sentimental attachment to China, and though largely dormant for two decades—except for conservatives who idolized Chiang—Nixon and Kissinger detected a reservoir of American good will toward the Chinese people. And Nixon particularly savored the thought of doing what liberal Democrats had only dreamed of doing.

Third, the central balance—Soviet-American relations—required additional stability. For the United States to flourish in a "post-hegemonic" world, effective means had to be found to contain the expansionistic tendencies of the Soviet Union. The most extreme, though least likely, threat, Nixon and Kissinger thought, came from the Soviet nuclear arsenal. With its achievement of nuclear parity, however, Moscow might now be willing to regulate the arms race and strengthen deterrence. And it was in the U.S. interest to prevent the Soviets from seeking to gain the credible perception of nuclear superiority. But Nixon and Kissinger fretted even more about the consequences of a highly armed Soviet Union engaged in provocative, bullying, erratic international behavior, whether in Berlin, the Middle East, Cuba, or some other area of tension. These actions could easily provoke a superpower confrontation that might escalate into a nuclear crisis. To reduce the likelihood of nuclear war Nixon and Kissinger wished to involve the Soviets in realistic negotiations designed, ultimately, to institutionalize deterrence. So critical was this issue that they were willing to detach it from other Soviet-American disputes. On the other hand, in order to persuade the Soviet Union to reduce regional tensions and to accept the legitimacy of the international order, they sought to enmesh Moscow in a complex web of incentives and punishments woven in Washington. As inducements to limit Soviet geopolitical ambitions the United States could offer technology, grain, credits, and other desired economic benefits. In addition, recognition of the Soviet Union as a genuine superpower, and acquiescence in the legality of existing European boundaries as well as Moscow's dominant position in Eastern Europe could further diminish American-Soviet tensions. In exchange Nixon and Kissinger had reasonable hopes for a Berlin settlement that guaranteed Western access; Moscow's assistance in helping the United States to withdraw gracefully from Vietnam; and a Soviet willingness to manage Third World crises. But if the Kremlin reverted to its imperialist ways the United States would move swiftly to withdraw economic favors, diminish Moscow's new international status through symbolic actions, and resist Soviet designs on the periphery. Indeed, depending on the circumstances, these rewards and punishments might be meted out simultaneously. As Kissinger later noted, the basic issue was "whether we will use them or they will use us."[68]

Fourth, the implementation of the Nixon Doctrine would presumably enable the United States to avoid combat in future Asian wars. While it would be necessary to provide allies with substantial military and economic assistance, it would ultimately be their responsibility to defend themselves. But, of course, neither South Korea nor South Vietnam had earlier been able to do so. Were Nixon and Kissinger, consequently, more prepared to accept the loss of valued allies than Truman or Kennedy? In fact, they hoped the question would remain moot, for if Moscow and Beijing accepted the legitimacy of the new equilibrium, then they would have little incentive to sponsor Third World aggressions. And purely local conflict could be handled by the Nixon Doctrine or by regional allies like Iran, who would enforce Washington's notion of stability. In this crucial sense events at the center and those on the periphery were mutually reinforcing. Superpower détente would help create more stable regional relations, and a superpower-managed stability along the periphery would, in turn, promote a political atmosphere conducive to the conclusion of additional functional agreements between the United States and the Soviet Union.[69]

The Nixon-Kissinger strategy of détente made global, anti-Communist containment appear, in contrast, rather lumbering and unimaginative. Nevertheless, as we saw in Chapter 1, cold war presidents had argued vigorously and usually successfully that containment required broad executive powers in making foreign policy. But Nixon argued that the implementation of détente necessitated even more presidential freedom. Tactically, détente placed a premium on speed, dexterity, and manipulation. Moreover, because he was convinced that significant segments of the foreign affairs bureaucracy, especially at the State and Defense Departments, wished to sabotage his strategy, Nixon imposed an extraordinary degree of secrecy and White House control on foreign policy formulation and implementation. No doubt Nixon's personality played a part in this process, but the strategy did, in fact, require tactics that only a highly centralized body could manage. At the very least it demanded a certain ruthlessness to orchestrate adeptly an international equilibrium of ideologically diverse states. Regional stability, for example, might depend on the willingness to sell sophisticated arms to the autocratic Shah of Iran or to tilt away from democratic India and toward the Pakistani dictatorship during the Bangladesh War. Or the stability of the central balance might require the United States to ignore what formerly would have constituted human rights violations in the Soviet Union and China. And, more extremely, the Nixon Doctrine might necessitate genuine *sangfroid* to place limits on the amount of assistance to be made available to endangered (and democratic) allies.

Even under the best of circumstances such tactical maneuverability would have been difficult to obtain and sustain in the American political system. Nixon did, for a short while, largely succeed in gaining effective control over important aspects of foreign policy. But it was his particular misfortune to attempt to achieve this tactical freedom at the very moment that Congress, after years of *de facto* deference to executive initiative, began to reassert its constitutional prerogatives in foreign affairs, and that the media, angered by a "credibility gap" that grew during the Vietnam War, started to subject American foreign policy to unprecedented scrutiny. But underlying these institutional changes was a more subtle issue. During the cold war, presidential supremacy in foreign affairs could be justified by reference to the mortal threat of international Communism. A policy of confrontation required a strong president. But in the early 1970s Nixon sought even more tactical freedom despite the fragmentation of the Communist bloc and the dawn of what he called an "era of negotiation." It seemed paradoxical, at best, that the president would need additional power to deal with a diminished threat.

In important respects, therefore, the Nixon-Kissinger reformulation departed from the cold war policy of global, anti-Communist containment. Their grand design envisioned the emergence of a stable, multipolar balance chiefly managed by the United States and animated by a shared sense of international legitimacy; the strategy entailed a reduction of U.S.-Soviet tension by engagement on a variety of issues as well as a Sino-American rapprochement; and the tactics demanded that the United States be free to act swiftly and adroitly, and perhaps even with amorality and deceit. The Nixon-Kissinger approach, like its cold war predecessor, identified the Soviet Union as the primary threat to international peace, but attempted to restrain it through a complex mix of incentives, rewards, and Soviet *self-*containment.

The public appeal of global containment from the late 1940s to the mid-1960s had in large measure rested on its simplicity. It appeared to be what was minimally required to "stop the spread of Communism," without triggering World War III. Moreover, it divided the world into easily understandable moral categories: the Free World and the Communist Bloc. In the context of U.S. public opinion this strategy successfully united the values of peace and strength. Yet global containment was conceptually flawed, because the strategy became an end in itself, and the grand design—a pluralistic world inhabited by a mellowed Soviet Union or a non-Communist Russia—disappeared into near invisibility. Containment, as it evolved, could promise only "more of the same."[70]

Nixon knew and Kissinger had written that "the acid test of a policy . . . is its ability to obtain domestic support" and that it involved two aspects: "the problem of legitimizing a policy *within* the governmental apparatus . . . and that of harmonizing it with the national experience."[71] In essence, Nixon and Kissinger attempted less to legitimate their policy within the bureaucracy than to circumvent existing structures by creating a tightly controlled, highly centralized, and loyal foreign policy apparatus. Nixon, who in domestic policy sought to transfer power from the executive departments to the White House in order to return some functions to the states, tried in foreign policy to wrest control of the most significant issues from State and Defense in order to implement his grand design. It would be difficult to overstate the resentments produced by these hard-ball tactics, and the so-called Pentagon spy ring that infiltrated the National Security Council staff in 1971 and 1972 was but an extreme manifestation of that outrage.[72] Nevertheless, Nixon and, to a large degree, Kissinger believed that their subtle, multifaceted, frequently audacious strategy would inevitably be sabotaged by timid, entrenched, bureaucratic interests. Nixon's response, somewhat ironically, was to construct a loyal new minority within the White House to outmaneuver his enemies in the governmental old majority.

Nixon's efforts to legitimate *publicly* his foreign policy—to "harmonize it with the national experience"—were critical to its success. "Scaring hell out of the American people" had been a favored tactic of cold war presidents to mobilize public support for a rather simple policy, but Nixon's reformulation required a more sophisticated approach. His legitimation strategy involved six main elements: (1) a declaratory history of postwar American foreign policy that emphasized the remarkable success of that record; (2) an explanation of the ways in which the world had changed since 1947 and how his policies appropriately addressed those changes; (3) a relentless effort to castigate isolationists who would entrust the fate of the world to other nations; (4) a series of surprises and televised spectaculars designed to show the public that "only Nixon" could have accomplished these amazing diplomatic breakthroughs; (5) a clearly Wilsonian promise of a "full generation of peace" and (6) a rather stern warning that the post-Vietnam world would challenge the character, will, and spiritual strength of the American people at least as much as the cold war.

Because declaratory history is a consensus-building technique, it does not seek to be comprehensive, complex, or controversial, and Nixon's version of postwar U.S. foreign relations was none of these things. Kissinger and, to a smaller degree, Nixon were aware that the Vietnam War had helped ignite a sweeping revisionist assault on the origins and development of the cold war by a number of American diplomatic historians and journalists. This challenge to long-accepted interpretations of U.S.-Soviet relations constituted further disturbing evidence of a breakdown of the old foreign policy consensus.[73] Nevertheless, Nixon's declaratory account of this history adhered closely to that of his cold war predecessors. Indeed, he drew on his foreign affairs experience to personalize the historical record of postwar American diplomacy. For example, at every stop on his February 1969 tour of Western Europe, Nixon recalled how as a member of the Herter Commission in 1947 he had traveled to Europe, studied its economic needs, and helped lay the foundations of the Marshall Plan.[74] He also repeatedly stressed that American aid, combined with European efforts, had been crucial in creating a "strong, prosperous, free Europe."[75] Similarly, while visiting several Asian countries during his around-the-world trip in July and August 1969, timed to exploit the Apollo moon landing, President Nixon reminisced about touring those nations as vice president in 1953, noting that U.S. aid had helped them grow stronger.[76] These statements were designed to indicate a reassuring sense of continuity—as embodied by Nixon—in American foreign policy to both foreign and domestic audiences. Nixon's declaratory history also emphasized that despite America's overwhelming strength in 1945—its atomic monopoly and economic preeminence—it had merely sought to contain aggression. Never seeking anything for itself, the United States had fought in four twentieth-century wars so that others could live in freedom.[77] In short, he portrayed an American foreign policy record that brimmed with generosity, altruism, and self-restraint. The declaratory histories of cold war presidents had focused on the "lessons" of the 1930s, but Nixon rarely invoked them. In view of his own age it would have been difficult to personalize them as he did the early postwar decades, yet he may also have sensed that these "lessons" had lost much of their previous grip on public opinion. Above all, however, the repeated references to the 1930s would have clashed with Nixon's primary historical challenge: to demonstrate the important ways that the world had changed since World War II. Thus Nixon conveyed a triple message: the American people should be proud of the U.S. foreign policy record, but significant international changes had occurred, and now the United States must fashion an appropriate diplomatic response.

It is interesting to note the manner in which Nixon characterized these changes. First, the "nuclear gap had been closed," and the United States would never again have superiority. Moreover, the Soviet Union had further enhanced its European offensive capability and had "closed the gap in military strength, particularly in the Mediterranean." But, Nixon added, "In describing this, this is no cause for fright. The United States is still infinitely strong and powerful."[78] Second, the great industrial nations of Europe, as well as Japan, had regained their economic strength. "Many of the policies that were necessary and right" at the conclusion of World War II "are obsolete today."[79] Third, "our adversaries no longer present a solidly united front; we can now differentiate in our dealings with them."[80] Fourth, the nations of Latin America, Asia, and Africa "have a new sense of pride and dignity and a determination to assume responsibility for their own defense."[81] And fifth, "we are moving with precision and purpose from an era of confrontation to an era of negotiation" in Soviet-American relations, "motivated by mutual self-interest rather than naive sentimentality."[82] In sum, nuclear parity, the economic resurgence of Western Europe and Japan, the fragmentation of the Soviet bloc, Third World nationalism, and new bases for U.S.-Soviet negotiations had brought about significant change. Nixon did not suggest that the Soviet internal system had or would soon be reformed, nor did he contend that its repressive nature posed an obstacle to a reduction in superpower tensions. Better relations, Nixon told the United Nations General Assembly in 1970, would be grounded in "a powerful common interest in avoiding nuclear confrontation," "the enormous cost of arms," "economic self-interest" in increasing "trade and contact," and "the global challenge of economic and social development" that "can give our competition a creative direction."[83] The general tone of President Nixon's public statements indicated that these changes, while making the world somewhat more complex, had also made it potentially less dangerous.

The real threat evidently came from within the United States—from those isolationists who, besides agitating for a dishonorable "bug out" in Vietnam, wished to compel America's withdrawal from the world. Here, of course, Nixon did borrow a term of opprobrium from the 1930s to tar his domestic enemies. As he had done to garner public support for his Vietnam policy, in legitimating his "stable structure of peace" Nixon claimed there were but two alternatives: his way and the approach of the isolationists. Drawn largely from the so-called better circles—the media and academe—these Cassandras were determined to betray America's rich international legacy by abandoning our allies to our adversaries. Nixon asserted that they sought to capitalize on the genuine "dangers of overinvolvement . . . to withdraw from the world," and he repeatedly claimed that at the end of "a long and unpopular war" the American people were particularly susceptible to the isolationists' seductions. But he warned that the "deceptively smooth road of the new isolationism is surely the road to war." On the other hand, "our foreign policy today steers a steady course between the past danger of over-involvement and the new temptation of under-involvement."[84] This provocative, confrontational, and simplistic paradigm, in effect, internalized the Manichaean cosmos of the high cold war. Nixon's rhetoric implied that as the world had grown more diverse the domestic environment had assumed the characteristics of bipolarity. And unlike the Soviet Union, with which the United States shared certain interests, Nixon's differences with the isolationists apparently remained intractable. Once again he was less interested in a new domestic consensus than he was in fashioning a "new majority" by impugning the new minority.

President Nixon, as we have seen, repeatedly stressed the responsible and moderate nature of his efforts to inaugurate "an era of negotiation." It is not lacking in irony, then, that Nixon, Kissinger, and Robert Haldeman's White House staff came to depend on theatrics, surprises, and televised spectaculars designed to awe and entertain a vast domestic audience. Haldeman, who had been a successful advertising executive in Los Angeles, had no particular love for the détente policy, but he saw an enormous public relations potential in it. Highly visible summit meetings with the Chinese and the Soviets, particularly if carefully planned, were bound to enhance Nixon's reputation as a great statesman. And while Haldeman and other White House image makers resented Kissinger's alleged attempts to upstage Nixon or to share the credit, they were willing to pay that price so long as the public perceived that "only Nixon" could have accomplished these feats.[85] For his part, Nixon frequently told the press that he would only hold summits yielding concrete results and not merely produce illusory "spirits" of this or that meeting. And, of course, in April 1972 he risked cancellation of the Moscow summit by mining Haiphong harbor. Nevertheless, a policy that aimed at creating a new international structure was implemented through a series of well-staged *tours de force*. Nixon, in fact, cultivated the notion of his indispensability to détente. For instance, in a January 1972 interview with Dan Rather of CBS News he claimed that his October 1967 article in *Foreign Affairs*, "raised the lid on what many think was the biggest surprise in history when I made the 90-second announcement that we were going to China."[86] In the long run these tactics whetted the public's appetite for more spectacles and additional agreements and damaged the chances to institutionalize détente domestically. This excessive personalization of foreign policy did not necessarily enhance its legitimacy.

Televised pyrotechnics constituted but the end result of enormous amounts of diplomatic preparation, activity noteworthy for its extreme secrecy. Heavy reliance on so-called backchannels permitted Nixon and Kissinger to dominate the foreign policy-making apparatus to a degree unmatched since Franklin D. Roosevelt. John Lewis Gaddis has suggested that notwithstanding this tactical secrecy the Nixon administration "set forth the broad methods of [its] strategy with . . . candor and clarity," primarily through the issuance of annual foreign policy reports from 1970 to 1973 that were quickly dubbed State of the World messages.[87] Divided into geographical and functional sections each of which would typically begin with a relevant public statement by Nixon, followed by a few paragraphs of commentary, these reports were painstakingly drafted, largely by Kissinger and his staff. Kissinger considered them to be "a conceptual outline of the President's foreign policy, . . . a status report, and . . . an agenda for action" that "could simultaneously guide our bureaucracy and inform foreign governments of our thinking."[88] Gaddis glowingly described them as "a serious and frank effort to explain the basic geopolitical assumptions behind the administration's approach to the world."[89] Interviews with several staffers who helped prepare these documents clearly indicated that Kissinger took them very seriously, frequently agonizing for days over individual words and phrases.[90] Immediately before the release of the initial report in February 1970, Nixon told William Safire that "it's a historic document, people will read it more and more as time goes by" and added, "a good theme to get across is that nobody else could have done this. Germ warfare, Okinawa, China—soon we'll have the genocide convention and I'll get it through Congress. But nobody else could."[91] These State of the World messages, then, were to be more (or less) than simply educative.

But Kissinger appears to have been disappointed in the reports' limited impact:

> To our sorrow we never managed to get across its basic purpose of raising fundamental questions and expressing a philosophy. Try as we might, the media would only cover the section on Vietnam, probing for hot news or credibility gaps, ignoring the remainder as not newsworthy.[92]

Running as each did to some two hundred pages these messages proved more useful as "rough guides for the bureaucracy,"[93] though Nixon attempted to convey their highlights to the public in short radio addresses delivered at the time of their release to Congress. Safire makes it clear that radio was chosen, because Nixon and his advisers felt that a nationwide television audience would be numbed by such reports. Perhaps the media was not alone in "probing for hot news." But perhaps the reports themselves were not quite as "candid" as Gaddis and Kissinger have claimed. Stanley Hoffmann, writing as a contemporary critic in 1972, more accurately described them as messages that "oscillate from pious generalities to highly tactical and piecemeal accounts of recent decisions." No honest description of the kind of international system envisioned by the Nixon Administration was offered nor was there any indication of the "newly allegedly 'clear definition of our purpose.'" Instead, what Hoffmann found was "a set of moral attributes: moderation, fairness, compromise—which do not become more precise just because we proclaim that we no longer strike moralistic poses."[94]

In fact, Nixon's decision to describe his grand design to the public as a "full generation of peace" significantly magnified the disturbing tendency that Hoffmann discovered in the State of the World messages, for, in his determination to harmonize his goals with the national experience, Nixon shrouded his *Realpolitik* vision in largely Wilsonian garb. It is true that he filled his public statements with caveats about the dangers and difficulties that lay on the road to peace and of the substantial differences of interest— not mere mutual misperceptions—that had divided the superpowers. Moreover, he refused to claim that either the world or the Soviet Union was growing more democratic. As Nixon told Eric Severeid of CBS News in January 1971, "we recognized the right of any country to have internal policies and an internal government different from what we might approve of. What we were interested in was their policy toward us in the foreign policy field."[95] And, of course, in his famous "pentagon of power" remarks in July 1971 President Nixon admitted that "the United States no longer is in the position of complete preeminence or predominance. That is not a bad thing. As a matter of fact, it can be a constructive thing."[96] Finally, Nixon repeatedly emphasized the crucial significance of U.S. military power in underwriting the new era of negotiation. As he told a Joint Session of Congress on his triumphant return from the first Moscow summit, "As we shape our policies for the period ahead, therefore, we must maintain our defenses at an adequate level until there is mutual agreement to limit forces. The time-tested policies of vigilance and firmness . . . are the only ones that can safely carry us forward to further progress."[97] It was the isolationists, according to Nixon, who in their antimilitarist zeal wished to unilaterally disarm the United States.

These and similar kinds of public statements do indicate a certain willingness to explain the grand design, in effect, as a multipolar, pluralistic, equilibrium maintained, in part, by American military strength. But much to the annoyance of Henry Kissinger, Nixon placed much more rhetorical emphasis on what he called a "full generation of peace."[98] Indeed, the words *balance* and *equilibrium* almost never appeared in Nixon's public discourse, no doubt because of his reluctance to employ these "un-American" terms to legitimate his foreign policy. Unfortunately, Nixon's constant references to a "full generation of peace," particularly in 1971 and 1972, far from candidly describing his grand design, ultimately became little more than a campaign slogan. Although he had occasionally used this phrase earlier, it did not play a central role in Nixon's speeches until the 1970 congressional elections campaign. Then, as part of a vigorous effort on behalf of Republican candidates, President Nixon began to assert that if the Vietnam War could be settled honorably, "we have in the world today an opportunity better than at any time since World War II . . . to have a generation of peace."[99] But this term, which was initially enlisted to win public support for Nixon's Vietnam policy, gradually became the centerpiece of his vision for the postwar world. In dedicating the Woodrow Wilson International Center for Scholars, surely an act heavy with symbolism, Nixon noted that Wilson "was a man born ahead of his time. We have reason to hope that he was not born ahead of our time." Though he had "failed to stem the tide of postwar isolationism" and "died a broken man," Wilson's dream of ending the "terrible world habit of war" may be on the verge of realization. While Nixon, the self-proclaimed realist, did not speak of Vietnam as "the war to end wars," he did claim that "the strong likelihood exists that there will be no need for a war to end wars, that instead, by taking one careful step at a time, by making peace for one full generation, we will get this world into the habit of peace."[100] Similarly, in summarizing the 1971 State of the World message for a nationwide radio audience, President Nixon recalled that "our goal is something Americans have not enjoyed in this century: a full generation of peace," and added that its creation "depends on our ability to make certain that each nation has a share in its shaping and that every nation has a share in its lasting."[101] To build a "full generation of peace," Nixon told a "Salute to the President" dinner in November 1971, was, "in truth, a great goal."[102]

Yet while Nixon publicly promised that support for his foreign policy would produce, in effect, perpetual peace,[103] he also expressed great concern that the United States would misuse this peace by growing soft and complacent. With the Soviet threat more muted and with global containment no longer an appropriate way to mobilize the public, Nixon, as the end of the Vietnam War appeared increasingly imminent, sought to find a new international mission for America. Nixon repeatedly reminded his audiences that "the pages of history are strewn with the wreckage of great civilizations in the past who lost their leadership just at the time that they were the richest, and at a time when they had the capability of being the strongest." "The challenge of our time," Nixon proclaimed, "was to not turn away from greatness."[104] At a press conference in August 1972 he put it as follows: "What we need in this country is a new sense of mission, a new sense of confidence, a new sense of purpose as to where we are going."[105] But Nixon found it very difficult to articulate the essence of that mission beyond the predictable homilies about the importance of "staying number one" and "playing a world leadership role." The real "mission"— that of conservative, central balancer—could not be mentioned. Rather, Nixon agreed with nineteenth-century American philosopher William James about the need to find "the moral equivalent of war: something heroic that will speak to men as universally as war does, and yet will be as compatible with their spiritual selves as war (is) incompatible."[106] Similarly, Nixon suggested that "America, in my view, will cease to be her true self when we cease to be engaged in an enterprise greater than ourselves."[107] He attempted to portray the post-Vietnam world as one that would test American "will and character," but aside from warning of the renewed danger of isolationism, he could not clarify the reasons for his concern.

In trying to harmonize his foreign policy with the national experience, Nixon spoke to the public with words drawn more from the political lexicon of Woodrow Wilson and Cordell Hull than that of George Kennan and Walter Lippmann. Perhaps Nixon had no choice but to rely on rather simple moral categories to describe his complex, necessarily expedient policies, for to do otherwise would have heightened public suspicions about Nixon's "tricky" tendencies and Kissinger's Central European background. Moreover, Nixon, despite an almost obsessive fascination with *Realpolitik*, could never wholly free himself from the grip of an essentially Wilsonian universe. It is important to reemphasize that the Nixon-Kissinger reformulation constituted an *adjustment* to new realities, realities that they thought might not prove permanent. In any case, despite occasionally candid statements about the real nature of his grand design, Nixon undertook no systematic effort at public education, relying instead on slogans and clichés to mobilize support. He spoke more openly about the strategy of détente and the Nixon Doctrine, but asked the public to accept on faith his reassurances that the implementation of these concepts would somehow guarantee a "full generation of peace." In this sense Nixon's perceived need to make an expediential, balance of power policy publicly palatable resulted in a rhetorical simple-mindedness reminiscent of cold war presidents.

A NEW FOREIGN POLICY CONSENSUS?

In Chapter 1 we recalled that the cold war consensus had possessed policy, procedural, and cultural components. Briefly stated, global containment, presidential supremacy in foreign affairs, and an ethic of national sacrifice in the service of anti-Communism all received widespread domestic acquiescence for about twenty years after World War II. Richard Nixon attempted to reconstruct a consensus by reformulating American foreign policy, by modifying, but hardly abandoning, the old cultural dimensions, and by reasserting presidential prerogatives in foreign affairs.

In transmitting his fourth annual foreign policy report to Congress in May 1973, Nixon noted that "One of my basic goals is to build a new consensus of support in the Congress and among the American people for a responsible foreign policy for the 1970s."[108] Did he achieve that goal? Did Nixon successfully legitimate the grand design, strategy, and tactics of his foreign policy reformulation? If Nixon's grand design consisted of an emergent, multipolar, stable equilibrium managed by the United States, then Nixon, as we have seen, did little to win its public acceptance. To harmonize his vision with "the national experience" Nixon repeatedly spoke of a "full generation of peace,"—subsequently extended to a "century of peace"—that his policies would allegedly guarantee. These words had undeniable appeal for a war-weary nation. What, after all, was the alternative? A "full generation of war," Nixon implied, would result from the rejection of his policies. Thus the fact that almost everyone could accept Nixon's goal of a "full generation of peace" proved largely irrelevant, for the phrase did not adequately describe the grand design.

It is, perhaps, not surprising that the strategy of détente, publicly discussed by Nixon with greater candor, became much more controversial and did so in large part because of its alleged failure to "harmonize with the national experience." More specifically, while the *process* of détente received widespread initial support, the concrete *results* of that process were quickly and quite effectively subjected to simultaneous liberal and conservative critiques.

The détente process, as publicly described by Nixon, held out the prospect for a less dangerous world. Heralding a new era of negotiation, it promised to end the paralysis that had gripped American foreign policy from Vietnam to the Middle East by exploiting the important international changes that were underway. At the very least this process would regulate the nuclear arms race by placing limits on superpower arsenals, reduce Soviet-American tension, allow the U.S. defense budget to shrink, normalize relations with the People's Republic of China, and avoid future Vietnams with the help of the Nixon Doctrine. Unfortunately, because of the lack of systematic public opinion data, it is difficult to assess popular support for these initiatives. Whereas Gallup closely tracked opinion about Nixon's Vietnam policy—a measure of this issue's persisting centrality—it did not ask the public to evaluate his overall foreign policy until June 1974, and in that poll 54 percent approved at a time when Nixon's presidential performance rating had tumbled to 24 percent.[109] On the basis of this admittedly fragmentary evidence it appears quite plausible to conclude that the détente process struck a positive chord with the public. Unlike George McGovern's foreign policy platform, which the Republicans successfully portrayed as dangerously irresponsible, Nixon's détente seemed to tap into the noninternationalist public's yearning for peace without unduly sacrificing strength. His landslide 1972 reelection, while primarily attributable to a prosperous economy and the likelihood of an imminent end to the Vietnam War, surely owed something to the popularity of détente.

In accounting for détente's subsequent domestic difficulties, as in explaining the congressional revolt against Nixon's post-Accords Vietnam policy, the importance of Watergate must be considered. The scandal gradually destroyed Nixon's ability to govern as it effectively replaced Vietnam as a national obsession. Détente thus passed from one shadow to the other, and by late 1973 virtually all of Nixon's foreign policy actions were widely perceived as cynical efforts to bolster his sagging political fortunes. His pre-Watergate public inferences that "only Nixon" could manage détente grew so blatantly insistent that at the June 1974 summit the Soviets openly sought to detach the president from the issue of improved superpower relations. In sum, Watergate certainly increased the domestic vulnerability of détente.

But Watergate alone did not create that vulnerability. It would have been exceedingly difficult for even an uninjured Nixon to make détente, as it was then understood, the foundation of a new domestic foreign policy consensus. By 1976 the policy had been rather tightly squeezed between a resurgent Right alarmed by the unrestrained growth of Soviet military power and a dissatisfied Left that found détente incapable of addressing a host of emerging global issues. President Ford, confronted with a shrinking domestic base, attempted to recapture the noninternationalist mass public by rechristening détente, "peace through strength."

Nixon and Kissinger had been aware from the beginning that the Right would find it difficult to accept the premises of détente, but felt that because of Nixon's own longstanding anti-Communist convictions it would have little choice but to support, or at least tolerate, this policy.[110] But as the process of détente unfolded and produced tangible superpower agreements, conservative critics, led at first by Senator Henry Jackson and then increasingly among Republicans by Ronald Reagan, Nixon, and Kissinger, were thrown on the defensive. In essence, they argued that the Soviet Union was systematically exploiting détente in order to achieve global domination.[111] As early as the summer of 1972 Jackson had forcefully criticized the "assymetries" of SALT I that allowed the Soviet Union to maintain a larger ICBM force than the United States. Further, the Senate put Nixon on notice that any SALT II treaty would have to address these concerns about numerical imbalances. That autumn Jackson introduced an amendment to an omnibus trade bill that made the granting of Most Favored Nation status to the Soviet Union contingent upon the liberalization of its Jewish emigration policy. The amendment sought to link U.S. economic benefits to the reform of the Soviet domestic system. Kissinger objected to this misapplication of linkage and argued that its passage would provoke Moscow. But Jackson was able to gain widespread congressional support for his amendment, not because these members doubted Kissinger's predictions, but because they feared the political ramifications of appearing to oppose Israel. Jackson and others also attacked another concrete result of détente: the "Basic Principles of Relations" document signed at the Moscow summit. Though privately regarded by the administration as but the first step of translating a functional network of relations into a legitimate world order, Nixon nevertheless hailed it in an address to a Joint Session of Congress as a "landmark declaration . . . that can provide a solid framework for the future development of better American-Soviet relations."[112] The agreement committed the superpowers to coexistence, an avoidance of direct military confrontation, the mutual disavowal of spheres of influence, and the exercise of leadership and restraint in regional conflicts. Conservative skeptics rather predictably put these principles in their own service to evaluate Soviet behavior in the Third World. Thus when Brezhnev threatened to send a military force to the Sinai during the October 1973 Middle East war, these critics argued that the Soviets had thereby violated the Moscow agreement. Soon Jackson and others began to argue that while détente had lulled America into a false sense of security, the Soviet Union had used it to achieve strategic superiority and to renew its determination to expand its global influence. Détente constituted appeasement—peace without strength.

Ford, fearing a Reagan nomination challenge from the Right, sought to accommodate some of these criticisms. His use of military force in the *Mayaguez* incident and his attempts to win congressional approval for "covert" aid to Angolan rebels were designed to restore American credibility after the fall of Saigon and to punish the Soviets for their African adventurism. His appointment of a very conservative Team B task force to estimate Soviet defense spending, in effect, acknowledged that earlier CIA figures had been misleadingly optimistic. His decision to postpone the completion of SALT II until after the 1976 election was based on a reasonable fear that Reagan would tellingly exploit the new treaty in the Republican primaries. And his acquiescence in a party plank highly critical of Kissinger further reflected Ford's fear of a conservative flight from his camp.

Yet while these attempts to refocus détente by emphasizing its competitive elements may have dampened some conservative criticism (though it scarcely eliminated them), they only provoked liberals in Congress, the media, and academe into launching a full-scale assault on both the substance and style of the Ford-Kissinger foreign policy. We will defer discussion of the "style" issue until later in this chapter and here concentrate on the substantive objections raised by the mainstream Left. By and large, liberals, while distressed by much of Nixon's Vietnam policy, applauded détente. Arms control, the opening to China, trade liberalization with the Soviet Union, a superpower code of conduct, and reductions in regional tensions—the "carrots" of détente—were welcomed. Indeed, liberal Democrats in the Senate, worried that attacks on détente would escalate in the wake of Nixon's resignation, held hearings in 1974 designed to allow Henry Kissinger to defend détente in a largely friendly forum.[113] Some had reservations about the specific details of actual agreements—for example, the very high levels in offensive systems allowed by SALT—but overall, liberals liked détente as publicly articulated by Nixon, and they accepted its major premises.

Nevertheless, particularly as the 1976 election drew closer, many began to question the adequacy and the direction of the Ford-Kissinger approach. At the root of their criticism lay the conviction that the world had changed even more than Ford and Kissinger were willing to admit. Thus they argued that American foreign policy, in its near obsession with the Soviet Union, had proven insensitive to a host of dramatic global developments. While liberal critics acknowledged the desirability of stable superpower relations, they contended that American foreign policy, with its focus on East-West relations, had become anachronistic. Impressed by the power of Third World nationalism, from North Vietnam's resiliency to OPEC's audacity, liberals claimed that U.S. foreign policy needed an agenda that reflected the growing importance of North-South relations. They criticized Kissinger's contemptuous dismissal of Third World demands for a New International Economic Order, his apparent satisfaction with the status quo in South Africa, and his very belated involvement in the Zimbabwe negotiations. Moreover, liberal critics, who at first had welcomed the Nixon Doctrine as a promise of "no more Vietnams," grew increasingly disenchanted with its emphasis on large-scale arms sales to "unsavory," yet friendly, regimes like Iran, Nicaragua, and the Philippines. Then too, they discovered to their disappointment that Kissinger could invoke the doctrine to support CIA activities in Angola at a time when they, again impressed with the apparent "lessons" of Vietnam, perceived the "disutility" of military force in peripheral areas—or at least that employed by the superpowers. Liberal critics also charged that Kissinger's geopolitical machinations inevitably had neglected the emergence of significant international economic issues. The newly formed Trilateral Commission chastised Kissinger for ignoring economic relations with America's traditional allies (and major trading partners). Kissinger responded by proclaiming 1973 the "Year of Europe," only to later be forced to make it the "Year of OPEC." Critics suggested that resource shortages, global inflation, ecological damage, the energy "crisis," and similar "transnational phenomena" required that the United States learn to "manage interdependence." Finally, there remained the more elusive theme of, for lack of a better term, the "national interest." Despite Nixon's occasional portrayal of Vietnam as an example of American overinvolvement, the Nixon Doctrine represented, as we have seen, an adjustment of means not ends. Indeed, neither Nixon nor Kissinger ever publicly suggested that U.S. interests were less than global or indivisible, and their characterizations (and Ford's) of Vietnam, Angola, and the Middle East as "test cases" of American credibility strongly echoed earlier assertions of cold war presidents. Yet liberal critics found it equally difficult to redefine the scope of U.S. interests. While some did envision a radical reduction in American commitments, particularly in the Third World, Nixon's rather obnoxious insistence that all liberal critics advocated isolationism grossly misrepresented the actual situation. In fact, not only were most of them opposed to a "continental defense," but they found it difficult to counsel even a policy of "selective engagement." Rather, on the eve of Jimmy Carter's election, most liberal critics were searching for ways to make continued U.S. global involvement less militaristic and more reform-minded, less Machiavellian and more moral, less unilateral and more cooperative.

The tactics that Nixon and Kissinger claimed were necessary to implement the détente strategy received an emphatically mixed reception. Initially the public, doubtless encouraged by the media's infatuation with Kissinger, seemed awed by the secret trips and overt theatrics surrounding the opening to China. On the other hand, many in Congress, already seething over the various deceptions hidden in Nixon's Vietnam policy, grew increasingly uncomfortable with the extreme secrecy, the backchanneling, and the radical centralization of decision making in the White House that appeared integral to détente. Far from establishing a national consensus supportive of such tactics, they were instrumental in fueling a congressional revolt, in raising howls of protest about an "Imperial Presidency," and in triggering calls for a more open, democratic foreign policy. While conservatives seemed much less concerned about Nixon's tactics than congressional liberals, their criticisms began to increase in direct proportion to their growing disenchantment with the *strategy* of détente. (Because this issue of a tactical consensus also relates to congressional-executive procedures, we will continue this discussion at the end of this chapter.)

This analysis leads to three conclusions: (1) Nixon achieved considerable success in publicly legitimating his grand design as a "full generation of peace" but in so doing he consistently misrepresented its true nature; (2) Nixon was initially able to legitimate the *process* of détente as an appropriate strategy but was unable to sustain a public consensus after the concrete results of détente proved increasingly controversial to the Right and irrelevant to the Left; and (3) the tactics developed by Nixon and Kissinger to implement détente alienated much of the bureaucracy, enraged many in Congress, and—in conjunction with Watergate—catalyzed public demands for a more moral, "American" foreign policy.

Nixon was less interested in reestablishing a cultural consensus in support of his foreign policy than he was determined to mold a new majority. Aware of the *Kulturkampf* unleashed by the divisive public and elite reactions to the Vietnam War and the Great Society, Nixon worked hard to exploit its political implications. In essence, he sought to build a post–New Deal electoral coalition held together by a set of widely shared social values. While certainly not unmindful of the crucial importance of a strong economy, Nixon nevertheless wished to tap Middle America's resentments toward big government, social engineering, countercultural excess, "crime in the streets," and similar phenomena. We suggested in Chapter 1 that, though easily exaggerated, an ethic of sacrifice in the service of anti-Communism had characterized cold war America. Nixon did not speak explicitly of an American way of life, but he did repeatedly assert that the "challenges of peace" would sorely test the will and character of Americans, much as earlier presidents had described the threat of Communism. In fact, Nixon transformed the old, external enemy of Communism into the new, domestic enemy of the noisy minority—those who would tell "real" Americans how to conduct their lives.

This provocative attempt to fashion a cultural majority only partly succeeded. Even as Nixon swept forty-nine states in the 1972 election Democrats strengthened their hold on both houses of Congress, and his rough-and-tumble efforts to play cultural politics, while doubtless satisfying to millions who harbored social resentments, only deepened the gulf between Nixon's supporters and enemies.

Moreover, there was no clear relationship between the nature of Nixon's foreign policy—other than Vietnam—and the character of his cultural majority. During the cold war it seemed appropriate that a policy of global, anti-Communist containment was undergirded by an American way of life. But détente would appear to have been at least as popular among Nixon's enemies as among his cultural supporters. Indeed, this descent into cultural politics diminished the likelihood of successfully legitimating the substance of his foreign policy by alienating those who might otherwise have applauded his efforts.

In Chapter 1 we also recalled that the major initiatives in American foreign policy from the late 1940s to the mid-1960s had been supported by an unusual degree of executive-legislative harmony. Frequently referred to as "bipartisanship," these decades witnessed a rather solid procedural consensus characterized by presidential leadership and congressional acquiescence in foreign affairs. Though seriously challenged by Republican criticism of Truman's handling of the Korean War and by the series of Bricker amendments that caused the Eisenhower administration some annoyance, this cold war procedural consensus was premised on the notion that the threat posed by international Communism in a nuclear era required a strong presidency. As a result Congress gave presidents very wide latitude in the conduct of American foreign policy. So long as they rather ritualistically "consulted" with the "bipartisan Congressional leadership" presidents during these years were paid an extraordinary amount of deference. Preferring ignorance to information in areas such as covert action, Congress would duly involve itself in foreign policy by passing—usually overwhelmingly—joint resolutions requested by the president.

Richard Nixon would have liked very much to have continued these procedures. Not only was he unable to restore the old procedural consensus that had begun to unravel by the late 1960s, but he also failed to establish the basis for any executive-congressional agreement on the conduct of foreign policy. Nixon, as we have seen, had emphasized the importance of international changes in his public efforts to legitimate détente. Similarly, he had sought to capitalize on the alleged negative changes triggered domestically by the Great Society to build his new majority. Curiously, however, Nixon never even tried to formulate new, mutually acceptable procedural arrangements with Congress. Doubtless the raw passions stirred by Vietnam would have greatly reduced the likelihood of an amiable outcome, yet Nixon exacerbated the situation through his confrontational tactics and his repeated insistence that his foreign policy absolutely required a strong president and an acquiescent Congress. In regard to Vietnam he argued that congressional criticism reduced North Vietnam's incentive to negotiate, endangered Vietnamization, and prolonged the stationing of U.S. troops in Southeast Asia. Nixon taunted his congressional opponents to demonstrate their convictions by cutting off funding, and when Congress finally did so in 1973, he ordered the Defense Department to shift money from other accounts to cover the shortfall. Two years earlier, after Congress had repealed the Gulf of Tonkin resolution, he derided it as superfluous and claimed that he, as commander in chief, would continue to prosecute the war as he saw fit. His periodic "consultations" were halfhearted exercises that merely informed Congress about decisions already made—often only minutes before they were made public. In effect, Nixon behaved as if "peace with honor" could be achieved if Congress would only "shut up."

Likewise, Nixon, as much through his actions as his words, conveyed the impression that only he could understand the complexities of global change and fashion an appropriately responsive American foreign policy. Ironically, the sophisticated mix of carrots and sticks that Nixon and Kissinger claimed were needed to modify Soviet behavior necessitated, if anything, increased congressional participation, for many of their initiatives required legislation. But Nixon claimed that a flexible, credible foreign policy depended on a president unburdened by a meddlesome Congress. As he told a White House reception for former POWs in May 1973, "Had we not had secrecy . . , there would have been no China initiative, there would have been no limitation on arms with the Soviet Union and no summit," and American prisoners would still have been held in North Vietnam.[114] In sum, although Nixon argued that significant changes abroad and at home required new foreign and domestic policies, he insisted that Congress play essentially the same role that it had meekly fulfilled during the cold war.

But a majority in Congress refused, and instead Nixon and Ford confronted a Capitol Hill revolt that eventually produced demands for executive-legislative "codetermination" in foreign policy making. We need not recount here the details of specific congressional actions to legislate restraints on presidential power in foreign affairs. The Jackson-Vanik amendment, the Eagleton amendment cutting off funds for U.S. military operations in Cambodia, the War Powers Resolution, the Clark amendment banning the CIA from aiding Angolan rebels, the Turkish arms embargo, and the 1976 Foreign Assistance Act providing Congress with extensive oversight of human rights abroad represent but the best-known examples in a broad-ranging challenge to executive supremacy. By the mid-1970s a "new" Congress had begun to take shape: skeptical of presidential prerogatives, newly democratized, and armed with its own policy-making machinery. It could, in fact, be plausibly argued that the Nixon-Ford years witnessed a more fundamental change in the procedures than in the substance of American foreign policy. But as Jimmy Carter assumed the presidency in 1977 these executive-congressional procedures for conducting foreign policy, far from being consensual, threatened to produce institutional gridlock.

NOTES

1. Henry Kissinger, *White House Years* (Boston: Little, Brown, 1979), 65.

2. Kissinger, *White House Years*, 65.

3. Joan Hoff-Wilson, "Richard M. Nixon: The Corporate Presidency," in Fred I. Greenstein ed., *Leadership in the Modern Presidency* (Cambridge, MA: Harvard University Press, 1988), 165.

4. Hoff-Wilson, 165.

5. Hoff-Wilson, 165.

6. Helmut Sonnenfeldt, personal interview, November 4, 1988.

7. Quoted in William Safire, *Before the Fall: An Inside View of the Pre-Watergate White House* (Garden City, NY: Doubleday, 175), 172.

8. Richard Nixon, "Inaugural Address," January 20, 1969, *Public Papers of the Presidents: Richard Nixon, 1969* (Washington, DC: Government Printing Office): 3.

9. Safire, 136. Nixon also wanted to use the speech to build congressional support for an ABM system.

10. Richard Nixon, "Address at the Air Force Academy Commencement Exercises in Colorado Springs, Colorado," June 4, 1969, *Public Papers of the Presidents: Richard Nixon, 1969* (Washington, DC: Government Printing Office, 1971): 432–435.

11. Safire, 141.

12. Safire, 172.

13. Richard Nixon, "Address to the Nation on the War in Vietnam," November 3, 1969, *Public Papers, 1969*: 908, 909.

14. See Andrew Z. Katz, "Public Opinion, Congress, President Nixon and the Termination of the Vietnam War," Ph. D. diss., Johns Hopkins University, 1987, 51.

15. Weekly Compilation of Presidential Documents, vol. 5, 1969 (Washington, DC: Government Printing Office, 1969): 1589, 1590.

16. Charles W. Colson, "The Silent Majority: Support for the President," *Richard Nixon: A Retrospective on His Presidency*, Hofstra University, Hempstead, New York, November 20, 1987. Jonathan Rieder correctly notes that "Middle America" did not really exist as a popular term before the 1960s. But out of this "maelstrom of defection" from the Democratic party there emerged this new social formation that could be juxtaposed to "limousine liberalism" (Rieder, "The Rise of the 'Silent Majority'" in Steve Fraser and Gary Gerstle eds., *The Rise and Fall of the New Deal Order* [Princeton: Princeton University Press, 1989], 244).

17. Kevin Phillips, *The Emerging Republican Majority* (New Rochelle: Arlington House, 1969).

18. Richard M. Scammon and Ben J. Wattenberg, *The Real Majority* (New York: Coward-McCann, 1970).

19. Colson.

20. Michael P. Balzano, Jr., "The Silent Majority: Support for the President," Nixon Retrospective, Hofstra University.

21. Donald F. Rodgers, "The Silent Majority: Support for the President," Nixon Retrospective, Hofstra University.

22. Safire, 172.

23. Alonzo L. Hamby, *Liberalism and Its Challengers: F.D.R. to Reagan* (New York: Oxford University Press, 1985), 325.

24. Safire, 542–52.

25. Safire, 551.

26. Hoff-Wilson, 176.

27. Quoted in Hoff-Wilson, 176.

28. Richard Nixon, "Radio Address on the Philosophy of Government," October 21, 1972, *Public Papers of the Presidents: Richard Nixon, 1972* (Washington, DC: Government Printing Office, 1974): 998.

29. Nixon, "Radio Address," 999.

30. Nixon, "Radio Address," 1000.

31. Kissinger, *White House Years*, 226.

32. Kissinger, *White House Years*, 227.

33. Kissinger, *White House Years*, 227.

34. Richard Nixon, "Address to the Nation on Vietnam," May 14, 1969, *Public Papers, 1969*: 370.

35. Nixon, "Vietnam Address," May 14, 1969: 371.

36. Richard M. Nixon, *RN: The Memoirs of Richard Nixon* (New York: Grosset & Dunlop, 1978):371.

37. Nixon, "Vietnam Address," May 14, 1969: 369.

38. Nixon, "Vietnam Address," May 14, 1969: 369.

39. Nixon, "Vietnam Address," May 14, 1969 370.

40. Nixon, "Vietnam Address," November 3, 1969: 902.

41. Nixon, "Vietnam Address," November 3, 1969: 906.

42. Nixon, "Vietnam Address," November 3, 1969: 906.

43. Nixon, "Vietnam Address," November 3, 1969: 909.

44. A. James Reichley, *Conservatives in an Age of Change: The Nixon and Ford Administrations* (Washington, DC: The Brookings Institution, 1981), 118.

45. Reichley.

46. Richard Nixon, "Informal Remarks in Guam With Newsmen," July 25, 1969, *Public Papers*, 1969: 546.

47. Nixon, "Guam Remarks," 548.

48. Nixon, "Guam Remarks," 548.

49. Nixon, "Vietnam Address," November 3, 1969, 905–06. In the first State of the World message the phrase "and the security of the region as a whole" was appended to the second point (Richard Nixon, "Message to the Congress. Transmitting the First Annual Report on United States Foreign Policy," February 18, 1970, in *Public Papers of the Presidents: Richard Nixon, 1970* [Washington, DC: Government Printing Office, 1972]: 141).

50. Robert S. Litwak, *Détente and the Nixon Doctrine: American Foreign Policy and the Pursuit of Stability, 1969–1976* (New York: Cambridge University Press, 1984), 126.

51. See Katz.

52. Richard Nixon, "Address to the Nation on Progress Toward Peace in Vietnam," April 20, 1970, *Public Papers, 1970*: 375.

53. Richard Nixon, "Address to the Nation on the Situation in Southeast Asia," April 30, 1970, *Public Papers, 1970*: 406, 407.

54. Nixon, "Address on Southeast Asia," 409.

55. Nixon, "Address on Southeast Asia," 409, 410.

56. Richard Nixon, "The President's News Conference of May 8, 1970," *Public Papers, 1970*: 414, 417, 423.

57. Reichley, 119.

58. Hamby, 307.

59. Richard Nixon, "The President's News Conference on January 31, 1973," *Public Papers of the Presidents: Richard Nixon, 1973* (Washington, DC: Government Printing Office, 1975): 55.

60. Nixon, "News Conference of January 31, 1973."

61. Nixon, "News Conference of January 31, 1973."

62. *Gallup Opinion Index, #92* (February 1973), 5–7.

63. Balzano, "The Silent Majority."

64. Quoted in Thomas M. Franck and Edward Weisband, *Foreign Policy By Congress* (New York: Oxford University Press, 1979), 15.

65. Kissinger, *White House Years*, 65.

66. Kissinger, *White House Years*, 56.

67. John Lewis Gaddis, *Strategies of Containment*; Litwak, *Détente and the Nixon Doctrine*; and Raymond L., Garthoff, *Détente and Confrontation: American-Soviet Relations from Nixon to Reagan* (Washington, DC: The Brookings Institution, 1985).

68. Gaddis, 293.

69. Litwak, 78–9.

70. Henry Kissinger, *A World Restored* (Gloucester, MA: Peter Smith, 1973), 326. Emphasis in original.

71. See, for example, Destler, *Our Own Worst Enemy* and Roger Morris, *Uncertain Greatness: Henry Kissinger and American Foreign Policy* (New York: Harper & Row, 1977).

72. Roger Morris, "The Foreign Policy Process," Nixon Retrospective, Hofstra University, November 19, 1987.

73. For a longer discussion of this theme see Richard A. Melanson, *Writing History and Making Policy: The Cold War, Vietnam, and Revisionism* (Lanham, MD: University Press of America, 1983).

74. Richard Nixon, "Remarks to the North Atlantic Council in Brussels," February 24, 1969, *Public Papers, 1969*: 134.

75. Richard Nixon, "The President's News Conference of March 4, 1969," *Public Papers, 1969*: 180.

76. For a characteristic statement see Richard Nixon, "Statement on the President's Visit to Thailand," July 28, 1969, *Public Papers, 1969*: 579.

77. See, for example, Richard Nixon, "Remarks at the Veterans of Foreign Wars Annual Convention in Dallas, Texas," August 19, 1971, *Public Papers of the Presidents: Richard Nixon, 1971* (Washington, DC: Government Printing Office, 1973): 911.

78. Richard Nixon, "Remarks at the Convention of the National Association of Broadcasters," March 25, 1969, *Public Papers, 1969*: 249.

79. Richard Nixon, "Annual Message to the Congress on the State of the Union," January 22, 1970, *Public Papers, 1970*: 9.

80. Richard Nixon, "Radio Address about Second Annual Foreign Policy Report to the Congress," February 25, 1971, *Public Papers, 1971*: 214.

81. Nixon, "State of the Union Address," 9.

82. Nixon, "1970 State of the Union Address," 9–10.

83. Richard Nixon, "Address to the 25th Anniversary Session of the General Assembly of the United Nations," October 23, 1970, *Public Papers, 1970*: 927–28.

84. See, for example, Nixon, "Radio Address on Second Foreign Policy Report," 214.

85. Personal interviews, Autumn 1988, Safire, 388, 390–91.

86. Richard Nixon, "'A Conversation with the President,' Interview with Dan Rather of the Columbia Broadcasting System," January 2, 1972, *Public Papers, 1972*: 7.

87. Gaddis, 305.

88. Kissinger, *White House Years*, 158–59.

89. Gaddis, 305.

90. Personal interviews, Autumn 1988.

91. Safire, 170.

92. Kissinger, *White House Years*, 159.

93. Kissinger, *White House Years*, 159.

94. Stanley Hoffmann, "Will the Balance Balance at Home?" *Foreign Policy* 7(1972): 73. Raymond Garthoff remarked on this theme several years later in this manner:

> This discrepancy between the private calculation and the public characterization, between the realistic management of power and the promise of "a new era" of "durable peace," ultimately came to haunt détente and undercut popular support as the excessive expectations it aroused were not realized. Nixon and Kissinger were reacting to what they saw as the conflicting imperatives of an external manipulation and wielding of power, and an internal political dynamic that required a simple and confident avowal of peace rather than education of the public in the complex ways of the world. (Garthoff, 29.)

95. Richard Nixon, "'A Conversation with the President,' Interview with Four Representatives of the Television Networks," January 4, 1971, *Public Papers, 1971*: 12.

96. Richard Nixon, "Remarks to Midwestern News Media Executives Attending a Briefing on Domestic Policy in Kansas City, Missouri," July 6, 1971, *Public Papers, 1971*: 807.

97. Richard Nixon, "Address to a Joint Session of the Congress on the Return from Austria, the Soviet Union, Iran, and Poland," June 1, 1972, *Public Papers, 1972*: 664.

98. Personal interviews, Autumn 1988.

99. See, for example, Richard Nixon, "Remarks in Fort Wayne, Indiana," October 20, 1970, *Public Papers, 1970*: 919.

100. Richard Nixon, "Remarks at the Dedication of the Woodrow Wilson International Center for Scholars," February 18, 1971, *Public Papers, 1971*: 188, 189.

101. Nixon, "Radio Address on the Second Annual Foreign Policy Report," 218–19.

102. Richard Nixon, "Remarks at a 'Salute to the President' Dinner in New York City," November 9, 1971, *Public Papers, 1971*: 1087.

103. In several 1973 speeches Nixon referred to a "century of peace and beyond."

104. Nixon, "New York Salute," 1090.

105. Richard Nixon, "The President's News Conference of August 29, 1972," *Public Papers, 1972*: 837.

106. Nixon, "VFW Remarks," 911.

107. Richard Nixon, "Remarks to Southern News Media Representatives, Attending a Briefing on Domestic Policy in Birmingham, Alabama," May 25, 1971, *Public Papers, 1971*: 675.

108. Richard Nixon, "Message to the Congress Transmitting Fourth Annual Report on United States Foreign Policy," May 3, 1973, *Public Papers, 1973*: 347.

109. Gallup Opinion Index 108, (June 1974): 3.

110. Sonnenfeldt interview.

111. See, for example, Garthoff.

112. Nixon, "Address to a Joint Session," 663–64.

113. United States Senate, Hearings before the Committee on Foreign Relations," Détente. 93rd Congress, 2nd Session, August 15, 20, and 21, September 10, 12, 18, 19, 24, and 25, and October 1 and 8, 1974.

114. Richard Nixon, "Remarks at a Reception for Returned Prisoners of War," May 24, 1973, *Public Papers, 1973*: 560.

CHAPTER 3

The Carter Administration

Jimmy Carter's narrow victory over Gerald Ford in 1976 represented the culmination of one of the most unlikely journeys in the recent history of American national politics. Not since the Civil War had either major party given the presidential nomination to a nonincumbent southerner, and no one from the Deep South had been chosen since Zachary Taylor of Louisiana had run for the Whigs in 1848. Furthermore, Carter became the first nominee in twenty-four years to lack congressional experience. In 1979 he recalled at a news conference that "a week after I was an announced candidate for President [in 1974], Gallup ran a poll and listed 36 people . . . [including] Ralph Nader and Julian Bond. . . . My name was not on the list. But I became the President."[1] The first Gallup poll of Democratic voters in 1976 placed Carter in a last place tie with Edmund Muskie and 4 percent behind Edward Kennedy, Hubert Humphrey, George Wallace, Henry Jackson, Birch Bayh, and George McGovern. Six months later he won the Democratic nomination on the first ballot in New York.

We will not retell the story of Jimmy Carter's "meteoric rise from obscurity,"[2] but a few points are worth emphasizing. His surprising primary electoral successes rested on his—and his Georgian staff's—ability to understand and exploit the new rules of the Democratic party's nominating process. In particular, Carter, more than any of his rivals, recognized the significance of the Iowa caucuses, and his early organizational groundwork there made him an instantaneously "serious" candidate. Second, he took advantage of another circumstance: the notable increase in public cynicism about a range of institutions in American life, prominently including the federal government. Overall institutional confidence fell from 43 percent in 1966 to 20 percent a decade later, while confidence in the presidency and the Congress plummeted to 11 percent and 9 percent respectively. Nixon's last approval rating bottomed at 24 percent, and Gerald

Ford's dropped from 71 percent in August 1974 to less than 40 percent by January 1975. Hamilton Jordan, Carter's chief political strategist, wrote the governor of Georgia a remarkably prescient memorandum in November 1972 that observed, "Perhaps the strongest feeling in this country today is the general distrust of government and politicians at all levels. The desire and thirst for strong moral leadership in this nation was not satisfied with the election of Richard Nixon. It is my contention that this desire will grow in four more years of the Nixon administration."[4] Needless to say, the immense agony of Watergate, as well as the spectacular revelations of CIA misconduct, and a series of congressional peccadilloes featuring an Argentinean exotic dancer and a secretary who could not type,[5] further eroded the public trust in Washington. Here, of course, Carter as the quintessential outsider, held an important edge over candidates saddled with Potomac baggage. Third, as Charles O. Jones correctly argues, there were policy circumstances in 1976 which favored a Democratic candidate like Carter who was willing and able to turn from the expansionist themes of the Great Society to more managerial issues like governmental efficiency, budgetary reform, and decentralization.[6] Finally, the circumstances of the mid-1970s were such that Carter's total lack of foreign policy experience (or even demonstrable prior interest) did not disqualify him from seriously seeking the presidency. Whereas in every presidential election between 1948 and 1972 the public had cited foreign policy as the most important problem facing the nation, a Gallup poll of October 1976 showed that 78 percent indicated that inflation and unemployment were the most pressing issues, while only 6 percent mentioned foreign policy. Equally noteworthy, in light of Carter's early identification with "good government" themes, was the fact that only 6 percent of those polled suggested that restoring public trust in government constituted America's biggest problem.[7] In sum, several rather unusual circumstances combined to favor the unknown, unblemished Jimmy Carter in 1976, yet the public's preoccupation with the health of the economy promised to make it the litmus test of his administration.[8]

THE PEOPLE'S PRESIDENT

For Jimmy Carter the fundamental task for his administration was the restoration of the faith of the American people in themselves, their government, and their government's foreign activities. This crisis of faith had produced a debilitating national disunity which Carter believed had been exacerbated by Vietnam, Watergate, and the CIA revelations. But the core of the crisis went deeper than these disturbing recent events: "The root of the problem is not so much that the people have lost confidence in government, but that government has demonstrated time and again its lack of confidence in the people. For too long political leaders have been isolated from the public. They have made decisions from an ivory tower."[9] Carter's solution was straightforward: "There is a simple and effective way for public officials to regain the public trust—*be trustworthy!*"[10] And, not surprisingly, Carter sincerely and stubbornly believed that he was uniquely qualified to restore the public trust and to end the divisiveness of American life.

President Carter and his advisers early settled on a four-part strategy to achieve this goal. First, he attempted to personify the essential decency of the American people. As he put it in his Inaugural Address, "You have given me a great responsibility—to stay close to you, to be worthy of you, and to exemplify what you are. Let us create together a new national spirit of unity and trust. Your strength can compensate for my weakness, and your wisdom can help to minimize my mistakes."[11] He was an average American, no smarter than most, who like many of his fellows had served in the Navy, tilled the soil, worshiped God, and raised a family. He, like them, was imperfect but was willing to learn, work hard, and do better. And, in contrast to his frequently disingenuous predecessors, Carter would "never lie" to the American people. Symbols, as well as rhetoric, were crucial to the strategy. Thus by carrying his own bags, walking with Rosalynn down Pennsylvania Avenue, dispensing with "Hail to the Chief," donning a cardigan for a fireside chat, fishing in humble streams, playing softball in Plains, and enjoying Willie Nelson, Carter revealed himself as a man of the people. He, of course, was hardly the first president to play "log cabin" politics, yet in the wake of Watergate and the "imperial presidency" Carter believed that circumstances required this approach.

Second, President Carter attempted to stay close to the electorate by establishing a direct relationship with the public. Unlike Lyndon Johnson and Richard Nixon, who grew fatally isolated from the people, Jimmy Carter would listen, and by listening would convince Americans that they could trust the president to care about their well-being. Typical was this remark made in April 1977:

> I believe that many political . . . and news media figures underestimate the competence and intelligence and sound judgement of the American people.

And when we've failed in the past number of years . . . it's been because the American people have been excluded from the process.

. . . And I want the American people to be part of the process from now on so that when I do speak the American people are part of it.[12]

He invited them to openly debate issues like the Middle East, energy and arms control, and, early in his term, publicly announced negotiating positions before offering them to other nations. He held frequent press conferences with the Washington news corps—two a month through 1978. He met over sixty times in the White House with local editors. Even more unusual was Carter's participation in a couple of call-in radio shows designed to answer questions from the people. But it was the "town meeting" format that President Carter used on almost twenty occasions that demonstrated most dramatically his concern with the average citizen. Not only would these town meetings typically take place at a high school or civic auditorium, but he emphasized his "just folks" unpretentiousness by spending the night at someone's home and by making his own bed as well. Taken together these gestures were meant to convey the image of a decent, honest, accessible, and compassionate man who happened to be president.

Third, Carter, like Nixon, recognized that the old Democratic New Deal coalition had been greatly weakened by the perceived excesses of the Great Society and a growing resentment among many voters toward the alleged intrusiveness, arbitrariness, and inefficiency of the federal government. Carter, in fact, shared this resentment and was additionally distressed by what he saw as the pervasive tendency of politicians from both parties to do the bidding of narrow, special interests. According to one of his inner circle of Georgians, "He doesn't like politicians. He really just doesn't like them. . . . He's not willing to risk his future on just the politicians. He knows that there are good ones and bad ones and so on, but he really does not like them. He's anti-politician."[13] And as a lifelong Democrat Carter was particularly distressed by the tremendous power exerted by certain groups on the legislators of his own party.[14] Moreover, he was aware of the increasing vulnerability of the Democratic party to the charge that it was the party of special interests and fiscal irresponsibility. On the basis of his own inclinations and his experiences in Georgia politics, Carter concluded that the public's faith in the federal government could be restored only if the presidency could serve as the repository of the public good. And he was convinced of his unique ability to discern and articulate the public good by circumventing established institutions and organizations. As Erwin C. Hargrove has suggested, Jimmy Carter considered "good policy"—comprehensive solutions to pressing national problems—to be the goal of enlightened political leadership.[15] At the same time he suspected that public policy—whether in Washington or Atlanta—had too often reflected political expediency and brokered interests. Carter and his advisers knew that issues like energy, tax and budgetary reform, and the Panama Canal treaties lacked natural constituencies, but they conducted intensive programs of policy campaigning and issue-by-issue coalition building on their behalf. Indeed, President Carter particularly relished tackling those complex and difficult problems that had either cowed or defeated his predecessors. Good policy, he confidently believed, would inevitably be created after he had listened to conflicting views, personally mastered the issues through diligent homework, and applied his impressive analytic powers to the complexities of the problem. While he was certainly aware of the political benefits that the adoption of his policies could provide, Carter's primary aim was to formulate good policy to demonstrate that America's democratic system could constructively respond to challenges and restore popular faith in the integrity of government by showing that the public good could triumph over narrow self interest.[16] Thus national unity would not be achieved through ideological appeals or by dividing the pie to "satisfice" politically potent groups, for Carter detested the Democratic party's penchant for interest group liberalism. Rather Carter expected that the sheer good sense of wise policy, if carefully conceived and efficiently managed, would mobilize public support. And even if the White House were forced to retreat from its initial policy positions and compromise with Congress, Carter evidently believed that the public would nevertheless appreciate his courage in confronting complicated problems.

President Carter enjoyed substantial public popularity through the summer of 1977 but by the following spring his approval rating had fallen well below 50 percent. When the press asked him to explain this significant decline Carter repeatedly attributed it to the intractibility of the issues that he had taken on, the difficulty of explaining their complexity to the public, and the disturbing reality that many citizens apparently doubted the very urgency of these problems. Carter's frustrations intensified during the summer of 1979 when he felt caught between a new energy crisis precipitated by the Iranian revolution and a public which was inclined to blame shortages on greedy oil companies. This situation provided the context for perhaps the most revealing speech of Carter's presidency, the so-called crisis of confidence or national malaise address of July 15, 1979. In it he highlighted the themes that had served as his *leitmotif* since the 1976 primary campaign. Characterizing the current condition of America as in "moral and spiritual crisis" Carter had "been reminded again that all the legislation in the world can't fix what is wrong with America," for it faced a nearly invisible threat that "strikes at the very heart and soul and meaning of our national will:"

> We can see this crisis in the growing doubt about the meaning of our lives and in the loss of a unity of purpose for our nation.
> The erosion of our confidence in the future is threatening to destroy the social and political fabric of America. . . .
> Our people are losing that faith, not only in government itself, but in the ability as citizens to serve as the ultimate rulers and shapers of our democracy.[17]

This crisis, Carter insisted, had its roots in the traumas of the 1960s and early 1970s: the assassinations of John and Robert Kennedy and Martin Luther King; the "agony of Vietnam" that had "shown our armies to be not invincible;" the shock of Watergate that threw the presidency into disrepute; a decade of inflation that shrunk "our dollar and our savings"; and by a "growing dependence on foreign oil."[18] Moreover, Carter admitted, "These wounds are still very deep. They have never been healed."[19] What must be done?

> First of all, we must face the truth, and then we can change our course. We simply must have faith in each other, faith in our ability to govern ourselves, and faith in the future of this nation. Restoring that faith and that confidence to America is now the most important task we face.[20]

President Carter then claimed that America faced a turning point in its history with two paths to choose: one that led to "fragmentation and self-interest," the other that promised "common purpose and the restoration of American values" like hard work, strong families, close-knit communities, and faith in God. "Energy," Carter argued, "will be the immediate test of our ability to unite this nation. . . . On the battlefield of energy we can win for our nation a new confidence." He concluded by reiterating his determination to act as a decisive leader and to listen even more intently to the American people.[21]

Carter, in this quite remarkable speech, admitted that good policy alone could not restore national unity and confidence, but that strong presidential leadership in touch with the public was required. Immediately after the address Carter did attempt to "be presidential" by firing a substantial portion of his Cabinet, and he did listen anew to the people by staging a series of town meetings across the country. Nevertheless, by making energy the test of national will, he, in effect, once again implied that good policy would restore Americans' faith in themselves and their government. Yet, as Carter admitted several months later, it was not good policy but the national outrage caused by Iran's seizure of American hostages that "galvanized the American public toward unity" as nothing had "in the last decade."[22]

Finally, President Carter and his advisers sought to restore public trust by articulating a foreign policy that reflected the character, values, and experience of the American people. Whereas Nixon's foreign policy design and his efforts to fashion a domestic new majority were logically and substantively separable, Carter saw foreign policy largely as the external manifestation of American life. To that end he framed a foreign policy that would convey to the world the decency, honesty, and candor that he wished to project to the American public. We will discuss Carter's foreign policy more fully in the chapter's remaining sections, but it should be emphasized that much of that policy was understood to be largely a continuation of domestic policy. In light of the tight connection that Carter drew between the internal and international realms, his appointment of Patricia Derian, a former Mississippi civil rights activist completely without foreign relations experience, to serve as Assistant Secretary of State for Human Rights Affairs, becomes more comprehensible, for he viewed this issue, in particular, as one that inevitably bridged foreign and domestic policy.

In sum, President Carter believed that he had inherited a nation that had been disillusioned and divided by a decade of war, scandal, and economic dislocation. He thought himself uniquely well qualified to restore public trust and unity by personifying the best features of the national character, by conducting an open and honest dialogue with the American people, by framing comprehensive policies that embodied the public good, and by offering a foreign policy reflective of enduring American values.

A COMPLEX NEW WORLD

Despite his own notable lack of foreign policy experience, Jimmy Carter made the Kissinger legacy a centerpiece of his 1976 campaign and leveled a series of substantive and stylistic charges against the secretary's stewardship. Most important, candidate Carter claimed that America's international image had been tainted by Kissinger's reliance on secret diplo-

macy, back channels, "Lone Ranger" decision making, and an amoral manipulation of power, and strongly implied that these proclivities were
intimately related to the Watergate mentality that had gripped the Nixon
White House. As a result neither Congress nor the American people had
been sufficiently involved in the formulation of U.S. foreign policy.
Carter criticized as well the content of some of Kissinger's contributions, suggesting that (1) the United States had paid excessive attention to the Soviet
Union, while simultaneously signing a SALT agreement that had set un-
equal and overly high limits on ICBMs; (2) the United States in its obsessive pursuit of superpower condominium had been insensitive to the legitimate demands for change from Latin American and African nations; (3)
human rights had been sacrificed to a policy that sold huge quantities of
arms to unsavory friends; (4) there seemed to be little concern about the
global threat of nuclear proliferation; and (5) the well-being of America's
democratic allies—Japan and Western Europe—had been largely ignored.
No doubt this grab bag of criticisms constituted, in part, an electoral strategy designed to separate Carter from what appeared to be the more unpopular aspects of the Kissinger record. James Fallows, an early Carter speechwriter who grew disenchanted with the administration, suggested as much
in his contention that

> 'history,' for Carter and those closest to him, consisted of Vietnam and Water-
> gate; if they could avoid the errors, as commonly understood, of those two
> episodes, they would score well. No military interventions, no dirty tricks, no
> tape recorders on the premises, and no 'isolation' of the President.[23]

But while Fallows's uncharitable testimony captures an important dimension of the Carter presidency, it nevertheless underestimates the degree to
which the administration's early initiatives embodied a world view different in several respects from both American cold war foreign policy and the
Nixon-Kissinger reformulation.

At the core of that view lay the conviction shared to varying degrees
by Carter and his senior advisers that the world had changed in decisive
ways since 1945 and that the United States's failure to respond adequately
threatened to condemn it to philosophical isolation. This critique had been
developed with the help of the Trilateral Commission. Founded by David
Rockefeller to express his concern about the Nixon-Kissinger alleged obsession with U.S.-Soviet relations, this group was to focus on U.S.-West
European and U.S.-Japanese issues and to explore the economic dimensions of rapid global change. Carter joined the commission and was intro-

duced to many of those whom he would later tap for senior administration posts. First, the era of unchallenged American economic and military global supremacy had ended and been replaced by a fluid, shifting configuration sometimes called "complex interdependence." Stanley Hoffmann, who often functioned as a friendly academic critic of the administration, likened this condition to a "vast omelet" in which "I may want *my* egg to contribute a larger part of the omelet's size and flavor than *your* egg—or I may want to break yours into it first, etc. . . . But we all end up in the same omelet."[24] In these circumstances no state could realistically expect to exert the sort of dominance characterized by the United States during the cold war. Second, Third World demands for a New International Economic Order reflected this new global reality and, if unaddressed by the industrial democracies, would increase the likelihood of nuclear proliferation. In this regard Carter had been impressed with the seeming implacability of Third World nationalism, in Vietnam and Algeria in particular, and believed that it was imperative to improve North-South relations. Third, the overall level of armaments in the world had reached alarming proportions as power had been diffused among more and more nations. Superpower relations had been gripped by a spiraling nuclear arms race, while the developing world had been inundated with a flood of sophisticated conventional weapons. Both of these developments had made international relations less stable. Fourth, despite its recent arms buildup, the Soviet Union had been gradually transformed into a generally status quo power saddled with massive internal problems and an increasingly unattractive ideology. National Security Affairs Assistant Zbigniew Brzezinski, even early in the administration, demonstrated more skepticism about Moscow's intentions than Carter and some of his State Department advisers, but in general there was a belief that the cold war, if not fully dead, had become comatose. Fifth, and closely related to the second point, Carter administration officials shared the conviction that military power—at least as employed by the superpowers to sustain their influence in the Third World—had lost much of its utility. Carter, of course, had appointed to top foreign policy positions many people who had helped conduct the Vietnam War and had been profoundly chastened by the experience. Indeed, only Brzezinski, among Carter's senior advisers, had remained away from Washington during these years, though he probably would have become NSC Director if Hubert Humphrey had won the 1968 election. At the same time, however, these officials had also been impressed by the failure of the Soviet Union to preserve its influence through arms exports to countries like Egypt and Syria. They concluded, therefore, that neither superpower could confidently employ military power against Third World nationalist movements without risking domestic repercussions or international embarrassment. Sixth, and finally, the Carter team identified several emerging "transnational" issues such as resource depletion, environmental degradation, and global inflation that posed insidious, long-term threats to the world community.

Contemporary critics frequently complained that the Carter administration lacked a grand design. Aware of the many public disagreements among his senior advisers that seemed to create inconsistency and indecisiveness as well as Carter's inclination to describe his foreign policy with lists rather than an overall vision, these commentators were hard-pressed to discover transcendent themes. In fact, however, Carter and his advisers did initially possess a grand design that, while poorly articulated, was nonetheless real. The administration's early foreign policy was animated by a vision that entailed the creation of a stable, just world order cemented by a mixed, but increasingly cooperative, superpower relationship; steadied by a serious, sustained "North-South dialogue" that would help accommodate the demands of the developing nations for greater participation in international political and economic decisions; and anchored by a relatively less powerful but more "mature" United States that would constructively exploit these massive global changes through good example and a willingness to cooperate with all nations.

Brzezinski, who knew of Carter's aversion to geopolitical thinking, attempted to translate this enormously ambitious, yet rather hazy, grand design into a list of strategic objectives. With the help of Samuel Huntington, a Harvard political scientist, and William Odom, an army officer and former Brzezinski student, he crafted a forty-three-page memorandum which formalized the themes of a 1976 paper that Carter had relied on in his campaign speeches. In late April 1977 Brzezinski presented the new document to the president, who liked it and proceeded to use it as the basis for administration foreign policy.[25] In its preface Brzezinski wrote of the need for "a *broad architectural process* for an unstable world organized almost entirely on the principle of national sovereignty and yet increasingly interdependent socially and economically."[26] He then enumerated ten goals to be accomplished during the next four years which together comprised a set of "working blueprints":

1. To cooperate with the industrial democracies in promoting closer political and macroeconomic coordination in developing a stable and open monetary and trade system. Among specific targets were

the reintegration of Greece into the NATO command structure, resolution of the Cyprus dispute, ratification of the Multilateral Trade Negotiations, and improved coordination of Western economic policies toward the Soviet Union and Eastern Europe.

2. To weave a worldwide web of relationships with new emerging regional "influentials" like Venezuela, Brazil, Nigeria, Saudi Arabia, Iran, India, and Indonesia, thereby widening, in keeping with historical circumstances, our earlier reliance on the Atlantic community.

3. To develop more accommodating North-South relations in order to increase Third World economic stability and growth, diminish Soviet influence, decrease hostility toward the United States, and reward those developing nations eager to have good relations with the industrial democracies. The most specific target was to ratify a new Panama Canal Treaty by the end of 1978 as a symbol of America's understanding of change in Third World and of its willingness to cooperate with these nations.

4. To push U.S.-Soviet strategic arms limitation talks into *reduction* talks and thereby lay the basis for a more stable relationship. At the same time the United States would rebuff Soviet incursions both by supporting friends and by ameliorating the sources of conflict which Moscow could exploit. Furthermore, the United States would counter Soviet ideological claims by assuming a more affirmative commitment to human rights. Finally, the administration would make détente more comprehensive and reciprocal. Specifically, the United States would work to complete SALT II by early 1978 and an arms reduction treaty (START) by 1980, achieve phased mutual and balanced force reductions by 1980, and begin discussing military restraints in the Indian Ocean.

5. To normalize Sino-American relations as a central stabilizing element in our global policy. The administration should try and establish full diplomatic ties by 1979 and thus lay the basis for a long-term cooperative relationship.

6. To obtain a comprehensive Middle East settlement in order to prevent the further radicalization of the Arab world and the reentry of the Soviet Union into the region's affairs.

7. To begin a peaceful transformation of South Africa toward biracial democracy, forge a coalition of moderate African leaders, and eliminate the Soviet-Cuban presence from the continent. Specifically, the United States should help achieve majority rule in Zim-

babwe by 1978, pressure South Africa to begin dismantling apartheid by 1980, and reach agreement with Moscow for the joint cessation of arms sales to Africa by 1979.

8. To restrict the level of global conventional and nuclear armaments, the United States would reduce by 15 percent, with the exclusion of transfers to NATO, Australia, New Zealand, and Japan, the 1976 dollar value of transfers. It should also cooperate to restrain nuclear proliferation and sign a series of nuclear testing treaties early in the administration.

9. To enhance global sensitivity to human rights by highlighting U.S. observance of such rights and by undertaking initiatives designed to encourage other governments to give a high priority to them. Thus the administration should adhere to five major human rights treaties, push for a full review of these issues at the Belgrade conference, propose human rights criteria for the International Financial Institution loan program, and expand our refugee programs for those fleeing oppressive left-wing and right-wing regimes.

10. To maintain a defense posture capable of deterring the Soviet Union from undertaking hostile acts or applying political pressure. Such would require the modernization and reconceptualization of its defense posture reflective of broad changes in the world, NATO's needs and Soviet Third World interventions. Thus the administration should examine U.S. overseas commitments and bases, seek greater budgetary flexibility, and try to standardize NATO equipment.[27]

According to Brzezinski, President Carter was "quite taken" with this outline, and referred to it regularly and praised it as "an unusually useful document." Evidently Brzezinski agreed, because he cites it in his memoirs as convincing evidence that the Carter administration did indeed possess "a central strategy, a defined philosophical perspective, and certain basic priorities."[28] For Brzezinski, "a more accurate indictment . . . is that we were overly ambitious and that we failed in our efforts to project effectively to the public the degree to which we were motivated by a coherent and well-thought-out viewpoint."[29]

During the 1976 campaign Carter had also asked Cyrus Vance to formulate specific goals and priorities for a Carter administration foreign policy, and he complied with a long memorandum in late October that, like Brzezinski's, emphasized issues that all three men had helped develop at the Trilateral Commission. Vance's memo advanced five "persuasive general foreign policy themes," the last of which bore directly on the problem of domestic legitimation:

1. U.S.-Soviet issues, while of central importance, should not be allowed to so dominate our foreign policy that we neglect other important relationships and problems. In dealing with the Soviets we should stand resolutely firm to protect key interests while working to further reduce tensions.
2. There should be a new sensitivity, awareness, and priority to the vast complex of North-South issues and an emerging set of global issues like energy population, environment, and nuclear proliferation.
3. Without unrealistically inserting itself into the internal operations of other governments, the United States should give important weight to human rights considerations in selecting foreign policy positions while continuing in international forums its unwavering stand in favor of the rights of free people.
4. The administration's foreign policy should be marked by gravity, not flurry. It should not try to do everything at once or solve all of the world's problems, and it should focus on long-term general objectives.
5. The new administration must make the Congress and the American people joint partners in foreign policy matters. The president should assume major public leadership on foreign policy, and make a major investment in educating the public to perceive the difference between its long-term and short-term interests, and the difference between the national interest and the interests of particular domestic groups and subconstituencies.[30]

The first three items broadly reflected the priorities of Brzezinski's "working blueprint," while the fourth one would be repeatedly violated by a president who quickly launched an incredible number of domestic and foreign policy initiatives. Vance's last suggestion certainly captured Carter's deep commitment to use the presidency to serve the public good.

Neither Brzezinski's nor Vance's memorandum explicitly constituted an integrated strategy geared to implement a grand design as, in contrast, had the Nixon-Kissinger reformulation. They were, rather, largely lists of objectives devoid of any self-evident connective tissue. But, in fact, Carter and his senior advisers were united in their determination for America to continue to play an active international role despite the Vietnam disaster.

Moreover, they agreed that to do so the United States needed to adjust pragmatically to a "complex, new world," while finding ways to remain relevant to other nations. These shared convictions produced an approach that mixed managerialism, moralism, and retrenchment.

Interviews that we conducted over the course of several years with senior- and middle-level Carter foreign policy officials confirmed what many commentators had suspected: These policy makers had in varying measures been profoundly wounded by their Vietnam experience, were extremely wary of making decisions that would suck the United States into another quagmire, but wished to carve out a constructive role for America in the post-Vietnam world that would mesh its unique strengths and experiences with new global realities.[31]

First, the United States, confronted by a newly diverse world of rapid change, would manage complex interdependence by encouraging the construction of what W. Anthony Lake, Director of the State Department's Policy Planning Staff, described as new "global coalitions . . . which will be in constant motion, coming together on one issue, but moving apart on another. Any state will belong to many different coalitions, with loyalties and interests that cut across traditional lines." Fortunately, this multifaced role was neatly tailored to America's domestic attributes, for "no other people have so well learned the workings of a pluralistic world and the political skills needed to keep it working. No other nation is composed of such diverse groups and shifting coalitions as the United States. Our domestic tradition is now our greatest international asset."[32] In this new world, where military power (at least among the strong) had lost much of its former utility, sophisticated managerial talents were now required to supervise the resolution of complicated transnational issues like economic growth and inflation, energy, nuclear proliferation, and the environment. Such a world would resist American efforts to impose solutions or dominate outcomes, but the United States could influence events by adroitly working in cooperation with other states.

Second, members of the Carter administration feared that the American public, wearied, disillusioned, and disgusted after a decade of war, scandals and assassinations, might well retreat into a bitter isolationism. At the same time they worried that the Vietnam War and Kissinger's unprincipled manipulation of U.S. power had led to the "philosophical isolation" of America in a hostile world. By emphasizing the role that human rights would begin to play in American foreign relations, both of these disturbing developments could be simultaneously addressed. Domestically, as we suggested earlier, a commitment to human rights would help restore the

American people's faith and trust in their government. Human rights could help erase the collective memory of horrors like My Lai, the secret bombing of Cambodia, Agent Orange, and CIA misconduct. More specifically, it could provide common ground for conservatives who complained that Kissinger had ignored Soviet human rights violations and liberals who deplored his permissive attitude toward brutal tyrants like the Shah of Iran, Anastazio Somoza, and Ferdinand Marcos. Moreover, as Brzezinski put it, "by emphasizing human rights America could again make itself the carrier of human hope, the wave of the future," and also "restore America's political appeal to the Third World.[33] President Carter, because of temperament and religious conviction, was particularly committed to this issue and seems to have been remarkably unconcerned about the potential geopolitical implications of this stance. There was, however, a general administration inclination to view human rights as a means to restore a domestic foreign policy consensus and to sustain U.S. international influence at a time of relatively declining American power.

Third, and perhaps most important, the Carter administration, like its Nixon-Ford-Kissinger predecessor, was searching for ways to restore a balance between diminishing resources and extensive international commitments. Carter's approach entailed a pragmatic, antidoctrinaire adjustment to this new reality through reducing commitments, shifting burdens, and accommodating rivals.[34] According to Leslie H. Gelb, Director of the State Department's Bureau of Politico-Military Affairs from 1977 to 1979:

> The environment we are looking at is far too complex to be reduced to a doctrine in the tradition of post–World War II American foreign policy. Indeed, the Carter approach rests on a belief that not only is the world far too complex to be reduced to a doctrine, but that there is something inherently wrong with having a doctrine at all.[35]

Doctrine, then, would be eschewed in favor of an approach in which every issue and commitment would be carefully examined "on its merits." Commitments could be shrunk by reducing U.S. arms sales and military assistance, by withdrawing troops from South Korea, by diminishing CIA covert activities, and by avoiding situations that might become other Vietnams. Burdens could be shifted by urging NATO and Japan to intensify their own defense efforts, by strengthening ties with China, and by relying more on emerging regional powers. And rivals could be accommodated by making détente more comprehensive, normalizing relations with erstwhile enemies like Vietnam and Cuba, and by defusing regional conflicts that might exacerbate U.S.-Soviet relations. The result was a foreign policy of geopolitical retrenchment that nonetheless reflected an optimism that an important American international role could be sustained through managerial competence and moral zeal.

The Carter strategy, with its stress on the management of shifting global coalitions and its focus on a long list of equally important policy objectives, surpassed in complexity not only the cold war strategy of global containment but also the Nixon-Kissinger reformulation. On that basis alone one might have expected from the Carter administration the same emphasis on dexterity, flexibility, and speed that Nixon and Kissinger had claimed required extreme tactical secrecy and centralization. But, of course, since the very identity of the Carter presidency depended on its firm rejection of the Nixon-Kissinger style, it could hardly emulate the tactical approach of the previous administration. Thus the Carter administration emphasized openness, honesty, and participation in spite of the dizzying complexity of its foreign policy agenda. As we will see in the next section, Carter repeatedly sought to win public support for his foreign policy by contrasting its democratic character to the deceptive tactics allegedly employed by recent presidents. Moreover, many of his early actions were clearly designed to demonstrate this difference as, for example, Carter's open letter to Andrei Sakharov, his public announcement of Cyrus Vance's SALT negotiating instructions prior to the March 1977 trip to Moscow, and the public unveiling of a Middle East peace strategy before discussing it with the relevant actors. The administration, by reinserting an "open covenant, an openly arrived at approach" into U.S. foreign policy, predictably offended other governments but, initially at least, seemed ready to pay that price in order to prove its moral integrity to the American people.

Like Nixon and Kissinger, Carter and his senior advisers were keenly aware that American foreign policy had lacked a firm domestic consensus since the mid-1960s.[36] Yet in contrast to Nixon and Kissinger, who largely regretted the passing of the cold war consensus, members of the Carter administration, with the partial exception of Brzezinski, tended to blame this consensus—and the policy of global containment which it had supported—for leading the United States into Vietnam. Leslie M. Gelb exemplified this attitude in a book published very soon after he left the State Department. In *The Irony of Vietnam: The System Worked*,[37] Gelb argued that the Truman Doctrine and the policy of anti-Communist containment that it sanctioned lay at the root of America's involvement in Vietnam. Presidents had not been dragged into Vietnam against their will nor had they been deceived by the foreign policy bureaucracy. Rather they had gone into Vietnam with their eyes wide open, because the doctrine and their convictions had demanded it. In short, Carter and most of his advisers wished to reconstruct a domestic foreign policy consensus but to do so with substantially different materials than those used to build the cold war base.

Carter recognized the importance of legitimating his foreign policy within the bureaucracy. He had, as we have seen, as a presidential candidate severely criticized Nixon's and Kissinger's efforts to subvert the State and Defense departments by centralizing power within the staff of the National Security Council. Nevertheless, Carter accepted most of Brzezinski's recommendations to create a decision-making process that seemed to grant primacy to the National Security Assistant and his staff. In practice, however, at least until late in the administration, Carter employed a multiple advocacy system whereby the president, after listening to the arguments of Vance, Brzezinski, Harold Brown, and sometimes Andrew Young, and others, would set policy. Because Carter found it useful to receive contradictory advice, he tended to underestimate the political damage caused by media accounts of policy disagreements.[38] Thus in an effort to infuse the policy process with openness, Carter risked creating a public perception of incoherence, which, in turn complicated his efforts to garner broad support for his foreign policy.

Very early in his administration President Carter attempted to explain his foreign policy to the bureaucracy by holding a rather unusual series of what were actually town meetings with large numbers of State, Defense, and CIA employees. After enumerating his objectives in exceedingly humble terms Carter then stood for questions from these bureaucratic audiences. Unlike his public town meetings, which continued throughout most of the administration, Carter did not repeat these forums, largely because he doubted their utility. Nevertheless, these exercises were designed to restore the morale of these agencies in the wake of their allegedly shoddy treatment by Nixon and Kissinger.

Similarly, Carter's efforts to legitimate *publicly* his foreign policy differed substantially from Nixon's. His consensus-building strategy in 1977 and 1978 involved six main elements: (1) a declaratory history of postwar American foreign policy that differed significantly from those of Truman, Eisenhower, Kennedy, Johnson, and Nixon; (2) an explanation of the ways in which the world had changed decisively since the end of World War II; (3) the repeated claim that his foreign policy reflected the character, values, experiences, and aspirations of the American people; (4) a portrayal of his foreign policy as courageously willing to deal comprehensively with extremely complicated issues in order to serve the long-term interests of the United States; (5) the assurance that America's strength allowed it to be generous and cooperative; and (6) the promise of an emergent world community characterized by greater justice and peaceful change. Nowhere in this public legitimation was there even a hint of retrenchment or retreat. Rather, at least during the administration's first two years, its rhetoric exuded optimism about the future.

The Carter administration's declaratory history constituted in several ways a revisionist account of post–World War II American foreign policy. In general, Carter said very little about that record and almost nothing about the historical themes that had been emphasized by every president since Truman. Those presidents had repeatedly invoked the events of the 1930s and their presumed lessons, as well as policy initiatives like the Marshall Plan, aid to Greece and Turkey, the North Atlantic Treaty, and the defense of West Berlin in order to celebrate America's firmness, prudence, and generosity. When on those very few occasions in 1977 and 1978 Carter did refer to the early postwar period, he contrasted its nature to the contemporary world. For example, in May 1977 he told the NATO Ministerial Meeting in London:

> In the aftermath of World War II, the political imperatives were clear: to build the strength of the West and to deter Soviet aggression. Since then East-West relations have become far more complex. Managing them requires patience and skill.
>
> Our sense of history teaches us that we and the Soviet Union will continue to compete. Yet if we manage this dual relationship properly, we can hope that cooperation will eventually overshadow competition.[39]

The use of a NATO forum to stress the management of complexity represented a significant departure from tradition, for presidents had routinely utilized these occasions to offer heroic accounts of the early cold war.

But even more noteworthy was Carter's indictment of important parts of America's postwar record. In his first major foreign policy address, President Carter directly criticized U.S. policy *aims* in Vietnam and implied that global containment had driven the intervention:

> For too many years we have been willing to adopt the flawed and erroneous principles of our adversaries, sometimes abandoning our own values for theirs. We have fought fire with fire, never thinking that force is better quenched

with water. This approach failed, with Vietnam the best example of its intellectual and moral poverty.

. . . [T]he unfortunate experience that we had in Vietnam has impressed on the American people deeply, and I hope permanently, the danger of our country resorting to military means in a distant place on Earth where our security is not being threatened.

Not since Franklin D. Roosevelt at Chautauqua in 1936 seemed to blame munitions makers and other profiteers for dragging the United States into World War I had a president so thoroughly condemned an American military effort. Carter's additional assertion that an "inordinate fear of Communism" had led the United States to "embrace any dictator who joined with us in that fear" threw the entire policy of anti-Communist containment into disrepute. He concluded this unorthodox account by arguing that America's traditional conviction that "Soviet expansion was almost inevitable" and "must be contained" had lost much of its validity in light of the "historical trends" that had "weakened its foundation."[40]

Finally, if Carter's declaratory history suggested that the United States's inappropriate fear of Communism and obsession with the Soviet Union had led it to abandon its principles and to define inappropriately its security interests, it also claimed that American foreign policy had historically paid too little attention to Africa and Latin America. This neglect had allegedly damaged U.S. relations with these continents and had further threatened the United States with philosophical isolation. Thus in February 1978 Carter told a town meeting that "until just recently our country played no significant role at all in Africa. Since I've been in office, we have greatly increased our interest, involvement, and influence in Africa." He emphasized this point by recalling that Nigeria had refused to permit Henry Kissinger to visit that country and by crediting Andrew Young for changing that situation.[41] Carter expressed similar sentiments in regard to South America and suggested that the Panama Canal treaties symbolized a new U.S. appreciation of that continent's stature.

In sum, the Carter administration's early declaratory history contrasted dramatically with previous presidential accounts of postwar American foreign policy. By ignoring certain U.S. actions and by indicting others, Carter sought to distance himself from the presumably discredited policy of global containment and its offspring, Vietnam, while simultaneously laying the foundation for his own foreign policy initiatives. We now lived in a complex new world, Carter repeatedly claimed, and historical analogies and lessons drawn from the 1930s and 1940s had lost their relevance as guides to the 1970s and 1980s.

Second, Carter sought to legitimate publicly his foreign policy by specifying the many ways in which the world had changed during the last three decades. In 1977 and 1978 President Carter and his advisers described this world as "new," "complex," and full of opportunities for the United States. In his Notre Dame speech Carter noted that "In less than a generation, we've seen the world change dramatically. . . . Colonialism is nearly gone. . . . Knowledge has become more widespread. Aspirations are higher." And although the world remained dangerously divided ideologically, economically, and racially, "America should not fear" this new world. "We should help to shape it" with "a new American foreign policy—a policy based on constant decency in its values and on optimism in our historical vision."[42] In October 1977 he told the United Nations General Assembly that "power is now widely shared among many nations with different cultures and different histories and different aspirations. . . . However wealthy and powerful the United States may be, however capable of leadership, this power is increasingly only relative. The leadership is in need of being shared."[43] In March 1978 Carter described a world that had "grown both more complex and more interdependent. There is now a division among the Communist powers. The old colonial empires have fallen. . . . Old ideological labels have lost some of their meaning. Over the past twenty years, the military forces of the Soviets have grown substantially, both in absolute numbers and relative of our own." Yet as he told a Nigerian audience the following month:

> Nothing can shake my faith that in every part of the world peaceful change can come and bless the lives of human beings. Nothing can make me doubt that this continent will win its struggle for freedom . . . from racism and the denial of human rights . . . want and suffering . . . and the destruction of war and foreign intervention.[44]

Thus while Carter acknowledged that the world would never be "perfect," he assured the "citizens of the world" in a United States Information Agency (USIA) telecast on Inauguration Day that "our desire is to shape a world order that is more responsive to human aspirations."[45]

Third, Carter believed that a foreign policy that reflected the values and aspirations of the American people could serve as a powerful tool in achieving national unity. Again and again he asserted that recent American foreign policy, both in its formulation and its content, had largely ignored the wishes of the public. If the people had been involved in discussing policy options instead of being deceived and dismissed by their government, "some of the mistakes that were so devastating to our country in the past" could have been prevented.[46] A more democratically made foreign policy, Carter suggested, would result in a wiser, more responsible foreign policy. Furthermore, if the people could choose an appropriate foreign policy, they would infuse it with a deep commitment to human rights. The American people would not support "the intrusion of American military forces into the internal affairs of other nations" unless "our security was directly threatened."[47] At the same time, Carter frequently recalled,

> We've been through some sordid and embarrassing years recently with Vietnam and Cambodia and Watergate and the CIA revelations, and I felt like it was time for our country to hold a beacon light of something pure and decent and right and proper that would rally our citizens to a cause.[48]

And since "we are not trying to send in troops to make other nations conform to us," "there has to be some means . . . for a President to exemplify or to personify what the American people believe. And my opinion is that the American people believe very deeply in the concept of human rights." Carter admitted that it would be difficult to measure tangibly the success of such a foreign policy, but he repeatedly assured the public that the policy was helping to improve the world, because "there's not a national leader on Earth who hasn't now in the forefront of his or her consciousness the question of human rights."[49]

Fourth, President Carter asked the public to support a foreign policy designed to tackle courageously a wide array of extremely complicated international problems. Issues like nuclear proliferation, conventional arms transfers, southern Africa, the North-South dialogue, and international trade were presented as urgent matters, but, in practice, Carter's public rhetoric focused on the Panama Canal treaties, the Middle East, and SALT. According to Erwin C. Hargrove, Carter deliberately took on hard cases, hoping to achieve domestic political benefits, yet willing to accept domestic criticism.[50] Overall he wished to project an image of policy competence, the leader of an administration prudently implementing preventive diplomacy to bring about a safer and more just world. As in the domestic realm, Carter tried to build policy coalitions to support these "comprehensive" initiatives, not on the basis of ideology or party loyalty, but because of their allegedly inherent good sense. Thus Carter inferred that the Panama Canal treaties symbolized not retreat or surrender but the generosity of a strong, confident nation unwilling to use its power to bully the weak; the Camp David Accords represented the triumph of reason and compromise over hatred and distrust; and the "deep cuts" SALT proposal of March 1977 went far beyond that contemplated by previous administrations in order to halt the nuclear arms race.

When each of these issues proved more intractable than Carter initially anticipated, he publicly argued that such delays were inevitable in light of their innate difficulties. For example, in response to repeated press queries about the protracted SALT negotiations, Carter described them as "complicated," "very complicated," "extremely complicated," and "extraordinarily complicated." But he sought to reassure the electorate that his administration could competently manage these complexities despite the fact that "he had a lot to learn." The period of détente had not ended, Carter reiterated, but because "we are now trying to address some questions that in the past have been avoided . . . I think the period of debate, disagreement, probing, and negotiation was inevitable. And . . . I have no regrets about the issues that have been raised that have proven to be controversial."[51]

Fifth, President Carter claimed that America's strength allowed it to champion human rights, practice preventive diplomacy, and deal constructively with the opportunities created by this complex, new world. There was, to be sure, some ambiguity in this message, for he repeatedly acknowledged that neither he nor the United States possessed the power or wisdom to solve all of the world's problems. Indeed, it had been the wrongheaded desire of previous administrations to dominate others, to oppose change, and to intrude into the affairs of other nations that had presumably begotten Vietnam. But President Carter nevertheless sought to camouflage the retreatist elements of his foreign policy behind an optimistic rhetoric that emphasized the "improved" role that the United States could play by generously cooperating with others.

Sixth, on those rather infrequent occasions that Carter publicly articulated the outlines of his grand design, he described it as "a wider framework of international cooperation suited to the new and rapidly changing historical circumstances."[52] Typically he would then list several issues that, if successfully confronted, would help to build a genuine world community. This reluctance to legitimate a comprehensive vision had multiple roots. Secretary of State Vance, who throughout 1977 and much of 1978, functioned as the president's primary source of advice, was deeply committed to a "case by case, step by step, stone by stone" approach and, like Gelb, Lake, and other State Department officials, wished to avoid imposing simple slogans on a complex global reality. That sort of thinking had presumably led directly to Vietnam. Carter, who had a genuine aversion to geopolitical abstraction, found Vance's attitude very congenial. Moreover, the grand design itself hardly suffered from an excess of conceptual clarity and would have been difficult for any president to capture compellingly for the public. At least some officials recognized the domestic liabilities of this incremental, nondoctrinaire approach. For example Paul Kreisberg, Vance's Deputy Director of the Policy Planning Staff (PPS), noted that it was a

> very subtle policy, and subtlety is a characteristic that is very hard to sell politically. It's hard to make a speech about change . . . which says there are fourteen major problems in the world, and we have to deal with them all. . . . [People] kept asking "Where are the priorities?," and the argument that the priority was the East-West struggle began to appear . . . more attractive [to the administration] by the end of 1978.[53]

Finally, according to the testimony of several senior advisers, Carter lacked deep and settled foreign policy convictions. He entered office committed to human rights but had not thought through the foreign policy implications. Rather, he viewed the issue primarily as a way to unite liberals and conservatives at home behind an appealing cause.[54] Carter possessed *inclinations* but few convictions. Nevertheless, these officials also believed that

> the Carter Administration was trying, maybe imperfectly, but valiantly, to devise a new consensus. . . . [W]hat the Carter Administration was trying to do at a minimum was to say, look, the world had changed dramatically, there are over a hundred new countries, there's economic interdependence, there's a whole series of problems that urgently need our attention . . . and our foreign policy has to be about a lot more things than it has been in the past.[55]

For PPS member John Holum this new domestic consensus was to be constructed on a "complex" foundation which included a "sensitivity" to change, especially in the Third World, a renewed concern for human rights, and arms control with the Soviet Union. But Holum admitted that no such new consensus ever emerged: "It was a tragedy that those new directions in foreign policy were so precariously based—they didn't have a popular foundation yet—that the whole thing could come unraveled over something like Iran."[56]

THE ARC OF CRISIS

Indeed, the "shocks" of 1979—the fall of the Shah and subsequent oil shortage, the Sandinista victory in Nicaragua, the discovery of the Soviet brigade in Cuba, the seizure of American diplomats in Teheran, and the Soviet invasion of Afghanistan—profoundly challenged the grand design and strategic objectives of the Carter foreign policy. Moreover, domestic shocks in the form of soaring inflation, rising unemployment, and a new energy crisis contributed to growing public and elite doubts about the ability of Carter to lead the nation. Polls showed approval ratings, especially for his handling of the economy and foreign policy, to be the lowest ever recorded.[57]

Although early in the administration Carter had been inclined to gravitate toward the advice offered by Vance—patience, prudence, and a step-by-step approach—these disturbing international events of 1979, as well as their astute political manipulation by domestic conservative critics like the Committee on the Present Danger and *Commentary*, accelerated Brzezinski's ascent in the foreign policy inner circle. That process had already begun the previous year, in part because of the continued Soviet arms build-up and its intensified "adventurism" in Africa, and in part because of Carter's disappointment with Vance's reluctance to be a more forceful public advocate for the adminstration's foreign policy. In addition, beginning in mid-1978 Brzezinski began to replace several original NSC staffers, like Jessica Tuchman Mathews, who had taken a "world order" approach with more East-West orientated people like Fritz Ermarth and F. Stephen Larrabee.[58] According to Ermarth, a former aide to Senator Henry M. Jackson,

> I was uncompromisingly of the view that the bear was coming out of his cage and was going to cause us no end of trouble. The United States was hourly falling behind in this challenge. My job was to cry alarm and mobilize resources, and that's what Brzezinski had me on the staff doing. There was no question about that.[59]

These personnel changes exacerbated the increasingly difficult State-NSC relationship, though Gelb's replacement in April 1979 as Director of Politico-Military Affairs with Reginald Bartholomew, a career Foreign Service Officer, was further evidence of the National Security Assistant's enhanced stature. The overall result was that Brzezinski seemed well placed to interpret the shocks of 1979 to a president who would soon face reelection.

Carter did not immediately nor wholly jettison the grand design and strategic objectives of 1977. Brzezinski, after all, had helped to formulate them. The shift in foreign policy outlook occurred haltingly and incompletely, though it became more pronounced after Afghanistan. Some senior State officials, Hodding Carter for example, doubted whether the president was even aware that the *Weltanschauung* had changed. The same, however, can not be said of Brzezinski, who by restoring an East-West focus to American foreign policy, tried to transform Jimmy Carter into another Harry Truman—in early 1948 an unpopular, but feisty, Democratic incumbent assailed by both Left and Right.

The "lessons of Vietnam" hovered like a mist around the Carter administration. Though rarely invoked explicitly, they informed many of its most important foreign policy statements. For example, on May 1, 1979, Secretary of State Vance delivered a speech in Chicago which, according to key aides, expressed his philosophy in an especially cogent manner. These officials further recalled that the wording of the following passage became the subject of a long and rather contentious discussion within the PPS. In the speech Vance asked:

> In seeking to help others meet the legitimate needs of their peoples, what are the best instruments at hand? Let me state first that the use of military force is not, and should not be, a desirable American policy response to the internal politics of other nations.[60]

In the words of one PPS member who participated in this debate:

> That word "desirable" was a compromise position between those who wanted to simply say that the use of military force is not an appropriate instrument, and those who felt that we could not rule that out in *every* circumstance. The great example that was given was . . . Saudi Arabia. The debate took place between the poles. And there was a lot of playing out of Vietnam in the course of that discussion both explicitly and implicitly.[61]

Vance himself apparently had difficulty in deciding the issue, and his indecisiveness highlighted a nagging problem for the administration: What *had* Vietnam "taught" America about military interventions? From the time of the Truman Doctrine's enunciation until the emergence of significant domestic opposition to Vietnam, presidents had reserved the right to intervene anywhere to "help free peoples" remain free. In essence, this meant that while the United States would abstain from military action in Eastern Europe (notwithstanding the rhetoric of rollback), it refused to rule out armed assistance for others, whether threatened from without or within. But, although the Truman Doctrine had given equal rhetorical priority to combatting external aggression and internal subversion, in practice, presidents invariably discovered evidence of outside support (usually Soviet) whenever they contemplated military intervention. Vietnam was no exception, and while the Johnson adminstration justified its policy in abstract, universalist terms, it consistently claimed that the war also represented an external (and illegal) aggression by Hanoi.

Vance sought to scale down the Truman Doctrine by explicitly reducing America's perceived stakes in *some* purely domestic upheavals. Military force would no longer be a desirable response to the internal politics of other nations, even, evidently, if free peoples were threatened by subversion. But if, for example, Islamic fundamentalists or Marxist revolutionaries toppled the Saudi monarchy and withheld petroleum, the United States, according to Vance's formulation *might* nevertheless be required to intervene—not to uphold some imperial principle of world order—but to ensure the economic survival of the West. According to this view, American security had not been at stake in Vietnam—a domestic revolution. But what if Western economic survival was not directly endangered by either domestic subversion or external aggression? Until Vietnam, presidents had assumed that all external aggressions threatened American security, but Vance's formulation seemed to alter the old equation. How would the Carter adminstration view, for example, a pro-Soviet coup in a Third World nation? Paul Kreisberg described the State Department attitude in the following way:

> I think that the notion that the Soviets were making a gain and that we had to draw lines and say "here, and no further" was really, from the State Department's point of view, alien to our basic thinking about the world. It implied that specific places around the world were turning points, and that if the Soviets gained influence in, for example, Ethiopia or South Yemen, or in any other given place, that this (a) was irreversible and (b) would transform fundamentally the strategic balance. [Our] approach was basically to say that the world is a place that is in constant flux, things are never totally black or white, and, on balance, Soviet influence has been diminishing in recent years in a whole series of countries that seemed to be firmly in the Soviet camp.[62]

Pluralism would thus render Soviet gains temporary and reversible in certain instances, but pluralism frequently required time to work, and in the meantime a policy of patience and restraint was susceptible to domestic American pressures for bold action.

Brzezinski was acutely aware of this problem and was more impressed than his State Department's counterparts with an additional danger: the psychological impact that the loss of a marginally important country might have on nations of vital significance. Although choruses of "Who Lost Iran?" and "Who Lost Nicaragua?" had not reached quite the crescendo of

"Who Lost China?" in the late 1940s, they were proving to be very damaging to the administration's desire to be perceived publicly as a pragmatic problem solver.

Moreover, the National Security Adviser had little patience with the State Department's agonizing that Vance's May 1979 speech represented. He had concluded by 1978 that too many in the Carter administration had overlearned the lessons of Vietnam by seeming to rule out the use of military force in *all* circumstances.[63] Even a pluralistic world might require American intervention in areas of questionable strategic significance in order to counter Soviet efforts to exploit and exacerbate turbulent situations. Brzezinski, in contrast to Vance, believed that the rapid and judicious use of force in places like South Yemen or Somalia could be justified in order to deny them to the Soviets or to bolster the morale of regional friends. In the words of a very close aide,

> I think that's one of the legacies of Vietnam—we are afraid to use power. The tragedy of Vietnam is that there are a series of people that were in the government who felt that the use of power was something alien to America, because it had been misused. I think that what we needed to do was to get at the selective use of that power instead of saying, "we can't do that."[64]

Carter, who had been initially inclined to side with Vance on this issue, gradually grew more sympathetic to Brzezinski's views until evidently embracing them in the aftermath of Afghanistan.

President Carter also gravitated increasingly toward Brzezinski on what one senior NSC official saw as the most fundamentally divisive issue of all that plagued the administration: whether or not the Soviet Union was a status quo power.[65] Indeed, it heavily influenced judgments about a host of problems including SALT and its linkage to Soviet behavior in the Third World, Nicaragua, U.S. support for the Shah, the meaning of the Soviet brigade in Cuba, the export of arms to China, and events in eastern Africa. On balance, Vance, whose top priority was superpower arms control, resisted placing regional and local issues in an East-West context, whereas Brzezinski showed a greater willingness to contain Soviet global pretentions through a variety of means including, if necessary, transforming SALT into a "carrot."[66]

By early 1980 the Carter administration, in reacting to the shocks of 1979 and the extremely damaging conservative attacks on it, unveiled what constituted a modified grand design and a new strategy that in important respects shared more with pre-Vietnam American foreign policy than with its own original world vision. Carter apparently continued to cling to the vision of an emerging cooperative global community but concluded that the Soviet invasion of Afghanistan, as well as Iran's seizure of the American diplomats, had severely damaged the likelihood that such a community would soon be realized. If the law-abiding and peace-loving nations of the world cooperated in punishing Moscow and Teheran for their transgressions, then the march toward global community could be resumed. The essence of the grand design remained valid, but its achievement would have to be postponed.

Carter's new strategy of containment comprised five main elements designed to punish the Soviet Union for its Afghan aggression and to deter it from launching additional invasions. First, the president pledged, in what the administration encouraged the press to call the Carter Doctrine, to take the necessary steps to protect the security of the Persian Gulf and southwest Asia. Second, the United States undertook a broad diplomatic effort to mobilize a host of nations, including China and members of the Islamic Conference and Non-Aligned Movement (minus Cuba), into a loose, anti-Soviet coalition. Third, the administration initiated an across-the-board effort to expand and modernize strategic general purpose forces, land, air, and sea capabilities, and the oft-delayed Rapid Deployment Force. Fourth, Carter cancelled or suspended an array of on-going negotiations with the Soviet Union involving, for example, the demilitarization of the Indian Ocean, the SALT II ratification, and the conventional arms talks. Indeed, the United States began to search for usable naval ports and arms recipients in eastern Africa, the Persian Gulf, and southwest Asia. Finally, the administration attempted to coordinate with NATO and Japan, with mixed success at best, a series of punitive measures against the Soviets, including a grain embargo, a variety of additional trade sanctions, and the boycott of the Moscow Olympic Games.[67] In designing this list Carter had asked all of the "relevant" bureaucracies to send him inventories of possible sanctions, and upon their receipt simply stapled them all together. Indeed, Carter's actions went beyond even Brzezinski's intentions who, unlike the president, appreciated the consequences of this massive shift in U.S. policy for Soviet-American relations. Whereas Carter fully expected to win quick Senate approval of SALT II early in his second term, Brzezinski suspected that some the administration's symbolic measures would provoke and humiliate Moscow without necessarily containing it, with the consequence of destroying the remaining vestiges of détente.[68]

In view of this *volte face* it is somewhat surprising that the resulting turmoil in the foreign affairs bureaucracy was not more widespread. Secretary Vance, of course, angrily resigned in April 1980 and delivered a blistering public attack on the administration's apostasy at the Harvard commencement in June. In his memoirs he described Carter's response to Afghanistan as having tipped the scales toward those favoring confrontation, but Vance himself believed that the Soviet action had "threatened the very basis" of superpower relations.[69] Vance resigned primarily because of his profound objections to the Iranian hostage rescue mission, though he had felt increasingly excluded from Carter's inner circle for more than a year. Brzezinski, for his part, had preemptively moved to mute criticism of this new policy within the NSC staff by beginning a house-cleaning operation in early 1979. Other would-be critics in the State Department like Gelb and Joseph S. Nye, Jr., Deputy Undersecretary for Security Assistance, Science, and Technology, also left the government that year. But perhaps the most significant factor in encouraging the bureaucracy to acquiesce in the new Carter approach was the growing fear of Ronald Reagan's election. Carter's hard line appeared eminently moderate in contrast to the Republican candidate's blusterings.[70]

President Carter's efforts to legitimate publicly his 1980 foreign policy involved six components: (1) a declaratory history of American foreign relations that emphasized the essential wisdom and continuity of that postwar record; (2) a predominately negative portrayal of international change; (3) a description of a complex, turbulent world that required a strong U.S. economy and military posture as the foundation for a truly cooperative global community; (4) the reassurance of American military superiority, after a period of neglect, due to his administration's far-sighted actions; (5) a plea for national unity at a time of unparalleled crisis; and (6) a series of theatrical exercises designed to underline the seriousness of the crisis and the administration's determination to confront it. On balance, this attempt to reconstruct a domestic foreign policy consensus bore a closer resemblance to the rhetoric of cold war presidents than to Carter's own previous behavior.

In contrast to his earlier revisionist accounts of past American actions, Carter now recited a much more traditional history that praised U.S. steadfastness in the face of Soviet aggressions. For example, in his 1980 State of the Union Address (he had not even wanted to deliver one in 1978 believing the custom to be imperial), Carter treated the last thirty-five years as a coherent unity in which "America has led other nations in meeting the challenge of mounting Soviet power." He recalled U.S. leadership in founding NATO, in containing Soviet challenges in Korea, the Middle East, and Berlin, and in facing the Cuban Missile Crisis. While describing Soviet-American relations as a combination of cooperation, competition, and confrontation, the president claimed that in invading Afghanistan, Moscow had taken "a radical and an aggressive new step . . . that could pose the most serious threat to the peace since the Second World War."[71] In April 1980 he proudly remembered how "in 1946 the United States stood firm against Soviet occupation of northern Iran, against Soviet-sponsored subversion in Greece, against Soviet demands on Turkey" and asserted that the Soviet Union continued today "to exploit unrest to expand its own dominion and to satisfy its imperial ambitions."[72] Deeming its "aggressive military policy . . . unsettling to other peoples throughout the world," he condemned the invasion of Afghanistan as a "deliberate attempt of a powerful atheistic government to subjugate an independent Islamic people." Carter predicted that if the Soviets remained in Afghanistan and extended their control to adjacent countries "the stable, strategic, and peaceful balance of the entire world will be changed."[73] In April, for the first time in his presidency, Carter invoked the events of the 1930s:

> It is extremely important that we not in any way condone Soviet aggression. We must recall the experience of 1936, the year of the Berlin Olympic games. They were used to inflate the prestige of . . . Adolph Hitler, to show Germany's totalitarian strength to the world in the sports arena. . . .
> The parallel with the site and timing of the 1980 Olympics is striking.[74]

And in February 1980, Carter pointedly quoted Harry Truman to the American Legion: "'It is not our nature to shirk obligations. We have a heritage that constitutes the greatest resource of this Nation. I call it the spirit and character of the American people.'"[75] In sum, Carter's linkage of the Soviets to the Nazis and President Truman to himself constituted a declaratory history that might have well been uttered in the 1950s.

Whereas the initial Carter rhetoric had welcomed international change and had emphasized the promising opportunities it provided the United States in helping to construct a better world, by 1980 President Carter usually portrayed it in largely negative terms. Thus in January he told Congress that his administration's policies had focused on three areas of change:

- the steady growth and increased projection abroad of Soviet military power
- the overwhelming dependence of Western nations on vital oil supplies from the Middle East
- the pressures of change in many nations of the developing world, including revolutionary Iran and a general uncertainty about the future.[76]

While he occasionally admitted that change could also bring benefits, Carter throughout the year stressed the centrality of global stability to his foreign policy objectives. Earlier optimistic references to "shifting coalitions" and getting on "the right side of change" ceased and were replaced by tones of concern appropriate to a world now described as in crisis.

By the last year of his administration Carter's complex world had grown turbulent and now required a strong U.S. economy and defense as its foundation. The vision of a truly cooperative global community remained, but the timetable for its achievement needed drastic revision. As he put it in February "we must face the world as it is. We must be honest with ourselves, and we must be honest with others."[77] Two months later he described that world as "not one world, but many. It's a more complicated world—. . . uncertain, suspicious . . . searching for balance."[78] In May he called it a "complex . . . turbulent" place and admitted that transforming it into a "global mosaic . . . will not be an easy task." Carter then emphasized that in such a world the two preconditions for an effective American foreign policy were "a strong national economy and a strong national defense."[79]

Whereas candidate Carter in 1976 had pledged to cut at least five billion dollars from the defense budget, in 1980, when running for reelection, he sought to take credit for reversing "a dangerous decline in defense spending" from 1969 to 1976, when "real defense outlays, that is constant dollars spent, declined every year." As he told the American Legion "only since 1977 have outlays for defense been increased every year. Our 5-year defense program through 1985 will continue this trend."[80] At a January press conference President Carter asserted that because he had "never doubted the long-range policy and long-range ambitions of the Soviet Union," his adminstration "had consistently strengthened the Nation's defense, after 15 years of a decrease in commitment."[81] As a result of these efforts "we remain the world's most powerful force, and the American people and the Congress are now united as one in keeping the United States second to none in military strength."[82]

Beginning with his Inaugural Address President Carter had repeatedly emphasized the importance of national unity to lay the foundation for a new American foreign policy and to formulate comprehensive solutions for urgent domestic and international problems. His crisis of confidence speech of July 1979 constituted an implicit admission of his failure to provide the leadership necessary to restore unity. The evidence suggests that Carter realized that the national outrage triggered by Iran and the Soviet Union in late 1979 had produced, at least in the short-run, a "rally round the president" effect that might conceivably be sustained through 1980. Carter attempted to use these twin crises to build the unity that had previously eluded him. Thus in mid-November 1979 he announced that "no act had so galvanized the American public toward unity in the last decade" as the taking of the American hostages. "We stand today as one people."[83] In early December Carter found the situation even more unprecedented, for "not since Pearl Harbor, some forty years ago, have we felt such a nationwide surge of determination and mutual purpose."[84] Two weeks later, in a truly remarkable statement, he suggested that "we must understand that not every instance of the firm application of the power of the United States is a potential Vietnam. The consensus for national strength and international involvement, already shaken and threatened, survived that divisive and tragic war."[85] Then, after the Soviet invasion of Afghanistan, Carter, in announcing a grain embargo, claimed that "I need the support of the American people. I believe that it's a matter of patriotism and . . . a matter of protecting our Nation's security."[86] On January 16, 1980, the president expressed pleasure "at the resolve and the courage and the unity of the American people."[87] Later that week, in dismissing the suggestion from David Broder that his appearance on "Meet the Press" had been timed with the Iowa caucuses in mind, he insisted that "our country is in a state of crisis."[88] But by May, with the Soviets still in Afghanistan and the American hostages still in captivity, Carter called for public understanding and support for a foreign policy that could not promise "instant success." Rather, "we must expect prolonged management of seemingly intractable situations and often contradictory realities."[89] In short, the "rally round the president" phenomenon had largely disappeared six months after the onset of crisis.

Finally, President Carter, who in 1976 had criticized the flamboyant style of Kissinger, now undertook a series of theatrical exercises designed to heighten the sense of urgency provoked by Iranian and Soviet actions. Of course, a certain theatricality had never been wholly missing from the Carter foreign policy. Recall, for example, the open letter to Sakharov, Vance's early "mission to Moscow," the elaborate Panama Canal treaties signing ceremony, the Carter-Begin-Sadat White House lawn party, and Carter's Middle East shuttle of March 1979. But these efforts were more than rivalled by such administration atmospherics as the president's Rose Garden strategy, whereby Carter vowed to remain in the White House until the hostage crisis had been resolved;[90] the dispatch of Clark Clifford, a living relic of the Truman Doctrine era, to the Persian Gulf; and the spectacle of the National Security Adviser aiming an AK-47 through the Khyber

Pass. Yet these efforts, though laden with heavy symbolism, seemed merely to emphasize Carter's immense frustration at failing to repatriate the hostages from Iran and dislodge the Soviets from Afghanistan.

A NEW FOREIGN POLICY CONSENSUS?

Did Jimmy Carter reconstruct the policy, procedural, and cultural components of a domestic foreign policy consensus? Did he successfully legitimate the grand design, strategy, and tactics of his foreign policy? To answer these questions we need to reemphasize the dramatic *policy* contrast, at least, between the "world order" initiatives of 1977 and "the neo-containment" actions of 1980. Did Carter rebuild a consensus around *either* of these policies?

Carter, like Nixon, remained exceedingly vague in his public statements about the nature of this grand design, but in contrast to his predecessor, who feared that the American people would not support an essentially *Realpolitik* vision, Carter's reticence stemmed from the genuine ambiguity of his design. What, after all, was a "truly cooperative global community" and what role would the United States play in it? President Carter did provide several clues to the American role: it would no longer rest on a rigid doctrinal foundation; it would tap its domestic experience to manage cooperatively shifting global coalitions; it would help resolve several nagging yet urgent regional and global problems; it would draw on its idealistic heritage to raise the global awareness of human rights; and it would not, of course, retreat into isolationism. But he failed to clarify exactly how this U.S. role would help realize a truly cooperative global community. Moreover, though many of his actions seemed designed to reduce or shift American commitments, he steadfastly refused to label them as such. Rather, the administration publicly claimed that by cooperating with, instead of seeking to dominate others militarily, the United States would actually *increase* its global influence. And though Carter implied that American interests were no longer indiscriminately global—Vietnam had not directly involved U.S. security—he refused to specify either their identity or their limits. Even worse, his public rhetoric about this crucial issue was sometimes dangerously confusing. Thus at a May 1978 news conference, after protesting that he was neither "preoccupied" with or "fearful" of the Soviets, he claimed that "we have a major vested interest in Africa. Our trade relationships are there. It's a tremendous developing continent. . . . In the past, we've not had an adequate interest there."[91] Did this statement mean that Africa now constituted a vital U.S. interest? Perhaps, but not apparently because of a growing Soviet presence there. Yet were America's *economic* stakes in Africa sufficient to deem the continent vitally important? It would have been difficult to make that case. This sort of sloppy, hyperbolic rhetoric repeatedly plagued Carter's efforts to articulate the foundations of American foreign policy.

If the grand design remained obscure, the accompanying strategy also proved difficult to legitimate. Time and again, when asked to explain his administration's strategy, President Carter would offer a long list of objectives drawn directly from Brzezinski's memorandum of April 1977. But he had enormous difficulty in demonstrating the relationship among the items listed, even though some of them seemed to contradict others, as, for example, détente and human rights. In this regard, James Fallows indicated his astonishment that Carter told him several times that liberty and equality were perfectly compatible concepts that could be pursued simultaneously.[92] So, perhaps, Carter believed Brzezinski's list constituted an integrated strategy.

But more likely Carter, suspicious of geopolitical abstractions in any case, simply found the notion of an integrated strategy to be largely irrelevant. In short, Carter attempted less to legitimate publicly a strategy than to win support for his managerial competence and his devotion to human rights. These were to serve as the bases for a reconstructed domestic foreign policy consensus. Neither, however, proved adequate to the task.

The "management of complex interdependence" had by the mid-1970s become a particularly fashionable phrase in the academic and foreign policy communities. Carter's tutelage at the Trilateral Commission had persuaded him of its desirability, and it gibed nicely with his own "problem-solving" inclinations. As president he surrounded himself with advisers similarly impressed with the phrase's import. These Trilateralists had been highly critical of Kissinger's reluctance to help manage the world economy, alliance relationships, and the North-South dialogue. The Carter administration believed that all of these things, as well as the phenomenon of pervasive global change, needed to be managed competently by the United States working in concert with others. And Carter especially thought that good policy in the international arena as in the domestic realm would help restore the American people's faith in their government and thereby help rebuild a consensus. The Carter administration did achieve two notable "management" successes: the Panama Canal treaties and the Camp David Accords. The latter substantially boosted the president's standing before a public who now perceived him as a peacemaker. But a large majority of the electorate saw the Panama Canal treaties not as the symbol of American strength and generosity that Carter had portrayed them, but as a dangerous act of weakness and appeasement. Carter, himself, on several occasions (before the hostage crisis and Afghanistan) called the ratification process the most unpleasant experience of his presidency. Moreover, as many analysts and participants have noted, he was forced to use up so much political capital that little was left in Congress when other problems, like SALT, needed to be managed later.

Then too, there seemed to be a nagging public perception about the administration's inability to deal competently with a host of foreign policy issues. An adminstration committed to the management of the world economy had immense trouble deciding on the fate of the dollar. An administration devoted to improving alliance relationships botched the neutron bomb issue, had difficulty persuading Western Europe and Japan to set meaningful energy import targets, and was openly ridiculed by West German Chancellor Helmut Schmidt. The North-South dialogue, as Carter was surprised to discover, carried with it a substantial price tag which the American people, beset by inflation, were unwilling to pay.[93] And when faced with two urgent examples of revolutionary change—in Iran and Nicaragua—the adminstration appeared as unable to "get on the right side" of it as its predecessors had been in Cuba and Vietnam. But more than anything else, in view of the relatively low priority given to foreign policy by the public in these years, it was the Carter administration's widely perceived failure to manage the American economy with competence that lowered rather than restored the people's faith in government. Carter's "misery index" of 1976, used to such great effect against Gerald Ford, would be brilliantly exploited in 1980 by Ronald Reagan.

If managerialism proved to be a slender reed on which to construct a new foreign policy consensus, so too did moralism. There were several reasons for the failure of human rights to provide a powerful core value around which the public could rally. First, as early as 1975, Carter, impressed with the broad-based domestic assault on the alleged amoralism of Kissinger's foreign policy actions, believed that human rights could unite liberals and conservatives behind an appealing banner. During the cold war anti-Communism had functioned in this manner, though liberals had insisted that, as the price for their membership in the coalition, U.S. economic development assistance be used to give anti-Communism a more positive dimension. Cold war presidents had, of course, frequently raised the issue of human rights but had done so almost exclusively in regard to the transgressions of Communist governments. Carter proposed to criticize the human rights behavior of all countries—including the United States, lest others claim him hypocritical—and to make U.S. aid and friendship contingent on that behavior. But after an initial flush of public and elite excitement about Carter's human rights rhetoric, the practical application of the policy provoked liberal and conservative ire as the adminstration attempted to deal "even-handedly" with nations that differed in strategic significance and over which the U.S. possessed differing degrees of leverage. According to the 1978 Chicago Council on Foreign Relations Survey (CCFR), whereas 67 percent of the public and 78 percent of the leaders thought that the United States ought to promote human rights abroad, only half of the public thought that Soviet treatment of its minorities was any "of our business," and only 40 percent agreed that the United States "should take an active role in opposing apartheid."[94] Among the elites, polls showed deep cleavages between "conservative internationalists," who criticized Carter for exerting excessive pressure on American "friends" in Manila, Managua, Santiago, Seoul, and Teheran, and for neglecting the human rights violations of Communist totalitarian regimes, and "liberal internationalists," who expressed the opposite sentiments. In summary, the attacks on Kissinger's "un-American" amoralism had actually constituted a *negative* consensus, and Carter's efforts to transform such criticism into a human rights policy quickly revealed the deep ideological divisions that a common dislike of Kissinger had partly disguised.

Second, in contrast to cold war anti-Communism, whose power had derived from the perceived enormity of the Soviet threat, human rights bore no apparent relationship to U.S. national security, except in the rather tortured sense that a "philosophically isolated" America would eventually become an endangered America. But the Carter administration failed to make even this case persuasively. Moreover, whereas anti-Communism had been used to justify a broad range of policies including nuclear deterrence, economic assistance, regional military alliances, and human rights, Carter's human rights approach lacked a compelling connection to many of his other initiatives, and thus remained more an irritating anomaly than an integral part of a coordinated strategy.

Finally, despite Carter's conviction that this issue could help restore the public's faith in the U.S. government after Vietnam, Watergate, and the CIA revelations, support for an active human rights policy was "a mile wide, but only an inch deep."[95] For example, the same CCFR 1978 survey that indicated that 67 percent of the public and 78 percent of the elites believed that American foreign policy should promote human rights abroad also showed that, when asked to list the two or three biggest international problems, a mere 1 percent of the public and 7 percent of the leaders chose human rights! Cold war anti-Communism could no longer provide a unifying core for U.S. foreign policy, but human rights, by itself, remained a peripheral concern for the public and the elites.

It is more difficult to judge the success of the Carter administration's efforts to legitimate its foreign policy tactics. They represented, it will be recalled, President Carter's overall approach to governing in the aftermath of Watergate—a general attempt to breathe openness, honesty, and decency into the entire policy-making process, including foreign affairs. This populist theme—while ridiculed by many foreign policy professionals as naive and dangerous—seems to have been broadly popular. The Bert Lance affair during the late summer of 1977 surely raised questions about the administration's commitment to elevated ethical standards, yet opinion polls throughout his presidency showed consistently that well over 70 percent of the public deemed Carter to be personally moral and admirable. Yet these same surveys indicated widespread dissatisfaction with his leadership abilities. It seems therefore, that these tactics proved both popular and largely irrelevant to the attempt to mobilize support for substantive policies.

The Carter administration then, could not reconstruct a foreign policy consensus on the basis of its early outlook and initiatives, and its dramatic *volte face* of late 1979 and 1980 in part represented a tacit acknowledgment of its failure. Yet as significant as these international shocks undoubtedly were in compelling this turnaround, the administration's behavior had also been strongly affected by the growing domestic political power of conservative and neoconservative counterelites. Groups such as the Committee on the Present Danger (CPD) and the American Security Council, along with their Congressional allies, had plagued the Carter administration from the beginning. Well-funded and well-connected, these organizations gained widespread media exposure for views that directly clashed with the administration's on a host of issues including SALT II, Africa, Central America, Soviet military strength and geopolitical intentions, the adequacy of the U.S. defense budget, and the advisability of the Panama Canal treaties. Moreover, Carter had seriously offended these groups by refusing to appoint a single member to his administration, preferring instead to surround himself with Trilateralists. He, in fact, came close to naming Paul H. Nitze to a top post, but after meeting with him in Plains, decided that his views were arrogant and inflexible.[96] The CPD had submitted fifty-three names to Carter and saw every one rejected, despite the group's heavily Democratic composition. When asked his opinion of Car-

ter's foreign policy team, Eugene V. Rostow, cofounder of the CPD, acidly replied, "My views are unprintable." Nitze expressed similar sentiments, noting that "every softliner I can think of is in government."[97] In addition, publications like *Commentary* and the editorial pages of the *Wall Street Journal* provided visibility for neoconservative intellectuals—many of whom had been liberal Democrats during the cold war—to undertake a merciless assault on the Carter agenda. As a result, Norman Podhoretz, Irving Kristol, Michael Novak, Peter Berger, and their confrères had begun to ridicule the administration's "world order" priorities well before the "shocks" of 1979. One particularly hostile statement by Carl Gershman, a Jeane Kirkpatrick protegé, neatly summarized the thrust of this dissent. Writing in *Commentary* in 1980 Gershman, apparently unimpressed by Carter's recent conversion, claimed that he had stocked the administration with a cabal of world order advocates, who, in their complete rejection of containment "had broken with thirty years of historical experience" and had repudiated the core of postwar American foreign policy. Furthermore, this new establishment

> had devalued the importance of national-security concerns . . . saturating American foreign policy with defeatism masquerading as optimism and "maturity" and "restraint," cravenly following international political fashion even if this meant denigrating the interests and values of one's own country, and worrying less about American security than about Soviet insecurity, in the nature of which virtually any Soviet action could be condoned or blamed on the United States.[98]

Composed mostly of members of the old cold war foreign policy establishment who had lost their nerve in the wake of Vietnam; radical intellectuals who prized equality more than liberty even if the price was totalitarianism; and neo-Wilsonian academics and foreign policy analysts who wished to breathe new purpose into an America staggered by Vietnam and Watergate, this elite, according to Gershman, formed the core of a "liberal-populist" governing coalition "wherein a southern president who campaigned as a populist staffed his foreign-policy bureaucracy with members of . . . the *new* foreign policy establishment."[99]

Ostensibly wracked by guilt and paralyzed by tendencies which bordered on isolationism and appeasement, at the heart of this group's outlook lay the conviction that military force was no longer a suitable foreign policy instrument for America to employ. Rejecting the bases of two generations of American foreign policy—the containment of Communism and the "lessons of Munich"—this new elite embraced the "lessons of Vietnam" as the foundation of a new American diplomacy. And from the primary Vietnam lesson—that containment was counterproductive, unfeasible, and unnecessary—this establishment, Gershman claimed, drew several corollaries. First, "world order" must replace "national security" as the organizing concept of American diplomacy. Second, the United States should adopt an attitude of "equanimity" toward changes in the world which previously would have been considered injurious to its interests. Third, because the Soviet Union was essentially a status quo power, American foreign policy ought not to be preoccupied with relations with Moscow. Fourth, to avoid isolation in a world filled with revolutionary change, America had to learn to become more flexible and less ideological in its dealings with the Third World. Finally, our moral strength, rather than a primary reliance on military power, should be used to help alleviate such "global problems" as hunger, racial hatred, and the arms race. For Gershman and his colleagues world order politics constituted a tragically naive departure in American foreign policy.

In place of such alleged wrongheadedness these articulate counterelites argued for, in effect, the reembracing of Soviet containment as the foundation of U.S. foreign policy, and they demonstrated notable success in wresting control of the agenda from the Carter administration. Indeed, the back-and-fill behavior of Carter during the last year of his presidency constituted an effort to placate these critics and to assuage a public that had grown increasingly alarmed by Soviet transgressions and frustrated by America's evident lack of international leadership. In part, of course, this public restiveness stemmed from the very success of the dissident counterelites in publicizing their message.

Yet Carter's rather frantic election year attempt to run as a Harry Truman, neocontainment underdog failed to impress the CPD and their allies. Unable to forgive his past sins, they doubted the depth and sincerity of his conversion. Moreover, these critics had found their own presidential candidate, someone who, unlike the "flip-flopping" Carter, seemed to possess long-standing, unshakable, anti-Communist convictions. With these conservative internationalists unappeasable and with many liberal internationalists highly critical of his lurch to the Right, Jimmy Carter was unable to reconstruct a domestic foreign policy consensus in the remaining months of his presidency. He tried to portray Ronald Reagan as a trigger-happy, dangerous radical and himself as a responsible moderate who would stand up to the Soviets without unleashing World War III. And, indeed, if foreign policy had been the sole issue in the 1980 election, Carter would have won. But only 15 percent of the voters ranked foreign policy as the most important problem, whereas 77 percent chose the economy. Double-digit inflation and rising unemployment—not foreign policy—combined to defeat Jimmy Carter. In sum, he did not bequeath to his successor a foreign policy consensus: détente was dead, the bear was prowling, a new cold war loomed, the public demanded billions more for defense. Yet neither these conditions nor this mood constituted a policy consensus. Elites remained deeply divided, and the public, while desiring a strong America, showed little inclination to support military interventions, even in the Persian Gulf.[100]

In contrast to Nixon, President Carter strove to reestablish a cultural consensus to undergird his foreign policy. Indeed, his intentions to relegitimate an ethic of sacrifice informed both his domestic and world order priorities of 1977 as well as his neocontainment efforts of 1980. Despite the optimistic tenor of his early presidential rhetoric, Carter nevertheless emphasized that the 1970s were a decade of limits: limits to what the president and the federal government could do, and limits to what the United States could do unilaterally in the world. To live gracefully within these limits, Carter intoned, Americans would need to restrict their appetites for government services and, especially, for petroleum. As in wartime all citizens would be called on to sacrifice for the common good. Yet Carter realized that sacrifices would not be made if the public sensed that special interests were receiving special privileges. He aimed, therefore, to devise comprehensive policies that would spread the burden evenly throughout the population. Similarly, his world order outlook implied a view that America could no longer dictate to or dominate other nations. Both multilateralism and nonintervention required restraint, maturity, and even a degree of sacrifice, for the wishes of others would be respected to a far greater degree than during the cold war. Carter's 1980 posture approximated more closely the pre-Vietnam ethic of sacrifice, for now Americans were asked to bear personal sacrifices in order to punish the Soviet Union, and some citizens—farmers, Olympic athletes, technology exporters, and nineteen-year-old males—were called on to perform special service for the nation.

Yet all of these efforts must be judged failures. First, the energy issue pitted producing states like Texas and Oklahoma against consuming states and collided with a public inclined to view the "crisis" as an oil industry conspiracy to raise prices. Carter proudly proclaimed that Congress' energy legislation had given him 65 to 70 percent of what he had asked and had far surpassed President Truman's accomplishments. But the compromises that Carter made in order to wage the "moral equivalent of war" appeared more like a meow than a roar, and undercut the president's crisis rhetoric. Second, neoconservatives seized on the "retreatist" dimensions of Carter's world order agenda and lambasted him for succumbing to a "culture of appeasement." America, they agreed, was in decline and had been for well over a decade. The failure in Vietnam, the nonreciprocal nature of détente, Watergate and the subsequent crippling of the presidency, the pathetic responses to OPEC and Third World radicalism, and, most important, our inability and unwillingness to counter the massive Soviet arms buildup were but the most dramatic examples of a profound and pervasive erosion of American power. This decline had to be perceived as part of a more general rotting of traditional liberal values. Employing moderate Democrats (or Republicans) like Madison and Tocqueville as benchmarks, critics decried the excesses of African-Americans, women, gays, and other minorities who sought more and more equality. The consequences of this "illiberal extremism" were painfully obvious: the fragmentation of the family, the eclipse of traditional religions, reverse discrimination, pornography, drugs, the spawning of an amoral psychoanalytic elite, and the growth of a culture of appeasement. Moreover, they condemned Carter for contributing to this decline by proposing a foreign policy agenda that, in demanding self-restraint while forgiving totalitarian transgressions, recalled the cravenness of interwar Britain. For them, Carter's ethic of sacrifice constituted disguised surrender. Finally, President Carter's belated reassertion of containment failed to resuscitate the old cultural consensus. Rather, his pleas for national unity at a time of crisis provoked the resentment of groups who felt unfairly victimized by the sanctions imposed on the Soviet Union. Farmers protested, athletes sulked, those required to register for the draft fretted, and neoconservative critics remained skeptical. Moreover, during a period of soaring inflation, even modest economic sacrifices appeared as terribly unfair burdens.

For someone who "just didn't like politicians" and who frowned on Congress as the seat of special interests, Jimmy Carter, more than any other modern president, consulted, informed, and even negotiated with legislators about foreign policy. There were two major reasons for this unprecedented effort to involve Congress in this process. First, as was true of so much of the administration's outlook, Carter and his advisers believed that after Vietnam, Watergate, and other examples of an imperial presidency run wild, it was necessary to rebuild popular and legislative trust in the executive. Vance, in his October 1976 memo had urged Carter "to make the Congress and the American people joint partners in foreign policy matters," and to use the presidency to educate both about the long-term interests of the United States. Carter, as we saw, sought to implement this advice by publicly announcing the Secretary of State's negotiating instructions in advance of his ill-fated trip to Moscow in March 1977. On the other hand, the White House demonstrated extreme secrecy in negotiating the Panama Canal treaties and in formulating its initial energy proposals (which certainly possessed foreign policy implications). In fact, the hostile Senate reception to the treaties compelled Carter to shift tactics dramatically in order to obtain ratification. The president, who early in 1977 had similarly provoked Congressional ire by preemptorily cutting twenty-nine water projects from his budget request, reversed course and undertook an intense and prolonged campaign of "horse-trading," "schmoozing," and "stroking." Forty-two senators and several House members visited Panama, and some even conducted negotiations with General Omar Torrijos after the treaties had been signed. Carter himself negotiated, often publicly, with Dennis De Concini, a freshman Democrat from Arizona, about a reservation that could have eviscerated the treaties. Rosalynn Carter lobbied the wife of Edward Zorinsky, a Nebraska freshman senator, as well as his friend, the Archbishop of Omaha. Yet despite Carter's enormous political investment, his appeals to the public failed to enhance the treaties' popularity; he could not marshal enough Senate votes; and the Senate leadership was forced to save him from disaster.[101] Moreover, the president's stature suffered serious damage as a result of these frequently self-demeaning actions.

In a similar fashion, the Carter administration engaged Congress in the SALT II process. In contrast to Nixon's handling of SALT, when only a handful of legislators monitored the progress of the talks, Carter appointed a diverse group of thirty senators and fourteen representatives as SALT II advisers. Nearly all the senators traveled to Geneva, participated in discussions with both the American and Soviet delegations, and reviewed the draft text of the treaty. As an agreement with the Soviets became imminent, Carter, in order to placate potential opponents, replaced Paul Warnke, his chief negotiator, with a less controversial figure. Unlike the Panama Canal treaties, whose contents were sprung on unsuspecting senators, the administration maintained constant liaison with Congress on SALT II. Nevertheless, none of these gestures prevented Henry Jackson from comparing the June 1979 Vienna Summit with Neville Chamberlain's 1938 journey to Munich, and Carter's withdrawal of the treaty from the Senate in January 1980 surely prevented its defeat.

Second, Congress, quite apart from Carter's willingness to involve it in making foreign policy, demanded to play a major role. By insisting on its alleged prerogative to codetermine human rights policy, to oversee intelligence operations, to veto a wide array of executive initiatives, including conventional arms sales and nuclear technology transfers, and to compel the executive to negotiate treaties with it, Congress reasserted its foreign policy rights in a manner unseen since the 1930s. In contrast to Nixon, who responded viscerally and vengefully to this revolt, Carter demonstrated surprising patience in attempting to fashion workable procedural arrangements with Congress. On only a single occasion did he publicly chastise it for unwarranted interference in foreign policymaking, and then he submerged his criticism within a general assault on the device of the legislative veto.[102] Indeed, Carter showed much more concern with Congress' reluctance to deal "comprehensively" with his domestic legislative program than with its repeated intrusion into the foreign policy process.

Yet the Carter administration nevertheless failed to construct a new procedural consensus. In part, the failure stemmed from the sweeping institutional changes that had recently occurred in Congress: the erosion of seniority, the multiplication of subcommittees often with overlapping jurisdictions, and the explosive growth of staffs. And, in part, it was rooted in more general developments: the accelerated decline of political parties and the proliferation of lobbies—some single issue, others with ties to ethnic groups and foreign governments. All of these changes helped to produce a dramatically more complex policy-making environment. In these circumstances the achievement of an executive-legislative foreign policy procedural consensus became more difficult.

But these institutional and para-institutional obstacles, though undeniably important, masked a more fundamental problem—the absence during the Carter adminstration of a *policy* consensus about such issues as the requirements of U.S. security, the conditions in which American military power should be sanctioned, the strength and intentions of the Soviet Union, and the nature of change in the contemporary world. In those relatively rare instances of broad policy agreement, institutional impediments were easily surmounted. For example, Congress generously funded the Camp David Accords, despite their expense and despite a raging domestic inflation, because they were perceived as intrinsically valuable. Carter, moreover, had obtained the agreements through a combination of secret and shuttle diplomacy and had not involved legislators in the process, yet Congress seemed unconcerned by this "Kissingerian" display. Similarly, the establishment of formal diplomatic relations with China proved domestically so popular that Barry Goldwater and a handful of senatorial conservatives, lacking the votes to wage a political battle against this action, retreated to federal court to protest the alleged unconstitutional abrogation of the Mutual Defense Treaty with Taiwan.[103] On the other hand, the security implications of Salt II and the Panama Canal treaties provoked deep disagreement in Congress, and Carter's endless attempts to find an acceptable *procedure*, especially with SALT, merely reflected the underlying *policy* dissensus.

NOTES

1. "Remarks and a Question-and-Answer Session with Editors and Broadcasters," September 21, 1979, *Public Papers of the Presidents, 1979, II* (Washington, DC: Government Printing Office, 1980): 1714.

2. Jules Witcover, *Marathon: The Pursuit of the Presidency, 1972–1976* (New York: New American Library, 1977), Martin Schram, *Running for President: A Journal of the Carter Campaign* (New York: Simon & Schuster, 1977); and Betty Glad, *Jimmy Carter: In Search of the Great White House* (New York: W. W. Norton, 1980): chapters 11–20.

3. Warren E. Miller, "Misreading the Public Pulse," *Public Opinion*, II (1979): 11; "Opinion Roundup," *Public Opinion* II (1979): 30–1.

4. Witcover, 111.

5. Recall, for example, the widely publicized exploits of representatives Wilbur Mills (D-AK) and Wayne Hays (D-OH).

6. Charles O. Jones, *The Trusteeship Presidency: Jimmy Carter and the United States Congress* (Baton Rouge: Louisiana State University Press, 1988), 17.

7. *Gallup Opinion Index*, 71 (September 1980): 24.

8. Jones, 18.

9. Jimmy Carter, *Why Not the Best?* (Nashville: Broadman Press, 1975), 154, 145.

10. Carter, 146.

11. Jimmy Carter, "Inaugural Address of President Jimmy Carter," January 20, 1977, *Public Papers of the Presidents, 1977, I* (Washington, DC: Government Printing Office, 1977): 2.

12. Jimmy Carter, "Remarks at a Luncheon for Members of the Democratic National Committee's National Finance Council," April 28, 1977 *Public Papers, 1977, I*: 736–7.

13. Jones, 1.

14. For example, in May 1977, in a pointed criticism of George Meany of the AFL-CIO, Carter suggested that "it would be good for special interests of all kinds —labor, business, environment, and others—to cooperate and express a partnership in things that are accomplished for the [public] good" (Jimmy Carter, "The President's News Conference of May 12, 1977," *Public Papers, 1977, I*: 865).

15. Erwin C. Hargrove, *Jimmy Carter as President: Leadership and the Politics of the Public Good* (Baton Rouge: Louisiana State University Press, 1988), chapters 1 and 2.

16. James Sterling Young, "Foreword" in Hargrove, xx.

17. Jimmy Carter, "Address to the Nation on Energy and National Goals," July 15, 1979, *Public Papers, 1979, II*: 1236, 1237.

18. Carter, "Energy and National Goals," July 15, 1979: 1237–8.

19. Carter, "Energy and National Goals," July 15, 1979: 1238.

20. Carter, "Energy and National Goals," July 15, 1979: 1238.

21. Carter, "Energy and National Goals," July 15, 1979: 1238–40.

22. Jimmy Carter, "Remarks at the 13th Constitutional Convention of the AFL–CIO," November 15, 1979, *Public Papers, 1979, II*: 2124.

23. Austin Ranney, "The Carter Administration," in Austin Ranney, ed., *The American Elections of 1980* (Washington, DC: The American Enterprise Institute, 1980), 5.

24. Stanley Hoffmann, *Primacy or World Order: American Foreign Policy Since the Cold War* (New York: McGraw–Hill, 1978), 111.

25. Hargrove, 120.

26. Zbigniew Brzezinski, *Power and Principle: Memoirs of the National Security Adviser, 1977–1981* (New York: Farrar, Straus & Giroux, 1983), 53.

27. Brzezinski, 52–4.

28. Brzezinski, 56.

29. Brzezinski, 57.

30. Cyrus Vance, *Hard Choices: Critical Years in America's Foreign Policy* (New York: Simon & Schuster, 1983), 441–2.

31. Background interviews, Washington, DC, 1981 and 1982.

32. W. Anthony Lake, "Pragmatism and Principle in U.S. Foreign Policy," Address to the Boston Council of World Affairs, June 13, 1977 (Washington, DC: U.S. Department of State, *Current Policy* No. 269).

33. Brzezinski, 3.

34. David G. Skidmore, "The Politics of Decline: International Adjustment versus Domestic Legitimacy during the Carter Administration," Unpublished essay, 1989: 10.

35. Skidmore, 18.

36. Background interviews, 1981 and 1982. Hodding Carter III, personal interview, March 23, 1989.

37. Leslie H. Gelb, with Richard K. Betts, *The Irony of Vietnam: The System Worked* (Washington, DC: The Brookings Institution, 1978).

38. Hargrove, 118.

39. Jimmy Carter, "Remarks at the First Session of the NATO Ministerial Meeting," London, May 10, 1977, *Public Papers, 1977, I*: 849.

40. Jimmy Carter, "Address at the Commencement Exercises at the University of Notre Dame," May 22, 1977, *Public Papers, 1977, I*: 956.

41. Jimmy Carter, "Remarks at a Question-and-Answer Session at a Town Meeting with New Hampshire High School Students," February 18, 1978, *Public Papers of the Presidents, 1978, I* (Washington, DC: Government Printing Office, 1979): 374.

42. Carter, "Notre Dame Address," 957.

43. Jimmy Carter, "Address before the United Nations General Assembly," October 4, 1977, *Public Papers of the Presidents, 1977, II* (Washington, DC: Government Printing Office, 1978): 1716, 1722–3.

44. Jimmy Carter, "Remarks at the National Arts Theatre," Lagos, Nigeria, April 1, 1978, *Public Papers, 1978, I*: 650–1.

45. Carter, "Inaugural Address," 4.

46. Jimmy Carter, "Question-and-Answer Session with a Group of Publishers, Editors, and Broadcasters," June 24, 1977, *Public Papers, 1977, II*: 1174.

47. Carter, "Publishers, Editors, and Broadcasters," 1166.

48. Jimmy Carter, "Remarks and a Question-and-Answer Session with a Group of Editors and News Directors," July 15, 1977, *Public Papers, 1977, II*: 1274.

49. Jimmy Carter, "Remarks and a Question-and-Answer Session with Members of the Advertising Council, Inc.," June 22, 1977 *Public Papers, 1977, I*: 1147.

50. Hargrove, 142.

51. Jimmy Carter, "The President's News Conference of July 12, 1977," *Public Papers, 1977, II*: 1239.

52. Carter, "Notre Dame Address," 960–1.

53. Paul H. Kreisberg, personal interview, June 13, 1981.

54. Hodding Carter interview.

55. John Holum, personal interview, May 27,1981.

56. Holum interview.

57. "Opinion Roundup," *Public Opinion II* (1979): 29.

58. Brzezinski had appointed to the NSC staff several advisers to losing or would-be Democratic presidential candidates of 1976.

59. Fritz Ermarth, personal interview, May 22, 1981.

60. Cyrus Vance, "Meeting the Challenges of a Changing World," Address before the Chicago Council on Foreign Relations, June 1, 1979" (Washington, DC: U.S. Department of State, *Current Policy* No. 383).

61. Background interview, 1981.

62. Kreisberg interview.

63. Three weeks after the 1980 election Brzezinski publicly denounced "do-gooders" in the administration and the Democratic party who had been "traumatized by the experience of Vietnam because their party 'was responsible for the policies that produced the debacle'" (*New York Times*, November 29, 1980: 1). Although critical of Ronald Reagan for his alleged desire to achieve military superiority, Brzezinski "asserted that his attempts to expand military strength had encoun-

tered 'a great deal of opposition within the administration' and within 'a party which was automatically fearful that any emphasis on competition meant you were wanting to revive the cold war.'" (20).

64. Background interview, 1981.

65. Hargrove, 153.

66. Yet after Afghanistan even Vance declared that "our relations with the Soviet Union have been and will be essentially competitive." Quoted in Garthoff, 968.

67. Garthoff, 972–4.

68. Garthoff, 967. Background interview, 1989.

69. Vance, *Hard Choices*, 394.

70. Background interviews, 1981 and 1982.

71. Jimmy Carter, "The State of the Union Address before a Joint Session of the Congress," January 23, 1980, *Public Papers of the Presidents, 1980–81, II* (Washington, DC: Government Printing Office, 1981): 195–6. Two weeks earlier he had stated flatly that the invasion was the greatest threat to world peace since World War II (*Public Papers, 1980–81, I*: 40).

72. Jimmy Carter, "Remarks and a Question-and-Answer Session at the Annual Convention of the American Society of Newspaper Editors," April 10, 1980, *Public Papers, 1980–81, I*: 633–4.

73. Jimmy Carter, "Address to the Nation on the Soviet Invasion of Afghanistan," January 4, 1980, *Public Papers, 1980, I*: 22.

74. Carter, "American Society Remarks," 635.

75. Jimmy Carter, "Remarks at the Annual Convention of the American Legion," February 19, 1980, *Public Papers, 1980–81, I*: 349.

76. Jimmy Carter, "Annual Message to the Congress on the State of the Union," January 21, 1980, *Public Papers, 1980–81, I*: 162.

77. Carter, "American Legion Remarks," 348–9.

78. Carter, "American Society Remarks," 632.

79. Jimmy Carter, "Address before the World Affairs Council of Philadelphia," May 9, 1980, *Public Papers, 1980, I*: 868, 869.

80. Carter, "American Legion Remarks," 347.

81. Jimmy Carter, "Interview on 'Meet the Press,'" January 20, 1980, *Public Papers, 1980, I*: 111.

82. Carter, "American Legion Remarks," 344.

83. Carter, "AFL-CIO Remarks," 2124.

84. Jimmy Carter, "Remarks concerning Candidacy and Campaign Plans," December 2, 1979, *Public Papers, 1979, II*: 2194.

85. Jimmy Carter, "Remarks to Members of the Business Council," December 12, 1979, *Public Papers, 1979, II*: 2233.

86. Jimmy Carter, "Remarks at a White House Briefing for Members of Congress," January 8, 1980, *Public Papers, 1980–81, I*: 42.

87. Jimmy Carter, "Remarks and a Question-and-Answer Session with Editors and News Directors," January 15, 1980. *Public Papers, 1980–81, I*: 88.

88. Carter, "Meet the Press," 109.

89. Carter, "Philadelphia Address," 873.

90. And until Edward M. Kennedy (D-MA) had been defeated.

91. Jimmy Carter, "The President's News Conference of May 25, 1978," *Public Papers, 1978, I*: 978–9.

92. James Fallows, "The Passionless Presidency," *Atlantic Monthly 233* (May 1979): 36.

93. Background interview, 1982.

94. John E. Rielly, *American Public Opinion and U.S. Foreign Policy, 1979* (Chicago: Chicago Council on Foreign Relations, 1979), 13–14.

95. Skidmore, 27.

96. Strobe Talbott, *The Master of the Game: Paul Nitze and the Nuclear Peace* (New York: Alfred A. Knopf, 1988), 149.

97. Quoted in Jerry W. Sanders, "Empire at Bay: Containment Strategies and American Politics at the Crossroads," *World Policy Paper No. 25* (New York: World Policy Institute, 1983): 7.

98. Carl Gershman, "The Rise and Fall of the New Foreign-Policy Establishment," *Commentary*, July 1980: 24.

99. Gershman, 20.

100. See, for example, William Schneider, "The Public and Foreign Policy," *Wall Street Journal*, November 7, 1979: 26.

101. William L. Furlong, "Negotiations and Ratification of the Panama Canal Treaties" in John Spanier and Joseph Nogee, eds., *Congress, the Presidency, and Foreign Policy* (New York: Pergamon Press, 1981), 103.

102. Jimmy Carter, "Message to the Congress on Legislative Vetoes," June 21, 1978, *Public Papers, 1978, I*: 1146–49.

103. *Goldwater v. Carter*, 617 F. 2nd 697 (DC Cir. 1979), vacated with directions to dismiss, 100 Sup. Ct. 533 (1980).

CHAPTER 4

The Reagan Administration

In contrast to Jimmy "Who?", an obscure former governor about whom little was known even after his election in 1976, Ronald Reagan entered the White House as the most recognizable president since Dwight Eisenhower. But unlike the general, whose fame rested on his military record and not on his largely mysterious political outlook, Reagan's long–standing notoriety derived from a distinctive political philosophy articulated and reiterated for over twenty years. Indeed, conservatives had dreamed of a Reagan presidency since the eve of the 1964 election, when he had delivered a memorable nationally televised speech in support of Barry Goldwater. Yet by 1980, after two failed bids for the Republican nomination and nearing his seventieth birthday, Reagan risked becoming another Harold Stassen. Political pundits, especially those who prognosticated "inside the beltway," were confident that as an ex-actor and a right-wing ideologue, Reagan could never be elected president, and it was widely reported that he was Jimmy Carter's favorite potential opponent. Despite the warnings of Edmund "Pat" Brown, whom Reagan had thrashed in the 1966 California gubernatorial election, the Carter White House believed that once Reagan's "real," that is, "extremist," views on social security, foreign policy, the environment, and other issues were effectively publicized, the electorate would be frightened into voting for the incumbent. Moreover, Carter's advisers evidently anticipated a campaign in which Reagan's legendary "gaffes" would multiply and expose him as unqualified and irresponsible. They attempted, in short, to imitate Lyndon Johnson's successful 1964 strategy against Goldwater.

But, of course 1980, for many reasons, was not 1964, and the most important difference was the woeful condition of the U.S. economy. With inflation, interest rates, unemployment, and gasoline prices soaring, the "misery index," which had served Carter so well against Ford, was used to even greater effect by Reagan. To these seemingly intractable economic problems Governor Reagan offered a simple, "supply-side" solution: cut taxes and slash domestic social spending. If these actions were taken, the artificially shackled economy would respond with robust growth. George Bush, independent candidate John Anderson, and President Carter all pointed out the impossibility of doing these things, while drastically increasing defense spending, without incurring massive budget deficits. Reagan nevertheless insisted that his program could square the circle by stimulating savings, investment, and productivity. In 1976 Carter had suggested that an overregulated economy and the runaway growth of the federal government needed to be checked. Four years later Reagan much more loudly conveyed a similar message and blamed Carter and the Democrats for producing these very evils. Carter, who had run against Washington in 1976, now found himself portrayed as part of the problem by another anti-Washington candidate.

Jimmy Carter had the ignominious distinction to be the first elected incumbent since Herbert Hoover and the first Democratic president since Grover Cleveland to be defeated. And to be drubbed by someone commonly believed too "ideological" to win the presidency only magnified Carter's loss. Yet post-election surveys indicated that Reagan owed little, if any, of his victory to foreign policy issues. Despite his insistence that American foreign policy under Carter had been characterized by weakness, retreat, confusion, humiliation, and naiveté, Reagan was perceived by a plurality of voters as trigger-happy and potentially dangerous. That the electorate nonetheless presented Reagan with a landslide victory reflected its willingness to take a chance at a time of acute economic distress.

WE THE PEOPLE

Notwithstanding the apparent gulf that separated Carter and Reagan during the 1980 campaign, the new president's priorities closely paralleled those pursued by his opponent since 1977: the restoration of the economy, national self-confidence, and America's standing in the world. But whereas Carter had sought to achieve these goals by offering a long list of "good" policies, by trying to embody the nobility of the national character, and by "speaking out" on human rights, Reagan relied on a simple, understandable, comprehensive, and unusually consistent political philosophy presented with the help of often dazzling rhetoric to mobilize support for his priorities. Far from disqualifying him from the presidency, his acting (and sports broadcasting) background provided a hugely valuable asset in communicating with the citizens of the "electronic commonwealth."[1] In contrast to Carter, a plodding speaker with a sing-song voice that "dropped like a wounded bird at the end of his phrases, frequently fading into total inaudibility,"[2] Reagan's mellifluous baritone, craggy good looks, and easy affability thrived behind microphone and camera. Though his improvised remarks and press conference performances often revealed a shocking lack of substantive knowledge, the mere prospect of a nationally televised presidential address invariably sent tremors of fear through congressional Democrats. Reagan's uncanny ability to deliver lines sincerely, narrate poignant stories, and publicly evince an impressive range of emotions—all firmly hitched to an unwavering public philosophy—combined to make him a formidable rhetorical president.

In a fundamental sense Ronald Reagan continued the domestic political project begun by Richard Nixon. Nixon before Watergate had begun to build a new coalition—the "real majority"—from groups that shared a common resentment of New Class liberals, Great Society excesses, federal social engineering, and creeping permissiveness. Reagan mined this populist vein throughout the 1970s, but did so more systemically, programmatically, and consistently than Nixon. By forging bonds among previously disconnected (or nonexistent) groups—the Moral Majority, working class "ethnics," neoconservative intellectuals, big and small business, "yuppies"—Reagan entered the presidency as the spearhead of a movement that seemed poised to replace the New Deal coalition as the dominant constellation in American politics. It was, to be sure, like its predecessor, a potentially unstable amalgam comprised of people with partly clashing political, economic, and social agendas. Issues like school prayer, abortion, and women's rights—immune to compromise—threatened to be especially disruptive. Yet in the short run, at least, this emerging coalition agreed with Reagan that "individual freedom is the touchstone of good government; government power, especially when it is centralized in Washington, is to be distrusted; free enterprise is the key to economic and personal liberty; the role of government is to assure equal opportunity, not to mandate particular results;"[3] and it is the unique responsibility of the federal government to provide a strong national defense.

President Reagan's initial priorities simply and neatly captured these convictions. The insidious growth of governmental regulations would be reversed in order to liberate the "entrepreneurial spirit" for investment and productivity increases. Dramatically reduced tax rates would stimulate savings, investment, and growth. Federal social programs would be dismantled, and their funds returned to state and local governments as block grants. Accelerated defense spending would enhance America's military capability and help restore national pride and international respect. Reagan paid lip service to more divisively controversial issues like school prayer, abortion, law and order, and "reverse discrimination," but almost always before carefully chosen conservative audiences, and never to obscure his economic and defense priorities.

In Nixon's version of America the honest, hard-working, patriotic new majority had found itself constantly menaced by a privileged, selfish, effete, unscrupulous minority—an enemy who remained permanently outside the mainstream. Reagan's more ideological populism could certainly have been used to darken further this discordant portrait. On occasion, as we will see in our discussion of Central America, Reagan did lash out at those who obstructed his policies, but as a general rule, in speech after speech throughout two terms, he sought support for his programs by rhetorically portraying an America brimming with love and kindness and populated with caring neighbors, eager to volunteer their help to the community, if only the government would unshackle them. One prescient commentator, a speech communication scholar, accurately dubbed this powerful rhetorical creation, "MisteReagan's Neighborhood," designed to unify the nation, impel action, and insulate the president from criticism.[4] Drawn from familiar themes rooted in the American "civil religion," Reagan's rhetoric wove a seamless tapestry of "morality, heritage, boldness, heroism, and fairness" that offered a compelling, if rather fanciful, vision of a genuine national community. Composed of "extraordinary 'ordinary' Americans who never make the headlines and will never be interviewed," Reagan's nation was fundamentally good and decent.[5] He characteristically defined the citizenry in terms of occupations as, for example, in the first Inaugural Address: "men and women who raise our food, patrol our streets, man our mines and factories, keep our homes, and heal us when we're sick—professionals, industrialists, shopkeepers, clerks, cabbies, and truckdrivers."[6] These constituted the everyday heroes of America, who, through teamwork and partnership, labored to construct a cooperative community.[7] Moreover, sick and tired as they had grown of excessive taxation, runaway inflation, and a burdensome, meddling federal government, these sturdy folk had in the 1980 election "sent a message" to Washington to lower taxes, curb federal spending, and return political power to "we the people." Time and again, like the narrator in an apocryphal Frank Capra film, Reagan told stories about Americans who, instead of passively awaiting governmental assistance, joyfully volunteered to build a better community. Thus economic and political freedom, far from unleashing greed and license, encouraged compassion and quiet heroism.

We the people, a more inclusive and magnanimous notion than Nixon's new majority, allegedly faced a genuine economic crisis in the early 1980s, and Reagan, of course, blamed the federal government for causing it—"tax and spend" legislators who enacted expensive laws and regulations, and bureaucrats who implemented and administered them. At the same time, however, he sometimes acknowledged that government had grown, at least in part, in response to the people's demands. For example, in February 1981 President Reagan noted that "*we all* had a hand in looking to government for benefits, as if government had some source of revenue other than our earnings."[8] Even he, the former New Deal Democrat, "had for a time accepted government's claim that [taxing and spending] was sound economics."[9] Many "well-intentioned but misguided people" had persisted in their wrongheadedness. Yet, Reagan—whose domestic community required no permanent enemies—seemed confident that someday soon they too—like he and "the people"—would mend their ways. For "the problem isn't who to blame; it's what to blame," and the problem was government, with its built-in "tendency to grow."[10]

In bold contrast to Carter, who wondered publicly about the sources of the contemporary national "moral and spiritual crisis," Ronald Reagan repeatedly pointed to individual acts of heroism as convincing proof that America remained a good and vibrant society. Secret Service agent Tim McCarthy, airliner crash rescuer Lenny Slotnick, Space Shuttle astronauts, community volunteers, and the marines in Beirut were invoked to demonstrate that "America never was a sick society." Indeed, "the heart of America is strong; it's good and true. . . . We're seeing rededication to bedrock values of faith, family, work, neighborhood, peace, and freedom—values that bring us together as one people, from the youngest child to the most senior citizen."[11] For Reagan, America constituted a genuinely moral community of individuals with shared values and a common purpose, and his ability to convey this appealing vision in human and understandable terms greatly contributed to his personal popularity.

And, not surprisingly, this uniquely virtuous community—this "shining city on a hill"—had been providentially instructed to bring freedom and peace to the rest of the world. According to Reagan, American foreign policy reflected the selflessness, goodness, peacefulness, and generosity of the American people. In fact, virtually everyone in the world allegedly shared the same values and aspirations as the members of the American community, though many had been frustrated by the actions of oppressive governments. Evil still existed—particularly in the Soviet Union (at least before 1988)—but Reagan evinced growing confidence that the rising tide of democratic revolutions would sweep away the remnants of totalitarianism.

Reagan's rhetorical vision reflected four underlying themes—antigovernment nationalism, communitarian individualism, free market radicalism, and Wilsonian internationalism—which together formed a seamless web that purported to dip deeply into the American experience, but, in fact constituted only one part of it.[12] First, in continually celebrating the American spirit, Reagan discovered a preexisting *nation* of individuals dedicated to the common interest and general welfare, waging a heroic struggle against a late-arriving, alien, corrupt national government held hostage by special interest groups. In March 1982 Reagan asked,

> Did we forget that government is the people's business, and [that] every man, woman, and child becomes a shareholder with the first penny of tax paid? . . . Did we forget that the function of government is not to confer happiness on us, but just to get out of the way and give us the opportunity to work out happiness for ourselves?[13]

In this manner, as Hugh Heclo correctly noted, Reagan revived "a rhetoric older than the Constitution itself—the country versus the court—the real nation perceived as morally superior to a corrupt government."[14] Furthermore, this concept of a nation of individuals pitted against overweening centralized powers in Washington gave voice to those "Main Street" Americans who had felt victimized by the Great Society, as well as the youthful dissenters of the 1960s who had urged the return of "power to the people." Second, with the theme of communitarian individualism Reagan sought to disarm liberal critics who claimed that his real goal was to reward the rich and brutalize the poor by crippling the federal government. But Reagan turned the tables by arguing that federal social engineers, suffering from moral relativism and secular humanism, were determined to impose their perverted form of community on a very reluctant citizenry. He contended that a genuine community rooted in the traditional values of family, God, self-help, free enterprise, and individual freedom constituted the real America: "a nation of neighbors and an economy of rugged individualists."[15] Third, in extolling the virtues of a free marketplace, Reagan attempted to sweep aside the flotsam of the 1970s—those "doubting Thomases," "doomsayers," "Malthusian pessimists," and "false prophets" who had ominously warned of a more straitened future. In place of this depressing collection of "handwringers," President Reagan offered an America of hard-working individuals, who asked only that the market be liberated from governmental interference. Allow the market to work its magic, Reagan implored, and the future will be filled with growth, not trade-offs. Just as he had shown much success in banishing the *l* word— liberal—from the American political vocabulary, so did he remove the *d* word—decline—from all but academic discourse. Finally, as we will see in greater detail in the next section, Ronald Reagan sought to make Wilsonian internationalism once again respectable. Notwithstanding his emphasis on the twin threats of totalitarianism and terrorism, Reagan's international rhetoric exuded the same remarkable optimism as his domestic oratory. In contrast to Carter, who seemed content to know that as a result of his public statements foreign leaders had been forced to think about human rights, President Reagan by June 1982 had proclaimed an era of democratic revolutions that would surely remove the dead hand of Communism forever. Not merely an exemplar of freedom, America, Reagan suggested, had a sacred duty to defend the rights of others. Only after the march of freedom had created democratic governments, free markets, and individual liberty everywhere could Americans rest. And just as the tide of history had swung in favor of we the people at home, who had demanded an end to oppressive government, so too did it now favor people abroad who were fighting to destroy repressive states.

It cannot be gainsaid that Ronald Reagan's peculiar brand of "feel good," "pain free" conservatism struck an enormously respondent chord in the American body politic. His early tax and domestic spending cuts, coupled with the ensuing unprecedented budget deficits, relegated those who wished to expand significantly federal social programs to the political sidelines. The issue of the 1980s became, rhetorically at least, not whether, but how to limit the size of the national government. In that sense Nancy Reagan's "Just Say No" antidrug campaign slogan typified Reaganism's general public posture toward nondefense expenditures. Moreover, in contrast to an older American conservatism, which had been traditionally vulnerable to charges of privilege and elitism, Reagan's was baldly populist in which we the people struggled against a Washington sodden with experts, special interests, social engineers, and secular humanists. Masterfully building on the accomplishments of Richard Nixon and George Wallace, but doing so with a "human face," Reagan claimed to speak for the millions who had for too long been patronized and coerced by an antidemocratic liberal establishment. And, again, unlike Tory conservatives who had dourly fretted about an unretrievable past and a dangerous future, Reagan dispensed with tragedy and offered a vision bubbling with optimism. Whereas Carter had soberly spoken of restraint, sacrifice, and complexity, Reagan promised Americans self-described "simple" solutions, unlimited economic growth, and technological salvation. Finally, his rhetoric of national assertiveness, particularly in regard to America's adversaries, neatly captured a public wearied by a decade of "bad news" from abroad. Thus, to offer but one colorful example, Reagan told the American Bar Association in July 1985 that "we're . . . not going to tolerate . . . attacks from outlaw States by the strangest collection of misfits, loony tunes, and squalid criminals since the advent of the Third Reich."[16] Whereas the "Blame-America-First Crowd" had allegedly been busy defending these unsavory types, Reagan (and we the people) saw the truth and spoke it.

Notwithstanding the apparently pervasive political appeal of these themes, however, none was immune to difficulties that could eventually threaten Reaganism's agenda. First, as Heclo, Budget Director David Stockman, and others suggested, the Reagan administration failed to develop any principled basis for either cutting or decentralizing federal social programs. Despite Stockman's initial insistence that a consistent sense of equity govern policy, the administration, with the connivance of Congress, allowed political expediency to determine budget priorities. It soon became clear to Stockman that it was the poor and other unorganized groups that were particularly victimized, while middle-class "entitlement" programs remained sacrosanct.[17] And although Reagan's electoral triumphs seemed to vindicate the administration's understanding of political realities, the growing gap between rich and poor throughout the 1980s, the emergence of a permanent underclass, and the disturbing phenomenon of homelessness served as reminders of Reaganism's potential vulnerability on the "fairness issue." Of more immediate political significance, however, was an issue that had begun to manifest itself as early as 1984—defense spending. On an abstract level, one would expect Reagan conservatives to find it increasingly difficult to argue simultaneously for a strictly limited national government and an enormous military establishment that, among other things, distorted the market and regulated important parts of the economy. More practically, the perpetuation of massive deficits and the remarkable diminution of the Soviet threat during Reagan's second term brought the long defense buildup to an abrupt halt.

Second, Reagan's sentimental vision of a national community of caring neighbors eager to volunteer, yet hamstrung by an arrogant, alien, corrupt federal government, was severely damaged by a series of private sector abuses culminating in Wall Street insider trading scandals and the savings and loan crisis. Not even Reagan could plausibly indict the federal government as the cause of those excesses or other instances of unbridled individual greed, nor could he blame Washington for provoking a national drug crisis that threatened the very "family" values so dear to the president. Furthermore, despite the apparent broad popularity of Reagan's limited government message, opinion polls throughout the 1980s indicated widespread support for public programs, particularly those perceived as personally relevant. At the same time, however, there remained a great reluctance to pay for these services with higher taxes. In this sense, the federal deficit constituted the "free lunch" that conservatives had traditionally dismissed as an oxymoron, but, in fact, the deficit enabled the public to fulfill its twin wishes of federal services and lower taxes. Unlike inflation and unemployment, the deficit had an abstract, eschatological quality that made it politically tolerable in the short run.

Finally, Reagan's optimistic Wilsonian international vision, like his domestic outlook, obscured, as we will see, some important operational dilemmas. For example, under what conditions would the United States employ military force to "expand freedom"? Would an American public, told by Reagan that sacrifice at home was unnecessary, support prolonged engagements abroad?

A SHINING CITY ON THE HILL

As a former governor of California, presidential candidate Ronald Reagan may have lacked foreign policy experience but he surely did not lack opinions about America's proper role in the world. He had been delivering these opinions, as well as those on domestic issues, since his days on the "mashed potato circuit" as a spokesman for General Electric, in "the speech" on national television in October 1964, and in a long series of five-minute weekly radio addresses after leaving Sacramento. In essence, Reagan's assault on the Carter foreign policy built on these earlier views, with an adjusted focus to take advantage of the president's current predicament. Like Carter in 1976, Reagan leveled a combination of stylistic and substantive charges against the incumbent designed to distance him from the recent American foreign policy record. Once again the functioning of the National Security Council staff emerged as a campaign issue with Reagan, who pledged to end the policy-making confusion of the Carter administration by ensuring the supremacy of the State Department. More tellingly, candidate Reagan claimed that: (1) while the United States had been "unilaterally disarming" in the 1970s, the Soviet Union had undertaken history's most massive arms buildup; (2) the Soviets had exploited the arms control process to threaten the United States with a window of vulnerability which would soon put at risk its entire land-based ICBM force; (3) President Carter had unwisely signed a "fatally flawed" SALT II agreement; (4) the Carter administration, in part because of its highly publicized human rights campaign, had abandoned many of America's traditional friends, while apologizing for the misdeeds of its adversaries; (5) the United States had placed excessive faith in multilateral organizations like the United Nations, which had repeatedly abused and humiliated it; (6) for well over a decade America's standing in the world and the respect afforded it had steadily fallen; and (7) an anemic, inflationary domestic economy had diminished America's ability to provide international leadership.

Upon its electoral victory in 1980 the Reagan administration faced a public that manifested several not wholly consistent foreign policy attitudes: a sense of vulnerability in the wake of the Soviet arms buildup; a preoccupation with Soviet military power; a disinclination for direct military involvement in conflicts abroad; and paradoxically a simultaneous desire for U.S. world leadership. The administration responded with a program that allegedly aimed to restore the domestic economy, end the era of Soviet military superiority, reward the United States' anti-Communist friends abroad, halt the spread of Soviet influence, and combat terrorism. Furthermore, it promised to accomplish these goals without triggering a nuclear war (some early statements notwithstanding), risking another Vietnam-type conflict, or incurring federal budget deficits.

Central to both Reagan's domestic and global grand design was the restoration of the American economy, and the administration focused its attention during 1981 on the federal budget and tax reductions. Indeed, apart from some rather heavy-handed declaratory signaling which reflected the administration's ideological inclinations—for example, opposition to the Law of the Sea Treaty, withholding payments to the UN, and shooting down two Libyan jets in the Gulf of Sidra—the Reagan presidency appeared devoid of a foreign policy. Secretary of State Alexander Haig's early efforts to "go to the source" of Central American instability met with serious resistance from the White House *troika* of Edwin Meese, Michael Deaver, and James Baker, and the president's only important foray into foreign policy involved his rescue of the Advanced Warning Air Control (AWACs) sale to Saudi Arabia before a skeptical Congress—a deal initiated by the Carter administration. In contrast to his predecessor Reagan delivered no major foreign policy addresses until the Caribbean Basin Initiative in January 1982.

Yet Reagan's early foreign policy rhetorical quiescence hardly meant that he lacked strong beliefs. Indeed, the president and his senior advisers shared a set of overlapping convictions best termed "conservative internationalism" that collided with the world order outlook of the early Carter years. First, and most fundamentally, they believed that Soviet-American competition remained the defining characteristic of contemporary international relations, a struggle that the United States was losing through a lack of effort. Second, they were confident that the Soviet Union, despite its formidable, even preeminent, military power, suffered from grave economic and social woes and was vulnerable to external pressure. Third, previous U.S. efforts to achieve détente had been naive, one-sided disasters and would continue to be so until the internal nature of the Soviet regime had been decisively altered. Fourth, the world was not nearly as diverse or complex as liberal cant fashionably claimed, and thus regional conflicts in Africa, Central America, and the Middle East should best be viewed as part of the East-West struggle. Fifth, recent administrations, in misguided attempts to accommodate Third World Marxist states, had abandoned traditional, if authoritarian, friends and thus strengthened Moscow's hand. Sixth, the Soviet Union and its clients had exploited America's "Vietnam syndrome" to expand their influence. The United States, they believed, had to give renewed priority to military and paramilitary policy instruments—a sharp increase in the defense budget, covert action, military assistance and arms sales—instead of vainly attempting to win friends through agreements like the Law of the Sea and the Panama Canal treaties. And, finally, they were convinced that because America's wounds had been self-inflicted, and not the product of inexorable forces such as the diffusion of economic power and high technology, its decline could be reversed and its global preeminence restored. Much would depend on rebuilding domestic confidence in the strength, morality, and wisdom of the United States.

Together these convictions constituted a grand design reminiscent of a world much like that of the 1950s—only better. This world would resemble the earlier decade inasmuch as a respected, powerful America would again exert global leadership, but now, having lost the cold war, the Soviet Union would no longer pose a serious threat. The United States could thus escape the security dilemmas that had traditionally bedeviled states. Surrounded by friends—some democratic, others authoritarian—the United

States would not need to manipulate an international balance of power to survive, for, with the cold war now history, international relations—traditional statecraft—would be largely obsolete. This enormously optimistic, yet quintessentially Reaganesque vision, went considerably beyond containment. George Kennan, it may be recalled, had argued that the patient application of pressure against the Soviet Union would eventually lead to its collapse or moderation, which, in turn, would usher in a multipolar world with the United States playing a major balancing role. Moreover, Reagan's initial design grew in time even more grandiose as he took advantage of favorable trends first in Latin America and later in Eastern Europe and the Soviet Union to proclaim a new age of democratic revolutions that would universalize the contagion of liberty. Reagan's address to the British Parliament in June 1982 asserted that "around the world today the democratic revolution is gaining strength" at a time when "a great revolutionary crisis . . . is happening . . . in the home of Marxist-Leninism—the Soviet Union." "Democracy," he suggested, "is not a fragile flower. Still it needs cultivating. . . . It is time that we committed ourselves as a nation—in both the public and private sectors—to assisting democratic development." For "freedom is not the sole prerogative of a lucky few, but the inalienable and universal right of all human beings."[18] Indeed, Reagan's grand design—while clearly indebted to Woodrow Wilson, some of the founders, and many nineteenth-century publicists—possessed certain advantages over earlier visions. During other revolutionary democratic ages—the 1790s and 1840s—the United States had the desire but not the power to assist fellow democrats, while after World War I the United States had enormous power but confronted a world beset by radical revolutionary change. Now this design stood a better chance of being realized, for U.S. power and favorable international trends were presumably converging. Thus Reagan's grand design entailed nothing less than a fully democratic world guided by a resurgent America in which peace and prosperity could flourish.

It proved difficult, however, to translate these overlapping convictions and this global vision into a coherent foreign policy strategy. Reagan's early immersion in winning public and congressional support for his economic recovery program, as well as a hands-off leadership style, left the White House *troika*, Secretary of Defense Caspar Weinberger, Director of Central Intelligence William Casey, and Haig vying for control over foreign policy, while a greatly weakened National Security Council staff provided very little coordination. As a result of this organizational confusion the early Reagan foreign policy consisted primarily of a collection of departmental initiatives, whose sole common thread was an antipathy to anything that smacked of "Carterism." Neither a formal decision-making apparatus nor a basic national security document existed until after Reagan confidant William Clark moved from State to the NSC in early 1982. Three months after his arrival a National Security Decision Directive, coordinated by former Secretary of the Air Force Thomas C. Reed, received the president's signature. This eight-page directive outlined the political, economic, diplomatic, informational, and military components of a comprehensive national strategy.[19] Its contents remain classified, though Clark and other senior advisers publicly offered a general description of what some of its architects dubbed "prevailing with pride." First, because the Soviet Union was an "economic basket case," the United Sates should exploit this situation by waging economic warfare. Détente had created powerful interests in the West whose well-being depended on expanding Soviet trade and investment. The Soviets, in turn, had manipulated those interests into helping prop up their faltering economy. In the future, the West had to ensure that its resources, credits, and technology could not be used in this manner. Rather, every effort should be made to deny the Soviet Union access to Western economic assets. Thus Weinberger took the lead in tightening controls over the Western export of critical goods, in ending Soviet industrial espionage, in opposing the extension of credits to Poland, and in demanding that West Germany cancel a contract with Russia for a natural gas pipeline. Moreover, he recommended that weapons systems be built not only for their military utility, but in order to maximize the economic burdens they would place on Soviet attempts to counter them.[20] As it turned out, not only did vigorous Western European and congressional resistance to the notion of economic warfare largely scuttle Weinberger's plans, but by the late 1980s Soviet-American trade had reached unprecedented levels as a "Détente II" was in full bloom.

Second, this document apparently endorsed an extremely skeptical approach to nuclear arms control. If not for the intrusion of domestic political considerations, first in the Federal Republic of Germany in 1981 and then in the United States the following year, the Reagan administration would probably have preferred to offer no arms control proposals at all. Moreover, as part of the "two-track" theater nuclear force agreement reached with NATO in December 1979, the administration was obliged to negotiate with the Soviets while making preparations to deploy Pershing II and cruise missiles in Western Europe. Huge anti-deployment rallies in West Germany helped pressure the administration to unveil in November 1981 a "zero-zero" option that would have forced the Soviets to remove their theater nuclear forces in exchange for a U.S. pledge to forego deployment of its new weapons. In view of the administration's well-known doubts about reaching agreements with a Soviet Union that "had broken every treaty it had ever made," many interpreted this offer as a propaganda ploy. Nevertheless, it did succeed in defusing the West German protests and, of course, ultimately served as the basis for the 1987 Intermediate Nuclear Forces (INF) treaty. It remains unclear if the zero-zero option was taken seriously by the administration in 1981, for some Defense Department officials subsequently found it very difficult to tolerate Moscow's acceptance of the offer. In a somewhat similar fashion Reagan's rejection of the SALT process in favor of the commencement of START, designed to reduce existing strategic arsenals, struck some observers as public relations hyperbole—especially his Eureka proposals of May 1982 that would have cut deeply into land-based missiles—but it stole the thunder from the nuclear freeze movement which, Reagan claimed, wished merely to sanctify a dangerous status quo. In any case, "prevailing with pride" evidently urged that serious negotiations be postponed at least until the U.S. force modernization and expansion program was well underway, for positions of strength needed to be constructed first.

Third, according to Clark, "the modernization of our strategic nuclear forces" would "receive first priority in our efforts to rebuild the military capabilities of the United States."[21] Whereas the final Carter military budget had emphasized general purpose forces—largely to help implement the new commitment to Persian Gulf security—Reagan's fiscal year 1983 increases focused on strategic forces. Specifically, the administration "accorded the highest priority to a survivable C^3I [command, control, communications, and intelligence] system."[22] This force modernization contained eleven major elements, eight of which were continuations of Carter initiatives, while the others—the B-1, air defenses, and sea launched cruise missiles—were Reagan innovations.[23] Taken together, these programs represented a strategic force buildup comparable to those of the Korean War and Kennedy years. Yet, somewhat surprisingly in light of the 1980 campaign rhetoric, little was done to deal with the "window of vulnerability," other than undertaking a search for a feasible basing mode—a search that ended with the recommendation to deploy the MX in existing Minuteman silos. More innovative was the decision to substitute the threat of escalation in space and time for the threat of escalation in weapons. Rather than climb a vertical ladder to deter nuclear war, the administration proposed "horizontal escalation," whereby threats of conventional counterattacks against major Soviet interests held out the prospect of "prolonged war" in which Western economic superiority would prove decisive.[24] Weinberger's FY 1984–1988 Defense Guidance singled out Cuba, Vietnam, and North Korea as likely targets for conventional retaliation.[25] Central to the strategy of horizontal escalation and prolonged conventional war was a naval expansion program aimed at achieving a six-hundred-ship fleet. Equally essential, of course, was the development of a domestic industrial base that could sustain U.S. forces in a war of long duration. That, in turn, depended on the restoration of the American economy.

Fourth, the Reagan administration proposed to launch a comprehensive informational offensive strongly reminiscent of Eisenhower's psychological warfare efforts of the early 1950s. Concerned that the Soviets had been winning the propaganda struggle—"nuclear pacifism" in West Germany and widespread Western acceptance of the doctrine of "moral equivalence" were seen as evidence of Moscow's success—it was determined to seize the moral high ground and expose the Soviet Union and its friends as ruthless, aggressive totalitarians. Several steps were taken to implement this part of the strategy. Jeane Kirkpatrick, whose *Commentary* article "Dictatorships and Double Standards" had been admiringly read by Reagan during the campaign, was made Ambassador to the UN, where she quickly earned a reputation as a formidable "Soviet basher."[26] Similarly, Michael Novak, a 1960s hippie-turned-conservative Catholic philosopher, became chief representative to the UN Commission on Human Rights—a post he used to promote a distinctly libertarian approach. President Reagan appointed Charles Wick, an old friend, to head the United States Information Agency with instructions to transform it into an active combatant in the struggle against Communism. The State Department through its Bureau of Public Affairs published a long series of reports that accused the Soviets of promoting terrorism, causing "yellow rain" in Southeast Asia, abusing human rights, systematically violating treaties and other international agreements, and a host of other transgressions. President Reagan, as we will see, unleashed a rhetorical barrage against Moscow culminating in his March 1983 evil empire speech. The administration, in an effort to exert pressure on Fidel Castro, asked Congress to fund "Radio Martí." Finally, plans were laid to create a National Endowment for Democracy (NED), an amalgam of American business, labor, academic institutions and the two major political parties, which was to disperse government funds abroad in order to promote political pluralism. Loosely based on cold war programs of the CIA, which had clandestinely channeled financial assistance to democratic (or at least anti-Communist) groups, the NED was to openly strengthen pluralism both within and without the Soviet bloc. It was, in fact, established in 1983 under the presidency of Carl Gershman, a former Kirkpatrick aide, who oversaw such activities as training teachers, opening schools, publishing textbooks in Afghanistan, helping Solidarity print underground publications in Poland, providing printing supplies for the anti-Sandinista paper *La Prensa*, and helping the opposition in South Korea. It also, much more controversially, made a $575,000 grant to an ultraright French group, the National Inter-University Union.[27] All in all these several initiatives were designed to put the Soviet Union on the ideological defensive and to win the "war of ideas" with Communism.

Finally, the Reagan administration gradually evolved a geopolitical project that at its core reflected the long-standing conservative aversion to containment. Ronald Reagan, in particular, a self-described admirer of James Burnham, had during the 1950s and 1960s spoken of the alleged moral bankruptcy of containment's reluctance to assist people struggling against Communist governments. The Eisenhower administration, Dulles's rhetoric notwithstanding, had found it impossible to implement rollback in Eastern Europe for fear of triggering a war with the Soviet Union. But by the early 1980s the Soviet empire stretched far beyond its traditional security zone to places like Ethiopia, Angola, South Yemen, Cambodia, Cuba, Nicaragua, and Afghanistan. As we have seen, most senior Carter officials initially suspected that the Soviet Union was overextended and that powerful indigenous nationalist forces would eventually loosen Moscow's grip on many of these areas. Moreover, because of their dread of another Vietnam quagmire, they opposed sending military assistance to anti-Communist organizations until, of course, the Soviet invasion of Afghanistan. The Carter administration's decision to help arm the Afghan rebels, in effect, constituted the genesis of what would become known as the Reagan Doctrine, a synthesis of rollback and the Nixon Doctrine, whereby the United States would provide modest funds for "freedom fighters" struggling to unseat Third World Communist governments. The Reagan administration came to view this policy as a low-cost, low-risk effort to chip away at the periphery of the Soviet empire. At the very least, it would greatly increase the price that Moscow would have to pay to retain its Third World clients, and it might even lead to the overthrow of these governments which, among other things, would destroy the validity of the Brezhnev Doctrine and adjust the global "correlation of forces."

In sum, the Reagan administration by mid-1982 had formulated a reasonably comprehensive strategy designed to realize its grand design. Though it represented in large measure an extension and a systematization of programs begun by Carter, as well as the highly moralistic tone of its predecessor, Reagan's strategy rejected the managerial and retreatist dimensions of that approach. Rather, "prevailing with pride" involved the reassertion of American global leadership and the maintenance of all existing commitments. There was, to be sure, disagreement among senior officials about whether this reassertion should be primarily unilateral, or the result of close allied cooperation, with Weinberger and NSC Director Richard Allen evincing acute impatience toward Western European "détenteniks" and believing that Carter's obsession with multilateral initiatives had needlessly paralyzed American foreign policy. Furthermore, these advisers dismissed the devolution strategies of Nixon and Carter as symptomatic of the post-Vietnam loss of will.

But how did the Reagan administration propose to underwrite these global commitments? After all, its predecessors had perceived a reality of shrinking resources and had adjusted accordingly. Cold war presidents had, as John Gaddis pointed out, faced similar dilemmas. In Truman's case, the vast defense expenditures required by NSC-68 (the 1950 study that recommended global containment to Truman) were to be financed through short-term deficits that would, his Keynesian advisers assured, be quickly eliminated by robust economic growth. Walter Heller delivered essentially the same message to Kennedy a dozen years later.[28] Neither president had seemed comfortable with the prospect of budget deficits and had been persuaded to accept them as temporary evils on the road to economic recovery and military expansion. Reagan, citing the theories of supply-side economists, reassured the electorate in 1980 that so long as federal social spending was controlled, tax rates could be slashed, defense expenditures significantly increased, and, in a few years, the budget brought into balance, as savings and investments acted to spur economic growth and increase tax revenues. Some critics, like Senator Daniel Patrick Moynihan (D.–NY) argued, in retrospect, that Reagan had known all along that huge deficits would be the inevitable result of this supply-side voodoo, and that he planned to exploit the issue in order to reduce drastically the size of the welfare state. But the difficulty with Moynihan's conjecture is that it overlooked the pressures that these deficits ultimately exerted on defense spending as well. Thus, although the defense share of the budget rose from 22.7 percent in 1980 to 28.7 percent in 1987, the defense budget in constant dollars actually declined by more than 10 percent between its peak in fiscal 1985 and 1989.[29] Indeed, it appears likely that Reagan and his original inner circle genuinely believed that a growing U.S. economy could afford "prevailing with pride" without the necessity of long-term deficits. As it turned out, during the Reagan presidency the national debt tripled to $2.8 trillion. Massive borrowing, much of it from foreign sources, allowed the Reagan administration to pursue its ambitious national security strategy.[30] Put differently, other countries could, by lending money to the United States, in effect, subsidize the cost of U.S. protection and thus disguise any hint of American retrenchment.

The Reagan administration employed tactics that emphasized the centrality of declaratory signaling, frequently in the form of powerful rhetoric emanating from the president and his foreign policy advisers. It waged an unrelenting war of words against its adversaries designed to expose them as liars, oppressors, hollow failures, terrorists, and the like, and to prove that the United States possessed the will to confront them. And yet, as Coral Bell correctly suggested, even before Gorbachev's accession to power in 1985, "all was actually quiet, *save on the rhetorical front*, in the central confrontation between the superpower[s]. . . ."[31] The result was a heavily stylized "second cold war" in which words were chosen with the same care usually accorded military weapons in a real conflict. At home, as we have seen, the Carter tactic had been to welcome the participation of the American people in debating and formulating foreign policy. Reagan, despite a comparably populist rhetoric, did not speak of an open, honest foreign policy but rather, one that expressed the innate strength of "we the people." And whereas Carter had sought to demonstrate his devotion to democratic participation through town meetings and call-in shows, Reagan surrounded himself with the more traditional trappings of presidential power. His majesty would presumably embody the grandeur of those "ordinary, extraordinary Americans."

As the leader of a self-described "revolution" determined to challenge the Washington status quo, Reagan undertook a rather systematic effort to assert presidential control over the entire federal executive bureaucracy, including the various foreign affairs and national security agencies. The central elements of this strategy involved: (1) extensive use of the appointment power to infuse the federal establishment with loyalists; (2) development of a cabinet council system and other interagency devices to focus the attention of these political appointees on the Reagan agenda; (3) strengthening the ability of the Office of Management and Budget (OMB) to implement presidential wishes; and (4) repeated articulation of broad principles of acceptably "conservative" ways to manage the federal government.[32] The absence of a foreign policy consensus since the mid-1960s had been reflected in the widespread house cleaning of those relevant departments and agencies by Nixon and Carter. Reagan, initially at least, made ideological affinity even more critical, while extending this practice to the domestic bureaucracies in a manner that Nixon must have envied.

This largely successful "infiltration" strategy certainly eased the task of legitimating the Reagan foreign policy within the bureaucracy, for there were now loyal soldiers in key positions eager to receive their marching orders from the president. On the other hand, Reagan's radically detached management style required a team of foreign policy advisers that had access to the Oval Office and whom the president could trust to translate his instincts and convictions into policy. These requirements, as we know, were rarely met. Rancorous bureaucratic in-fighting, fully as bitter as that which had plagued the Carter administration, infected the Reagan White House until the last year of his presidency. Weinberger and Haig, and then Weinberger and George Shultz, opposed each other on a variety of issues including, most fundamentally, nuclear arms control and the conditions in which U.S. conventional arms should be employed. And when Weinberger and Shultz did agree that weapons ought not to be sold to Iranian "moderates," both were overriden and excluded by a renegade NSC in a truly bizarre attempt to free American hostages in Lebanon and illegally re-supply the Nicaraguan "democratic resistance." Indeed, the internecine warfare between administration pragmatists and ideologues dragged on until Reagan, deeply shaken by public reaction to the Iran-*contra* debacle, purged most of the remaining ideologues from the foreign policy apparatus.

But, particularly during his first term, when Reagan seemed more able to "be Reagan," his speechwriting office was remarkably effective in using presidential rhetoric to legitimate his foreign and domestic policies to both the federal bureaucracy and, as we will see, the wider public. Like theologians absorbing and interpreting a sacred text, Reagan's wordsmiths drew on "the speech" of 1964 for inspiration. Consisting of a central, simple claim—that powerful governments weakened the character of free people—this text was memorized by the speechwriters and served as the foundation for the half-million words annually uttered by President Reagan. It was, for speechwriter Al Meyer, "the conscience of the presidency." According to chief writer Bentley Elliott, "What I personally did to sound like Reagan was to spend the three weeks before I went to work for him reading all his speeches and making . . . sheaves of notes—on war, on blacks, on rhetoric, on [the] economy." Reagan, in turn, employed the resulting rhetoric to transform his cabinet into "willing evangelicals who carried the word to the specialized bureaucracies and their clienteles."[33] While foreign policy pragmatists like Shultz, Frank Carlucci, and Colin Powell may have ultimately steered a course inimical to Weinberger, Kirkpatrick, and other "evangelicals," they did so only after accepting the outlines of Reagan's original agenda.

We concluded the last chapter by suggesting that Carter largely failed to reconstruct the substantive procedural and cultural components of a domestic foreign policy consensus. How did President Reagan attempt to publicly legitimate the grand design, strategy, and tactics of his foreign policy in view of the fact that it bore a great resemblance to the post-Afghanistan approach of his predecessor?

Reagan's public legitimation efforts consisted of six elements: (1) an oft-repeated declaratory history of American foreign policy that likened the 1970s to the 1930s as decades of economic decay at home and appeasement of totalitarianism abroad; that extolled the period from 1947 through the mid-1960s as an era of strength, wisdom, generosity, prudence, firmness, and achievement; and that, as the administration gradually compiled its own record, portrayed the 1980s as a second golden age; (2) the reassurance that the setbacks of the 1970s were but aberrations that could be easily reversed with little pain or sacrifice from the American people; (3) the assertion that because the contemporary world bore a strong resemblance to that of the early postwar decades, its problems were thus susceptible to simple solutions; (4) a moralistic depiction of international relations that prominently featured a struggle between good and evil, and a portrayal of Reagan's foreign policy as one committed to defending and promoting the universal value of individual liberty; (5) the claim that the American political community and the world community (or parts of it at least) were similar in structure and aspiration; and (6) the increasingly confident promise of an emergent fully democratic world.

In contrast to Carter's unusually ahistorical early rhetoric, Reagan's brimmed with powerful historical images and lessons. By comparing the 1970s to the 1930s, Reagan and his advisers were following a tradition of creating distance from one's immediate predecessors. Again and again administration officials portrayed the 1970s as a decade of doubt, defeat, deceit, and despair, comparable only to the 1930s as an era of embarrassment for the United States. Secretary of State Alexander Haig, for example, claimed that during the 1960s and 1970s "the cohesion of America's foreign, defense, and economic policies disintegrated" in the face of Vietnam, Watergate, and prolonged economic distress, and while the American people wasted their time debating the utility of military power, the Soviets embarked on a vigorous military modernization program.[34] In 1982 Haig described the 1970s as "a decade when negotiations often seemed to be a substitute for strength," for the United States had been "dominated by the psychology of Vietnam and rising domestic resistance to military programs."[35]

President Reagan peppered his speeches with the same sentiments. In 1983 he described to the American Legion the international situation that he had inherited as president as "truly alarming for all who cared about America and the cause of peace and freedom" and suggested that only a "truly bipartisan effort" could "make things right again."[36] The president spoke to a group of high school students in January 1983 with even fewer qualifications: " . . . [W]hat we're doing with our present buildup of the military is overcoming several years in which we virtually, unilaterally disarmed. We let our arms go. We canceled things like the B–1 bomber and so forth."[37]

Reminiscences about the "lessons" of the 1930s occurred repeatedly in the president's improvised responses to questions. Barely six weeks into his first term, in an interview with Walter Cronkite, he linked his situation to that of Franklin Roosevelt's on the eve of World War II:

> I remember when Hitler was arming and had built himself up—no one's created quite the same military power that the Soviet Union has, but comparatively he was in that way—Franklin Delano Roosevelt made a speech in Chicago. . . . And in the speech he called on the free world to quarantine Nazi Germany. . . . [B]ut the funny thing was that he was attacked so here in our own country for having said such a thing. Can we honestly look back now and say that World War II would have taken place if we had done what he wanted us to back in 1938 [sic]?[38]

Reagan cited the "quarantine the aggressors" speech again and again, particularly during the years of the large U.S. defense buildup. He also liked to tell a story about the state of America's war-readiness in the late 1930s. During war games in Louisiana, he recalled, "We had soldiers that were carrying wooden rifles, and we were simulating tank warfare with cardboard tanks." Compare that to another oft-told story about the alleged condition of U.S. armed forces in 1980: "We had aircraft that couldn't fly and ships that couldn't leave port. Many of our military was on food stamps because of meager earnings, and re-enlistments were down. Ammunition was low, and spare parts were in short supply."[39] Sometimes the president explicitly connected the 1930s to those in Congress who opposed his defense spending requests:

> The calls for cutting the defense budget come in nice, simple arithmetic. They're the same kind of talk that led the democracies to neglect their defenses in the 1930s and invited the tragedy of World War II. We must not let

that grim chapter of history repeat itself through apathy or neglect. This is why I'm speaking to you tonight—to urge you to tell your Senators and Congressmen that you know we must continue to restore our military strength.[40]

While not actually accusing his predecessors of appeasement, Reagan habitually identified himself with FDR—not the Roosevelt of Yalta to be sure—but the vigilant president who had warned the world of the Nazi threat while the West slept—and thus insinuated that his critics were recommitting the mistakes of the 1930s.

The administration's characterization of the 1970s no doubt reflected widely shared popular perceptions. It outlined a declaratory history that was simplistic and tendentious. Moreover, to score rhetorical points with the public, Reagan and his advisers ignored significant, but less helpful, events of that decade. For example, whatever else may be said of the Carter foreign policy record, the Camp David Accords, formal diplomatic ties with the People's Republic of China, the Panama Canal treaties, and a rapprochement with much of southern Africa surely qualified as solid achievements. Yet Reagan's declaratory history of the 1970s conveniently omitted them. Note this telling exchange in May 1983 when Reagan was asked to evaluate these aspects of the Carter legacy:

> **Interviewer:** Four years ago when the Carter administration was in its third year, they had completed the Camp David agreement and the treaty from that; the SALT II treaty was about to be negotiated; normalization with China had taken place; and the Panama Canal treaty had been approved. Can you name several [tangible things] that you've achieved?
>
> **Reagan:** Well, in the first place, China relations had been normalized by the visits of a previous president. . . . And he carried on from there. And I'm not at all sure that he added to what had already been accomplished. With regard to the Camp David agreements, yes, they started, and we're proceeding within the framework of those agreements, because those agreements were simply to begin negotiations . . . but we're the ones who've gone a step beyond that with regard to trying to have an overall peace in the area. That had never been proposed.[41]

Its inaccuracies aside, this soliloquy underlined the purpose for which the administration used the history of the 1970s: to frighten and anger the public into supporting its foreign policy priorities.

Yet while Reagan officials indiscriminately condemned the U.S. diplomatic record of the 1970s, they enthusiastically praised the achievements of Truman, Eisenhower, and Kennedy. It was clear that the Reagan administration wished to identify with the feats of these presidents. For instance, in asking Congress to authorize aid to the *contras* in April 1983 Reagan quoted extensively from the Truman Doctrine and contended that "President Truman's words are as apt today as they were in 1947 when he, too, spoke to a joint session of the Congress."[42] The president also invoked the words of Eisenhower, repeatedly citing a letter in which Eisenhower argued that negotiations were the only alternative to nuclear destruction. Thus cold war presidents were recalled for their restraint as well as their activism. In order to fend off congressional criticism of his dispatch of marines to the Beirut airport, Reagan compared his actions to those of Eisenhower, who in 1958 had "used a bipartisan congressional resolution to send 8,000 American soldiers and marines to Lebanon. When order was restored, our military came home."[43]

President Reagan and his advisers supplemented these largely anecdotal references to past leaders with a somewhat more systematic public account of the cold war—an account that, in its unambiguous celebration of American achievements, stood in stark contrast to the more complex and critical analyses of contemporary diplomatic historians. Secretary of State Haig captured this approach fully when he recalled in April 1982 how the United States, after drifting into a disastrous isolationism in the 1920s and 1930s, had been determined to avoid this mistake after World War II by "eagerly" founding a new international order. "American resources, American perseverance, and American wisdom provided the crucial underpinnings of this international order," and "the successful application of American power" had brought "economic health and political stability to Western Europe and Japan."[44] Moreover, as President Reagan suggested to the British Parliament in 1982, the Western democracies in the 1940s and early 1950s had shown unique restraint in refusing to use their nuclear monopoly for territorial gain.[45] A few months later he reiterated this theme in a national television address designed to mobilize public support for the MX missile. Reagan reminded his television audience that at the end of World War II, with the United States the only undamaged industrial power, with its military power at its peak, and with an atomic monopoly, "We didn't use this wealth and power to bully; we used it to rebuild. . . . We had deeply held moral values," and "Our strength deterred . . . aggression against us."[46] Just as American power had kept the peace in that earlier era, so the MX—now dubbed "Peacekeeper"—was to do likewise in the 1980s.

It was perhaps appropriate that Jeane Kirkpatrick, the administration's best-known professor, was the only official to admit even the slightest possibility of other historical interpretations. Yet she did so only to disparage them. Thus, in a speech to the knowledgeable National Committee on American Foreign Policy she observed that NATO was "forged as a direct response to the actual, imminent danger to Western Europe of Soviet subversion and aggression. *No amount of historical revisionism can explain away facts of Soviet expansion into Europe.*"[47] There was a certain irony here, for Ronald Reagan's declaratory history embraced policies that he had once vilified. While his administration articulated a history that fell well within the old containment consensus of the cold war years, Reagan, for most of that era, had been a disciple of James Burnham and other conservative critics of U.S. foreign policy. What Reagan now called "restraint" and "generosity" Burnham had labeled "appeasement" and "naiveté." Both had called for an offensive strategy that went well beyond containment to overthrow Soviet client governments in Eastern Europe and ultimately the Soviet Union itself. Yet the administration's declaratory history did not aim to convert the electorate to Burnham's brand of "liberation theology." Curiously, despite his clear indebtedness to Burnham, the president did not defend the Reagan Doctrine by disparaging the accomplishments of containment. Despite early efforts of Reagan's NSC staff to develop a forward strategy, in 1981 and 1982 the administration was publicly attempting to mobilize support for a massive defense buildup without deepening popular perceptions of a trigger-happy president. By portraying the cold war as an era of U.S. strength and world order, administration officials sought to allay public fears of a dangerous new arms race.

Yet the shadow of Vietnam intruded into this tidy history of U.S. foreign policy. In general, Reagan and his advisers tried to say as little as possible about the Vietnam war, usually lumping it with Watergate as an event that had produced national disillusionment and self-doubt. Occasionally, when speaking to especially friendly audiences, this circumspection yielded to more visceral sentiments. During the 1980 campaign Reagan had told the American Legion that it was "time to recognize that ours was in truth a noble cause."[48] Jeane Kirkpatrick proclaimed to the same group two years later that "I don't think that we were driven out of Vietnam—I think we left. I think that's an important distinction and one we should not lose sight of."[49] In February 1987 Reagan suggested that U.S. troops came home without a victory not because they had been defeated, but because they had been denied permission to win."[50] Overall it was the press and not the administration that raised the issue. For example, a reporter asked Reagan only six weeks after his first inauguration to compare the situation in El Salvador to Vietnam in the early 1960s, and the President replied rather disjointedly,

I don't believe it is a valid parallel. I know that many people have been suggesting that. The situation here is, you might say, our front yard; it just isn't El Salvador. What we're doing, in going to the aid of a government that asked that aid of a neighboring country and a friendly country in our hemisphere, is trying to halt the infiltration into the Americas by terrorists, by outside interference, and those who aren't just aiming at El Salvador, but, I think, are aiming at the whole of Central and possibly later South America—and, I'm sure, eventually North America.[51]

Not until 1985, on the occasion of the tenth anniversary of Saigon's fall, did Reagan offer a more elaborate defense. He told a news conference in April that

that was the great disgrace, to me, of Vietnam—that they were fed into this meatgrinder, and yet no one ever had any intention of allowing victory.

Well, the truth of the matter is, we did have victory . . . .

But what happened? We signed the peace accords, . . . and we made a pledge to [Saigon]. And when the North Vietnamese did violate the agreement and the blitz started . . . and then the administration in Washington asked the Congress for the appropriations to keep our word, the Congress refused. We broke our pledge. . . .

And so, we didn't lose the war. When the war was all over and we'd come home—that's when the war was lost.[52]

But the American public's overwhelmingly negative memory of Vietnam clashed with the administration's and certainly constrained President Reagan's foreign policy options, especially in Central America. Opinion polls showing huge majorities opposed to sending U.S. troops to El Salvador and Nicaragua no doubt helped convince the administration to aid the *contras* as an alternative to direct military involvement. It subsequently began to turn the Vietnam issue to its own advantage by arguing that only congressional support of the *contra* program would preclude the chances of another Vietnam. But this legislative tactic only partially succeeded, for public backing of *contra* aid remained around 30 percent, and congressional enthusiasm for it was divided at best.

By the late 1980s the Reagan administration had compiled a historical record that it eagerly incorporated into its declaratory statements. In October 1987 Reagan reminded a West Point audience that "from the beginning, our administration has insisted that this country base its relations with the Soviet Union upon realism, not illusion. This may sound obvious. But when we took office the historical record needed restatement. So restate it we did."[53] In April 1988 the president recalled that

at first, the experts said this kind of candor was dangerous, that it would lead to a worsening of Soviet-American relations. But far to the contrary this candor made clear to the Soviets the resilience and strength of the West. . . .
 And now this approach to the Soviets . . . has borne fruit.[54]

History had vindicated his strategy, as he told students at the University of Virginia in December 1988, for "as I suggested in 1982, if the West maintained its strength, we would see economic needs clash with the political order in the Soviet Union."[55] Or, as he put it in his Farewell Address,

That's what it was to be an American in the 1980s. We stood, again, for freedom. I know we always have, but in the past few years the world again, and in a way, we ourselves—rediscovered it. . . .
 The fact is, from Grenada to the Washington and Moscow summits, from the recession of '81 and '82, to the expansion that . . . continues to this day, we've made a difference.[56]

For Reagan, then, the events of the 1980s had legitimated his approach to both foreign and domestic policies and had ushered in a new "golden age" of American achievement.
 President Reagan also sought to legitimate his foreign policy by reassuring the American people that its goals could be realized with little pain or sacrifice. The 1980 Republican platform neatly captured the apparent gap between the dire nature of the current crisis and the instruments available to confront it. After intoning that "the United States faces the most serious challenge to its survival in the last two centuries," this document then recommended a drastic tax reduction, ending the grain embargo against the Soviet Union, and the abolition of draft registration.[57] The massive increases in the defense budget between 1981 and 1985, apart from the resources that it *may* have drawn away from social spending, hardly constituted a national sacrifice, because, as we have seen, it was largely financed with foreign funds. Moreover, as Reagan himself repeatedly argued, even with this significant defense buildup, the proportion of the federal budget and the gross national product devoted to the military remained well below that of the 1950s and 1960s. Increases in defense spending—in itself a declaratory signal of future intentions—coupled with the president's famous rhetorical "candor" about Communism, the Soviet Union, and Third World adversaries, would together reverse the tide. Of course, as Coral Bell shrewdly observed, "since the image of U.S. military weakness was created chiefly by words (mostly from the Reagan camp . . .) it is logical

that more words from the same sources should have been effective in read-justing that somewhat distorted image."[58] Surely that helps to explain how Reagan, a mere four months into his presidency, could announce that "the people of America have recovered from what can only be called a tempor-ary aberration. There is a spiritual revival going on in this country, a hun-ger on the part of the people to once again be proud of America—All that it is and all that it can be."[59]

But, in fact, Reagan did not demand sacrifice, because he knew that such rhetoric would inevitably provoke a public weary of twenty years of "bad news" and seriously disillusioned with the risks and burdens of global leadership. Certainly the public was tired of watching America get "pushed around," but it also dreaded the prospect of another Vietnam. It did not want to be frightened, as Reagan's early loose talk about nuclear war made clear. It wanted, rather, to be praised, encouraged, and reassured, and Reagan skillfully responded to those needs, in part because he was, by temperament, uncomfortable with struggle and sacrifice.

Third, Reagan sought to legitimate the various elements of his foreign policy as "simple" responses to deceptively simple problems. In direct con-trast to Carter, who had described a new world of dizzying complexity that grudgingly yielded complicated solutions, Reagan emphasized the essential continuity of the post-1945 era. The only significant disjunction had oc-curred in the 1970s, when America had been beset by guilt and self-doubt, but that period, Reagan claimed, had largely ended with his election. His postwar world had been characterized by three fundamental realities: an aggressive Soviet Union determined to expand its influence, a prudent, selfless America leading the West against oppression, and billions of peo-ple around the globe struggling for individual freedom. Here again Reagan rhetorically identified himself with the American people who, unlike un-named "experts" despairing of the world's intractability, understood these simple truths. The world, of course, Reagan admitted, was not entirely static—changes had occurred since 1945. But in contrast to Carter, who strived to "get on the right side" of changes largely uncontrollable by the United States, Reagan saw change in terms of democratic revolutions tailor-made for American leadership. Even Reagan's legendary inability to keep his facts straight seemingly appealed to a public who wanted answers, yet felt inundated by information overload.

President Reagan was particularly successful in employing this "simple-mindedness" to legitimate his nuclear arms control strategy. By the late 1970s the arms control "process" had begun to encounter formidable do-mestic obstacles. It had grown incredibly complex as the array of "sublimits" written into the SALT II treaty demonstrated; it had become oddly detached from other aspects of Soviet-American relations; even its proponents appeared increasingly pessimistic that the process could defuse the arms race; and the public seemed less willing to accept the logic of Mutual Assured Destruction (MAD), which promised more of the same perceived insecurity, and more interested in reducing the nuclear arsenals of the superpowers.[60] Carter had tried to respond to these difficulties, but found his options narrowed by domestic critics eager to junk SALT II and by a series of devastating international shocks. Several Reagan officials, particularly in the Defense Department, were, in fact, opposed in principle to any arms control agreements with the Soviets. In short, by the early 1980s the domestic politics of arms control had produced a strategic stalemate,[61] and some of Reagan's early initiatives—for example, the zero-zero option and the Eureka proposals—seemed to invite Soviet rejection. But, in fact, Reagan gradually unveiled an arms control approach that addressed the concerns of the public, and that ultimately broke the domestic stalemate by, in effect, stating that his strategic modernization program would send a signal of firmness and determination to Moscow that would pressure the Soviets into concluding verifiable arms *reduction* agreements with the West. Whether the Soviets signed the zero-zero INF treaty and began to show great interest in drastic decreases in nuclear weapons because of Reagan's "simple" approach, or for their own reasons—after all, they had responded to U.S. pressure in the early 1960s in a vastly different way—cannot yet be determined. But the American public responded positively to a process that now promised to reverse the arms race and bring greater security. Appropriately it was a Reagan slogan—"trust but verify"—that captured the public imagination by brilliantly blending idealism and realism toward the Soviet Union. And though "experts" shuttered at the destabilizing potential of the Strategic Defense Initiative (SDI), more than two-thirds of the public supported Reagan's idea of a population defense against nuclear weapons, because it confronted the moral ambiguity and apparent illogic of MAD. While Reagan may not have viewed SDI as a bargaining chip, subsequent Soviet negotiating behavior suggested that their fear of it worked to soften their positions. Again, we cannot be certain about the cause, but the result—the prospect of a START treaty—won widespread public approval.

There were limits, however, to the effectiveness of Reagan's rhetoric of simplicity. Its success in arms control resulted from its very appealing goal and from its fidelity to Reagan's public persona as a firm man of peace. Selling arms to Iran proved to be a very different matter. Characteristically, Reagan attempted to offer a "simple" explanation:

[The Iranian initiative] was undertaken for the simplest and best of reasons: to renew a relationship with the nation of Iran, to bring an honorable end to the bloody six-year war between Iran and Iraq, to eliminate state-sponsored terrorism and subversion, and to effect the safe return of all hostages.[62]

But much of the public found this far from simple explanation wholly incomprehensible. In the month following this revelation the president's approval rating tumbled dramatically from 67 percent to 46 percent.[63] Not even Reagan could legitimate a policy that, despite its noble intention of freeing American hostages, appeared both immoral—selling arms to a terrorist state—and illegal—siphoning the profits to the *contras*. Reagan's tortured efforts to distinguish the hated Iranian regime from unnamed moderates sounded unconvincing, for the president had never before engaged in these fine, lawyerly distinctions. The world, he had repeatedly claimed, was simple. And whereas Reagan's previous factual confusions had seemed almost charming—for his grand design remained clear—his professed inability to remember key aspects of the Iranian affair appeared to the public as either woeful incompetence or outright prevarication. In retrospect, his rather miraculous recovery from this disaster was closely tied to the continuing improvement in Soviet-American relations. Some of his hard-line advisers even came to suspect that Reagan's allegedly headlong rush to détente in 1987 reflected a desperate desire to save his presidency.[64]

Fourth, President Reagan portrayed the world in highly moralistic terms and sought to demonstrate that his administration's foreign policy embodied this reality. That much he shared with Carter—which distinguished them both from Nixon—but unlike Carter, who failed to integrate human rights into a coherent strategy, Reagan firmly harnessed moralism to his strategic purposes. At first, this moralism appeared little more than a warmed over anti-Communism. For example, Reagan's original nominee for Assistant Secretary of State for Humanitarian Affairs, Ernest LeFevre, testified that he knew of no non-Communist violator of human rights, and Jeane Kirkpatrick's convenient distinction between totalitarian and authoritarian governments appeared to rationalize American support for right-wing military dictators. Reagan himself routinely contrasted the goodness of the American people to the evil of Communist regimes and terrorist organizations. These features never entirely disappeared from the administration's rhetoric—indeed many of Reagan's more ideological supporters welcomed them—but over time they were supplemented with more positive statements that aligned American foreign policy with those struggling to create democratic, capitalist systems. Many observers believed that the administration was the lucky beneficiary of a trend toward democracy in Latin America begun by Carter, and Reagan's initially pro-Marcos actions raised doubts about his commitment to Philippine democracy. But these suspicions were overshadowed, at least among the public, by Reagan's fierce democratic rhetoric that proclaimed America "a shining city on the hill," drenched with virtue, and possessed of universally sought values. As he put it in early 1985, "Our mission is to nourish and defend democracy, and to communicate these ideals everywhere we can."[65] "Freedom is the universal right of all God's children."[66] Simply by being itself America could serve as a global inspiration.

But America would be more than an exemplar of liberty—it would help to defend the rights of others. In what quickly became known as the Reagan Doctrine, the president asserted that "we must not break faith with those who are risking their lives—on every continent, from Afghanistan to Nicaragua—to defy Soviet-supported aggression and secure rights which have been ours from birth, . . . [for] support for freedom is self-defense."[67] In the next section of this chapter we will look more closely at administration efforts to legitimate its policies toward Grenada and Central America, but here it should be noted that the Reagan Doctrine, as described to the public, proclaimed both a moral obligation and a national security imperative—self-defense—to assist anti-Soviet "freedom fighters." This deft synthesis of principle and power distinguished the Reagan administration from the legitimation efforts of its immediate predecessors.

The Carter administration had sought to show that the American political experience would prove useful in helping the United States manage those shifting, global coalitions that constituted "complex interdependence." But this rhetorical effort was short-lived—perhaps because it seemed rather abstract and arid. Reagan too tried to forge a link between the domestic and the international realms. As we have seen, he repeatedly claimed that the United States exemplified universally shared values. In a less philosophical manner, however, he also argued that the democratic parts of the world constituted an enlarged American "neighborhood," composed of the same kinds of God-fearing, hard-working "ordinary, extraordinary" people that could be found on Main Street, USA. For example, in early 1982 he suggested that

the people of the Caribbean and Central America are in a fundamental sense fellow Americans. Freedom is our common destiny. . . . We are brothers historically as well as geographically. . . . [Now], more than ever, the compassionate, creative peoples of the Americas have an opportunity to stand together . . . to build a better life for all the Americas.[68]

And in February 1985 Reagan identified the "freedom fighters" of Nicaragua as "peasants, farmers, shopkeepers, and students. . . ." In short, they were neighbors, the kinds of people "we've aided . . . around the world struggling for freedom, democracy, independence, and liberation from tyranny."[69] This metaphor of an extended neighborhood, global in scope, yet rooted in the American experience, had, of course, been used by other presidents. Not only had Franklin D. Roosevelt announced a Good Neighbor Policy, but during World War II had likened his Four Policemen idea to neighborhoods patroled by friendly cops. To reduce the world to the familiar, whether done by Roosevelt or Reagan, seemed designed to make foreign policy personally relevant to the public. It could, of course, also encourage the unfortunate notion that the world was a replica of Main Street.

Finally, Reagan repeatedly asserted that his grand design—or "dream" as he called it—involved nothing less than the realization of a fully democratic world. This simple, appealing, and powerfully articulated vision, sharply contrasted with the rather murky (or disguised) designs of Carter and Nixon. Carter claimed that he had made American foreign policy moral once again, and that as a result, other leaders had been compelled to weigh the human rights consequences of their actions. But Reagan implicitly denied that American foreign policy had ever been less than totally moral—except during the 1930s and 1970s—and predicted that a tidal wave of democratic revolutions would continue to flood the world. These grandiose assertions, if made by someone else might have seemed absurdly hypocritical or utopian, yet when uttered by Reagan, they appeared to flow naturally and easily from deeply held convictions.

THE "RESCUE MISSION" AND THE "DEMOCRATIC RESISTANCE"

At the root of the dissensus that had plagued American foreign policy since Vietnam lay a disagreement about the nation's security requirements. A central manifestation of that dispute concerned the issue of the use of force abroad. Where, for what purpose, and under what conditions should the United States deploy combat troops? And, as a related theme, which friendly groups and governments should receive American military assistance? In fact, this ongoing argument had focused much less on the central front in Europe and more on the so-called periphery where U.S. interests appeared more ambiguous.

The Reagan administration's desire to roll back Soviet influence from its new outposts was bound to reopen these unresolved issues. In this section of the chapter we will examine the administration's efforts to legitimate, bureaucratically and publicly, two specific applications of the Reagan Doctrine: the Grenadian "rescue mission" of October 1983 and its long-standing support for the Nicaraguan "democratic resistance." These examples neatly illustrate the ways in which the legacy of Vietnam shaped and constrained the Reagan administration's behavior.

If "prevailing with pride" initially functioned as its global strategic blueprint, the Committee of Santa Fe's July 1980 report foreshadowed the essence of the administration's approach to Latin America. Authored by several regional specialists such as Roger Fontaine, Lewis Tambs, David C. Jordan, and Lt. General Gordon Sumner, Jr., all of whom would obtain posts in the new administration, this document bluntly rejected President Carter's Latin American policy as indecisive and naive. In addition it charged that the effort "to socialize the Soviets and their Hispanic-American puppets" was "merely a camouflaged cover for accommodation to aggression."[70] The report claimed that Latin America was being "overrun by Soviet supported and supplied satellites and surrogates," and argued that "decisive action, such as the occupation of the Dominican Republic in 1965" had been "replaced by retrograde reaction, as exemplified by the Carter-Torrijos treaties of 1978, and by anxious accommodation," such as President Carter's cancellation of the sea-air exercise "Solid Shield '80" after the Panamanian president objected.[71] The Committee of Santa Fe urged instead that the United States "take the strategic and diplomatic initiative by revitalizing the Rio Treaty and the Organization of American States; reproclaiming the Monroe Doctrine; tightening ties with key countries; and aiding independent nations to survive subversion."[72] It concluded that "in war there is no substitute for victory; and the United States is engaged in World War III." Thus, "containment of the Soviet Union is not enough. . . . Only the United States can, as a partner, protect the independent nations of Latin America from Communist conquest and help preserve Hispanic-American culture from sterilization by international Marxist materialism."[73] The Reagan administration's desire to exert pressure on Cuba, Nicaragua, and Grenada flowed logically from this analysis.

The Carter administration had greeted with ambivalence the nearly bloodless coup d'état that ousted the Grenada government of Eric Gairy on

March 13, 1979, and installed Maurice Bishop's New Jewel Movement. The State Department had been appalled by Gairy's human rights record, which featured the frequent use of the so-called Mongoose Gang to assault and sometimes murder his political opponents. According to one U.S. official he was "a blemish not only on the face of Grenada, but also on the Caribbean. [His] departure was probably a blessing for Grenada. It is unfortunate that his removal was by extraconstitutional means, but let's face it, this is probably the only way he would have gone."[74]

The new regime—ominously called the Peoples Revolutionary Government (PRG)—soon began to worry Washington, for in April it had received two arms shipments from Cuba, and Bishop repeatedly accused the United States of plotting to assassinate him and return Gairy to Grenada. By summer 1979 the PRG had clearly become a "problem" for mid-level officials at State. Indeed, Brzezinski's first reaction to the coup had been to consider blockading the island, and he soon began to see the entire region as a "circle of crisis."[75] According to one Carter adviser, there was not "an island in the Caribbean that couldn't go the way of Grenada in five years. Beyond these geopolitical concerns the administration grew increasingly disturbed by serious PRG human rights violations and its refusal to hold elections. Bishop and other senior PRG officials frequently engaged in provocative anti-U.S. rhetoric, and Grenada's UN representative refused to support a resolution condemning the Soviet invasion of Afghanistan.

It was this last action that led the Carter administration to reduce official contact with Grenada. It had never accepted the credentials of Grenadian ambassador-designate Dessima Williams, but now it instructed the U.S. envoy, Sally Shelton, to cease visits to the island, though she met several more times with Bishop in Barbados. Yet the Carter administration never viewed Grenada as a major issue. Neither the president nor his secretaries of state ever mentioned it publicly; Grenada was handled at the level of assistant secretary.

The Reagan team, on the other hand, entered office determined to isolate, punish, and perhaps even overthrow Bishop. Its multifaceted policy was evidently coordinated at the most senior governmental levels. Soon after becoming secretary of state, Alexander Haig ordered officials at the Bureau of Inter-American Affairs to make sure that Grenada would not receive "one penny" from any international financial institution (IFI).[76] Accordingly, Grenada was added to an informal "hit list" of countries that the State Department tried to prevent for political reasons from receiving IFI loans. In the words of one analyst, "Whenever a loan for one of these countries comes under consideration at an IFI"—in 1981 the list reportedly included Vietnam, Cuba, Nicaragua, Afghanistan, and Grenada—experts prepared "a negative critique in the technical, economic language that IFI uses to evaluate proposals." Then U.S. officials relied on these critiques "to lobby against the loan with the . . . IFI and other countries' foreign ministers and representatives on [the] IFI's executive board."[77] Apparently the U.S. executive director to the International Monetary Fund (IMF) used these "technical" arguments to try to deny loans to Grenada in 1981 and 1983.

In November 1979 the PRG announced plans to construct an international airport at Point Salines to encourage tourism. The Carter administration, while skeptical, did nothing, but Reagan's advisers feared that the airport's ten thousand-foot runway would be used by Cuban and Soviet military planes and tried vainly to persuade the European Economic Community (EEC) to refuse the PRG's request for assistance. Arguing that large loans to Grenada would add excessively to its external debt, United States officials evidently helped convince the IMF to reduce the loans from $9 million over three years to $3 million for one year. In August 1983 the United States again tried to stop or at least reduce a three-year IMF loan of $14.1 million to Grenada, but this time the other executive directors supported the staff's decision to offer the aid.[78] More than two years earlier, in June 1981, the State Department had put intense pressure on the Caribbean Development Bank to eliminate Grenada from a $4 million U.S. grant for basic human needs projects.[79] Moreover, the United States pressured the World Bank's International Development Agency to refuse a Grenadian request for a $3 million loan.[80] Yet, despite these vigorous efforts, the PRG was notably successful in obtaining international assistance. For example, the $23 million it received from Cuba, East Germany, the EEC, and Canada in 1982 was more than twice the amount that President Reagan proposed for the entire eastern Caribbean in his Caribbean Basin Initiative.

Covert operations against the Bishop government had been discussed by the Carter administration in the wake of Grenada's UN vote on Afghanistan, but after reviewing options the president apparently "rejected all but propaganda measures." In July 1981, however, the CIA approached the Senate Select Intelligence Committee with a plan to cause the PRG economic hardship. In February 1983 an unnamed CIA official denied that it sought to oust Bishop: "We may cause a little economic trouble, a little publicity, and [give] aid [to opposition groups], but we don't overthrow governments."[81] One member of the committee, however, characterized the proposal as "economic destabilization affecting the political viability of the government." In any case, the scheme found little support among the senators. Lloyd Bentsen (D-TX), for example, exclaimed, "You've got to be kidding!" when told of the plan.

Military pressure, however, was exerted against Grenada. From August 1 to October 15, 1981, the United States staged Caribbean maneuvers. In large part, of course, they were designed to intimidate Cuba. On Vieques Island, a military installation near Puerto Rico, more than two hundred thousand U.S. and NATO personnel not only invaded "Red," described as "a mythical island interfering in the region and shipping arms to Central America," but also "Amber and the Amberdines," which, according to the Defense Department, was "our enemy in the Eastern Caribbean where U.S. hostages were in need of rescue." According to the fictional scenario, the U.S. troops, after rescuing the hostages, would remain on Amber to "install a regime favorable to the way of life we espouse."[82]

The administration applied rhetorical pressure too. In June 1982 Stephen D. Bosworth, principal Deputy Assistant Secretary of State for Inter-American Affairs, told a House subcommittee that U.S.-Grenadian relations could not improve unless the Bishop government (1) halted its unrelenting stream of anti-American propaganda and false statements about U.S. policies and actions"; (2) moved to "restore constitutional democracy, including prompt, free, and fair elections"; (3) returned to "the high standard of human rights observance that is typical" of the Caribbean Commonwealth (CARICOM) states; and (4) practiced "growing nonalignment rather than continuing its present role as a surrogate of Cuba."[83] President Reagan had made passing reference to "the tightening grip of the totalitarian left in Grenada" when announcing the Caribbean Basin Initiative in February 1982, but he lingered longer in remarks made in Barbados on April 8, 1982, while on a "working vacation": "El Salvador isn't the only country that's being threatened with Marxism, and I think all of us are concerned with the overturn of Westminster parliamentary democracy in Grenada. That country now bears the Soviet and Cuban trademark, which means that it will attempt to spread the virus among its neighbors."[84] Then, in a speech on Central America and El Salvador to the annual meeting of the National Association of Manufacturers in Washington on March 10, 1983, Reagan presented Grenada in the context of a geopolitical nightmare:

> Grenada, that tiny little island—with Cuba at the west end of the Caribbean, Grenada at the east end—that tiny little island is building now, or having built for it, on its soil and shores, a naval base, a superior air base, storage bases and facilities for the storage of munitions, barracks, and training ground for the military. I'm sure all of that is simply to encourage the export of nutmeg.

People who make these arguments haven't taken a good look at a map lately or followed the extraordinary buildup of Soviet and Cuban military power in the region or read the Soviets' discussions about why the region is important to them and how they intend to use it.

It isn't nutmeg that's at stake in the Caribbean and Central America; it is the United States national security.

Soviet military theorists want to destroy our capacity to resupply Western Europe in case of an emergency. They want to tie down our attention and focus on our own southern border and so limit our capacity to act in more distant places, such as Europe, the Persian Gulf, the Indian Ocean, the Sea of Japan.

Those Soviet theorists noticed what we failed to notice: that the Caribbean Sea and Central America constitute this nation's fourth border. If we must defend ourselves against [a] large, hostile military presence on our border, our freedom to act elsewhere to help others and to protect strategically vital sealanes and resources has been drastically diminished. They know this; they've written about this.

We've been slow to understand that the defense of the Caribbean and Central America against Marxist-Leninist takeover is vital to our national security in ways we're not accustomed to thinking about.[85]

Finally, and most spectacularly, in a nationwide address on national security on the evening of March 23, 1983, the President unveiled aerial-reconnaissance photographs of Cuba, Nicaragua, and Grenada:

On the small island of Grenada, at the southern end of the Caribbean chain, the Cubans, with Soviet financing and backing, are in the process of building an airfield with a 10,000-foot runway. Grenada doesn't even have an air force. Who is it intended for? The Caribbean is a very important passageway for our international commerce and military lines of communication. More than half of all American oil imports now pass through the Caribbean. The rapid buildup of Grenada's military potential is unrelated to any conceivable threat to this island country of under 110,000 people and totally at odds with the pattern of other eastern Caribbean states, most of which are unarmed.

The Soviet-Cuban militarization of Grenada, in short, can only be seen as power projection into the region. And it is in this important economic and strategic area that we're trying to help the Governments of El Salvador, Costa Rica, Honduras, and others in their struggles for democracy against guerrillas supported through Cuba and Nicaragua.

These pictures only tell a small part of the story. I wish I could show you more without compromising our most sensitive intelligence sources and methods. But the Soviet Union is also supporting Cuban military forces in Angola and Ethiopia. They have bases in Ethiopia and South Yemen, near the Persian

Gulf oil fields. They've taken over the port that we built at Cam Ranh Bay in Vietnam. And now for the first time in history, the Soviet Navy is a force to be reckoned with in the South Pacific.[86]

Thus by the spring of 1983 the Reagan administration had elevated Grenada to the status of a serious security threat to the United States and its allies. Its strategic position in the eastern Caribbean allegedly formed the third point on a geopolitical triangle that stretched to Cuba and Nicaragua; its new airport would soon allow the Cubans and Soviets to threaten vital Caribbean sealanes; and Havana could use the island as a military bridge to Africa, and as an ideological bridge to the eastern Caribbean. Finally, the administration even raised the spectre of another Cuban missile crisis. For example, Nestor D. Sanchez, Deputy Assistant Secretary of State for Inter-American Affairs, claimed in February 1983 that Grenada's new military facilities "would provide air and naval bases . . . for the recovery of Soviet aircraft after strategic missions. It might also furnish missile sites for launching attacks against the United States with short and intermediate range missiles."[87]

The administration had virtually ended formal diplomatic relations with Grenada in 1981 by excluding it from the list of states to which the U.S. ambassador in Barbados was accredited. Occasionally, however, Grenadian Foreign Minister Unison Whiteman or an assistant was able to meet with mid-level U.S. embassy personnel in Bridgetown. Bishop wrote several letters to President Reagan asking for more normal diplomatic relations, but all went unanswered. Rumors about a U.S. or U.S.-supported invasion of Grenada, usually fueled by PRG statements, had routinely swept the island since the 1979 coup, but Reagan's March 23, 1983, speech seems to have genuinely alarmed Bishop. At this point it is likely that Fidel Castro personally urged Bishop to try to talk to President Reagan. In any case, at the invitation of Transafrica, self-described as "the Black American Lobby for Africa and the Caribbean," and with the support of the congressional Black Caucus, Prime Minister Bishop came to Washington in early June 1983 to attempt to see the president. Not only was he prevented from doing so, but he was apparently rebuffed by the State Department as well until two senators, Claiborne Pell (D-RI), and Lowell Weicker (R-CT), intervened on his behalf. Soon thereafter, Bishop met for forty minutes with National Security Adviser William Clark and Deputy Secretary of State Kenneth Dam.[88] Bishop termed the meeting "a useful first step in the recommencement of dialogue between the governments," and evidently promised to hold elections within two years. He added that the talks had "delayed" an invasion but admitted that "we do not think the threat has been entirely removed."[89] U.S. officials declined to characterize the talks.

On October 19, after a serious split developed in the PRG leadership, Bishop was killed by troops loyal to his opponents. An entity calling itself the Revolutionary Military Council (RMC), apparently led by General Hudson Austin, declared a twenty-four-hour shoot-on-sight curfew. Six days later nineteen hundred U.S. Marines and Army airborne troops, accompanied by three hundred men from a handful of Caribbean countries landed on Grenada, the first time since 1965 that U.S. forces had participated in a Caribbean military action. President Reagan, accompanied by Prime Minister Eugenia Charles of Dominica, soon appeared on television to announce the operations and the reasons for it. Reagan explained that the United States had responded to an "urgent, formal request from the five-member Organization of Eastern Caribbean States (OECS)," plus Barbados and Jamaica, "to assist in a joint effort to restore order and democracy" on Grenada. He emphasized that "this collective action" had "been forced on us by events that have no precedent in the eastern Caribbean and no place in any civilized society." First, "a brutal gang of leftist thugs" had "violently seized power," thereby threatening the "personal safety" of between eight hundred and one thousand U.S. citizens, including medical students and senior citizens. Second, the "rescue mission" had been carried out to forestall further chaos." Finally, Reagan proclaimed his wish "to assist in the restoration of conditions of law and order and of governmental institutions" to Grenada.[90]

We will not pass judgment on the factual accuracy of Reagan's statement, although it apparently contained several discrepancies,[91] but rather examine the administration's efforts to legitimate its actions.

The primary impetus for the pressure campaign against Bishop came from the State Department, initially orchestrated by Haig, and later by Shultz, and Assistant Secretary for Inter-American Affairs, Langhorne Motley. It was strongly supported by a variety of mid-level political appointees, many of them Latin American specialists at State and the NSC, including Nestor D. Sanchez, Roger Fontaine, Otto Reich, and Constantine Menges. Weinberger and the Joint Chiefs of Staff (JCS) had no objections to staging Caribbean maneuvers to intimidate the PRG (and the Sandinistas).[92] But whereas the State Department and National Security Adviser Robert McFarlane strongly advocated the "rescue mission," representatives of the JCS resisted State's desire even to begin contingency planning for the evacuation of U.S. citizens. After Bishop's murder they reluctantly agreed to do so, but Weinberger evinced little enthusiasm for the actual intervention, apparently fearing that it would whet the administration's appetite for risky operations in Central America.[93]

In light of the psychological warfare that had been waged against the PRG for more than two years, the Reagan administration needed to allay the widespread suspicion that this operation was not simply a unilateral invasion by the "northern collosus." Thus Reagan and his spokespersons repeatedly emphasized that the United States had been "invited" to participate in a multinational humanitarian action. Secretary Shultz, Deputy Secretary of State Kenneth Dam, the U.S. ambassador to the Organization of American States and others offered elaborate justifications, but Jeane Kirkpatrick and Ronald Reagan delivered the most comprehensive defenses. At the UN Security Council on October 27, Kirkpatrick began by challenging an alleged perspective about world politics that "treats the prohibition against the use of force as an absolute; and the injunction against intervention in the internal affairs of other states as the only obligation of states under the U.N. Charter." Rather, Kirkpatrick argued, "the prohibitions against the use of force in the U.N. Charter are contextual, not absolute. They provide ample justification for the use of force against force in pursuit of other values also inscribed in the Charter—freedom, democracy, peace." Thus, "the Charter does not require that peoples submit supinely to terror, nor that their neighbors be indifferent to their terrorization."

In evaluating the U.S. actions, one must begin, not with the October 25 landing, the ambassador suggested, but with the character of the Bishop government and the group that supplanted it. Bishop's government came to power in a coup, refused to hold elections, and "succumbed to superior force" when, "with the complicity of certain powers . . . it first arrested, then murdered Bishop and his ministers. Thus began what can only be called an authentic reign of terror in Grenada." Political violence then, in short, had gripped the island well before the arrival of the task force on October 25.

Furthermore, the people of Grenada had been subjected to "foreign intervention" because Maurice Bishop had "freely offered his island as a base for the projection of Soviet military power in this hemisphere. The familiar pattern of militarization and Cubanization was already far advanced in Grenada." In effect, "Grenada's internal affairs had fallen under the permanent intervention of one neighboring and one remote tyranny. Its people were helpless in the grip of terror."

But why was the U.S. action different from other interventions that, under the guise of restoring self-determination, actually deny it? Because, she answered, "we in the task force intend . . . to leave Grenada just as soon as law is restored, and the instrumentalities of self-government—democratic government—have been put in place." But don't all contemporary governments claim to be democratic? What will ensure that this new Grenadian government will represent the authentic expression of the people any more than the "gang of thugs" from which the island was delivered? "There is," Kirkpatrick asserted, "a simple test," because free institutions—a free press, free trade unions, free elections, representative, responsible government—will be clearly in evidence.

Kirkpatrick then attempted to show that the "U.S. response was fully compatible with relevant international law and practice." Reagan's "brutal gang of leftist thugs" now became "madmen" and "terrorists," who, the United States reasonably concluded, could at any moment decide to hold one thousand U.S. citizens hostage in a duplication of Iran. The ambassador admitted that in normal circumstances "concern for the safety of a state's nationals in a foreign country" does not justify military measures against that country. But in the Grenadian case no new government had replaced the old one; anarchy prevailed; and terrorists had wantonly endangered the lives of its citizens, foreign nationals, and the security of neighboring states. In these circumstances, Kirkpatrick claimed, military action to protect endangered nationals is legally justified.

Second, the OECS concluded that the heavily armed "madmen" who had engineered the coup possessed an oversized army—one and one-half times the size of Jamaica's—supported by more than six hundred armed Cubans and had ambitions for using Grenada as a center for subversion, sabotage, and infiltration. Lacking sufficient security forces, the OECS asked the United States to join the effort to restore order to Grenada and to remove it as a security threat.

Finally, Kirkpatrick vehemently denied that the U.S. action was somehow counterrevolutionary. "The issue was not revolution . . . nor was it the type of government Grenada possessed," for neither the OECS nor the United States had ever attempted "to affect the composition or character" of the Bishop government. Rather, the military power that Grenada had "amassed with Cuban and Soviet backing had fallen into the hands of individuals who could reasonably be expected to wield that awesome power against its neighbors." At the same time, however, "the coup leaders had no arguable claim to being the responsible government," as the failure of other states to recognize them, the governor-general's aid request, and their own declarations made clear. Kirkpatrick concluded that "in the context of these very particular, very unusual, perhaps unique circumstances, the United States decided to accede to the request of the OECS for aiding its collective efforts aimed at securing peace and stability in the Caribbean region."[94]

That same evening President Reagan addressed the nation in an effort to defend his policies in Lebanon and Grenada. He claimed that the nation's will was being tested by Soviet-backed terrorism in both the Middle East and the Caribbean. After asserting that the United States as a global power had a variety of vital interests in the Middle East, the president warned that "if terrorism and intimidation succeed, it'll be a devastating blow to the peace process and to Israel's search for genuine security." Pointing to a massive Soviet military presence in Syria he asked, "Can the United States, or the free world, for that matter, stand by and see the Middle East incorporated into the Soviet bloc?"

Then Reagan turned to Grenada and reminded his audience that Maurice Bishop, "a protegé of Fidel Castro," had overthrown a government elected under a "constitution left to the people by the British," sought Cuban help to build an airport, "which looks suspiciously suitable for military aircraft including Soviet-built long-range bombers," and alarmed his neighbors with a large army. Bishop, in turn, was ousted and subsequently killed by a group "even more radical and more devoted to Castro's Cuba than he had been." Now "Grenada was without a government, its only authority exercised by a self-proclaimed band of military men." Concerned that upwards of one thousand U.S. citizens on Grenada might "be harmed or held hostage," the president recounted how he had ordered a marine flotilla headed for Lebanon to be diverted to "the vicinity of Grenada in case there should be a need to evacuate our people." Then the OECS sent "an urgent request that we join them in a military operation to restore order and democracy to Grenada. These small peaceful nations needed our help." Hence Reagan acceded to their legitimate request and to his own concern for the U.S. citizens on the island. Resurrecting a theme from his inaugural address, he asserted that "the nightmare of our hostages in Iran must never be repeated."

President Reagan raised another issue connected with the landing, but did not quite offer it as a reason for the intervention: "[W]e have discovered a complete base with weapons and communications equipment which makes it clear that Cuban occupation of the island had been planned." A warehouse of military equipment, stacked with enough weapons and ammunition to supply "thousands of terrorists" had been discovered. The president was unequivocal: Grenada "was a Soviet-Cuban colony being readied as a major military base to export terror and undermine democracy. We got there just in time."

Nor did Reagan leave any doubt about the relationship between Lebanon and Grenada: "Not only has Moscow assisted and encouraged the violence in both countries, but it provides direct support through a network of surrogates and terrorists. It is no coincidence that when the thugs tried to wrest control of Grenada, there were 30 Soviet advisers and hundreds of Cuban military and paramilitary forces on the island."[95]

Initial congressional reaction to the operation was largely negative. The Senate was not in session on October 25, but in the House several representatives voiced sharp criticism. For example, Don Bonker (D-WA) accused the administration of "a cavalier attitude about using military force to deal with diplomatic problems" and claimed that "it flies in the face of the president's condemnation of Soviet interference in other countries."[96] Howard Wolpe (D-MI) called the action an example of "gunboat diplomacy in direct contradiction to American ideals, traditions, and interests."[97] Edward J. Markey (D-MA) asked the president: "where does all this military intervention end? Are the Marines going to become our new Foreign Service officers?" And George Miller (D-CA) maligned Reagan for refusing to meet with Maurice Bishop in June.

The next day, in the Senate, Gary Hart (D-CO) introduced a resolution to invoke the War Powers Act and "vowed to oppose any further extension of U.S. military involvement in this small island country."[98] The rest of the Senate, though, had virtually nothing to say about Grenada, and John Melcher (D-MT) warned that the intervention "should not distract us from the timely and urgently needed correction of a disastrous Lebanon policy."[99]

The Democrats continued the offensive in the House on October 26. Bob Edgar (D-PA) argued that American lives were not endangered in Grenada, that the people of Grenada had not been consulted, and that the Congress had been circumvented. Noting that bloody coups-d'état were a common occurrence in the world, he asked, "Are we to send in our marines and rangers every time there is an international disturbance?"[100] Major R. Owens (D-NY) called the invasion "illegal, immoral, and a wasteful expenditure of resources and human lives" and predicted that "the United States will now become a scapegoat" as the poor and unemployed throughout the Caribbean will blame this country for their condition.[101] Jim Leach (R-IA) reminded his colleagues that "our most loyal ally, Great Britain, strongly objects to our decision." Questioning the legality of the action, Leach complained that "we have reconstituted gunboat diplomacy in an era when the efficacy as well as the morality of great power intervention have come increasingly into question."[102] Gus Savage (D-IL) was even more blunt. He recalled Prime Minister Charles's briefing of the Black Caucus the previous day and, terming her "this puppet of the president" who "represents 'Aunt Jemimaism' in geopolitics," claimed that the intervention had raised "to an international level Reagan's ante-bellum attitude towards blacks in this country."[103]

Most Republicans had immediately leaped to the president's defense, but by October 26 even some Democrats began to offer support. Most notable in this regard was Dante Fascell (D-FL), soon to become chairman of the Foreign Affairs Committee. Although deploring the administration's failure to consult Congress prior to the invasion, he stated that "under the circumstances which existed in that region, which is virtually in our backyard, I believe the U.S. was justified."[104] Speaker Thomas P. ("Tip") O'Neill's (D-MA) first reaction was to urge national unity while the fighting was in progress, though he soon suggested that unless U.S. citizens had been in actual danger, the invasion would represent gunboat diplomacy.

As the medical students began returning from Grenada on October 26, however, and as U.S. forces began to uncover evidence of Cuban and Soviet weapons, criticism of Reagan diminished markedly. Tim Valentine (R-NC) exclaimed: "What a beautiful sight to see . . . our youthful countrymen kiss the soil of South Carolina with praise and thanks on their lips. Thank God for our Armed Forces."[105] And Dan Burton (R-IN) echoed: "We have heard the terms 'warmonger' and 'gunboat diplomacy' used. Well, last night we saw the results of that action. Students were getting off the plane. They were kissing the ground. They were saying 'God bless America.' They were thanking the president for sending in the marines and the rangers."[106] For William S. Broomfield (R-MI), the ranking Republican on the Foreign Affairs Committee: "It appears obvious . . . that the Soviets and Cubans had definite plans for turning Grenada into another Cuba. With yet another base in that area, the Soviets could continue to export revolution and terrorism to the small countries of the region."[107]

On October 28 the Senate voted sixty-four to twenty to invoke the War Powers Act in Grenada, but most of those who favored the resolution were careful to explain that their support did not imply criticism of the invasion. A few senators such as Gary Hart and Paul Sarbanes (D-MD) did use the resolution as the occasion to attack Reagan's action, but even Senator Hart tried to narrow its meaning: "This amendment . . . has nothing to do with whether the U.S. citizens were in danger. It does not question the authority of the president. . . . Whether we could have adopted some different remedy . . . is not an issue." The House also voted overwhelmingly (403 to 23) on November 1 to apply the War Powers Act to Grenada on these restricted legal grounds.

But when Steven D. Symms (R-ID) rose in the Senate to insert into a laudatory resolution a passage that would have described the rescue mission as "swift and effective action in enforcing the Monroe Doctrine," Majority Leader Howard Baker (R-TN) indicated that the White House preferred not to alter the resolution's language.[108] This extremely telling exchange provided an insight into the Reagan administration's dilemma. On the one hand, it wished to use the Grenada operation to help dissolve the "Vietnam Syndrome" and to put other regional "undesirables" on notice, but it did not want to alienate further friendly governments in the Caribbean and Central America. "Getting there just in time" to prevent the Sovietization of the Caribbean was one thing, invoking the Monroe Doctrine was something else again.

Despite the administration's elaborate efforts to portray the Grenada intervention as a humanitarian rescue mission, a compassionate response to an urgent request for help by small, friendly, democratic neighbors, and the successful foiling of a Soviet-Cuban colony, the American public supported the action because it was swift, conclusive, and relatively free of cost. Several polls conducted in the immediate aftermath of the operation affirm the overwhelmingly pragmatic nature of the public's reactions. The November ABC-*Washington Post* survey, for example, showed 71 percent in favor and only 22 percent opposed to the Grenada landing. Yet although most people—50 to 35 percent in the *New York Times* poll taken after Reagan's October 27 speech—thought the United States had intervened to protect U.S lives rather than to overthrow a Marxist government, most people also believed that the U.S. citizens in Grenada had not been in a "great deal of danger." And in a *Newsweek*-Gallup canvass more respondents favored the withdrawal of U.S. troops as soon as the safety of the U.S. nationals was assured than those who wanted the troops to stay until Grenada was able to install a democratic government. Consistent with this finding was a *New York Times*-CBS survey that indicated that the public was opposed by a 60 to 21 percent margin to U.S. support for the Nicaraguan *contras*. Furthermore, at the same time that the public supported the president on Grenada, a plurality—47 to 43 percent—continued to believe that he was "too quick to employ U.S. forces," and another plurality—49 to 44 percent—felt more "uneasy" than "confident" about Reagan's ability to handle international crises. The public, in short, liked the Grenada invasion because it worked, but was unwilling to read "broader lessons" into the affair.

Nevertheless, despite this public assessment and despite the judgment of those like Alexander Haig, who later claimed that Grenada could have been captured by the "Providence police force,"[109] Reagan repeatedly invoked the episode as one of his greatest achievements, a turning point in American foreign policy that had successfully challenged the Brezhnev Doctrine. But rhetoric aside, Reagan officials, as we will see, showed a curious reluctance to use the success in Grenada as a springboard to direct military action in Central America.

The Reagan administration, as it frequently reminded the public, had inherited from Carter a Central American situation marked by pervasive instability. In El Salvador leftist guerrillas had recently failed to topple the military government in a "final offensive" but seemed ready to try again. The Carter administration's efforts to encourage political reforms had not been notably successful, and right-wing death squads were suspected of murdering four American nuns in late 1980. In Nicaragua, Carter officials had watched Somoza fall in July 1979 to a revolutionary coalition subsequently dominated more and more by the Sandinistas.[110] Yet despite the avowed radicalism of this group, the Carter administration, recalling how Eisenhower's rough treatment of Castro had allegedly pushed Cuba toward Moscow, tried to establish normal relations with it. A leading Sandinista, Daniel Ortega, visited the White House, and Carter afterwards asked Congress to authorize a $75 million loan to the new Nicaraguan government. A lengthy debate ensued, and though the administration eventually sent $118 million in direct aid and encouraged $262 million in multilateral assistance, it had to compete with a rapidly growing Cuban presence in Nicaragua. The CIA uncovered evidence of large arms shipments from the Sandinistas to the Salvadoran guerrillas, Farabundo Martí Liberación Nacional (FMLN), thereby endangering the continuation of U.S. aid. By January 1981 it had become increasingly obvious that Nicaragua wished to reserve its closest relationships for Cuba and the Soviet Union, while rhetorically branding the United States as the "enemy."

The twin legacies of the Vietnam War and the Cuban Revolution would also help to shape and constrain the Reagan administration's policies in Central America. Many of these officials agreed that Eisenhower had mishandled Castro by allowing him to consolidate his power before attempting to oust him in a "covert/overt," half-hearted invasion. Yet largely because of the limits imposed by fears of another Vietnam, the Reagan administration evolved a policy toward Nicaragua that in its bogus secrecy and limited support for proxies came to resemble an eight-year-long Bay of Pigs.

Secretary Haig had not desired such an outcome. From the beginning he had wanted to "go to the source" of Central American instability—Cuba—and in June 1981 had submitted to the NSC a specific proposal to bring "the overwhelming economic strength and political influence of the United States, together with the reality of its military power, to bear on Cuba by a naval blockade and other military actions." He "stood virtually alone," however, and the plan was rejected because (1) Weinberger feared another Vietnam quagmire, and the JCS feared a Soviet counteroffensive against a vulnerable U.S. asset; (2) the administration doubted that such actions could be publicly justified without prior Cuban provocation; (3) some State Department officials thought that Castro would continue to "export revolution" despite a blockade; and (4) the White House *troika* did not want to divert public attention from Reagan's economic priorities.[111]

Two months later, in a surprising move perhaps facilitated by the fact that Reagan had not yet filled key State positions with political appointees, Assistant Secretary of State for Inter-American Affairs Thomas Enders, began a series of meetings with the Sandinistas to reach an agreement that would renew U.S. economic aid (halted in April) if Managua stopped arming the FMLN. Specifically, Enders proposed that (1) Nicaragua would cease its support of Central American insurgents; (2) Nicaragua would reduce its armed forces from twenty-three thousand to fifteen thousand; (3) the United States would promise to enforce its neutrality laws and to refrain from interfering in Nicaraguan internal affairs; (4) Washington would resume economic aid; and (5) both countries would expand cultural relations. Enders told the Sandinistas of U.S. concerns about political pluralism, a mixed economy, and their close ties with Moscow and Havana but, significantly, in light of subsequent demands, did not include them in the proposal.[112] It appears unlikely, however, that Enders could have in any case persuaded the administration to support the scheme. He had already provoked resentment by excluding key officials from planning discussions and had travelled secretly and alone to Nicaragua.[113] Moreover, hard liners at the White House doubted that the Sandinistas would fulfill their promises—they were, after all, Marxist-Leninists—and these suspicions were fueled by reports that the commandantes "had continued to express support for the FMLN." In any case, the Nicaraguans, instead of directly responding to Enders' proposals, complained about U.S. naval exercises off the Honduran coast, the termination of aid, and Washington's reluctance to stop training exile groups. The Reagan administration, in search of a pretext to end negotiations, interpreted the Sandinista response as a final rejection. Yet Enders, in his eagerness for secrecy, had failed to leave a clear documentary trail, thereby complicating later administration attempts to demonstrate publicly that it had exhausted diplomacy before adopting stronger measures.[114]

Due largely to the presistence of John Carbaugh, an aide to Senator Jesse Helms (R-NC), the 1980 Republican convention had adopted a plank that supported "the efforts of the Nicaraguan people to establish a free and independent government." On March 9, 1981, Reagan signed a Presidential Finding, authorizing the CIA to help interdict arms flowing from Nicaragua to Central American guerrillas. CIA Director William Casey used this authority to begin organizing Nicaraguans opposed to the Sandinistas. Since late 1980 the Argentine military had been training some of Somoza's ex-Guardsmen in Honduras, and at an August 1981 meeting in Guatemala, U.S. officials persuaded these groups to unite and form the Nicaraguan Democratic Force (FDN).[115] Reagan's signing of National Security Decision Directive (NSDD) 17 on November 23, 1981, made support for the *contras* official U.S. policy by authorizing $19 million for a five-hundred-member force to counter "the Cuban infrastructure in Nicaragua" that was "training and supplying arms to the Salvadoran guerrillas." Haig vehemently objected to the decision, arguing that it failed to address the larger problem of Soviet-Cuban intervention and correctly predicting that it would commit the administration to replacing the Sandinistas with a more congenial government.[116]

In March 1982 ex-Guardsmen trained by the CIA blew up two bridges in northern Nicaragua. This act not only had the effect of strengthening the administration's commitment to armed struggle, but also caused the Sandinistas to intensify their repression of suspected sympathizers, thereby winning additional converts to the FDN. The House Permanent Select Intelligence Committee had voted to approve U.S. covert actions as long as their sole aim was arms interdiction. When news reports claimed that the *contras* wished to overthrow the Nicaraguan government, the House, in December 1982, adopted the first Boland amendment, 411–0, to prohibit expending U.S. funds for that purpose. Meanwhile, the Reagan administration, to its great annoyance, was also burdened with a regional initiative by Mexico, Panama, Colombia, and Venezuela—the "Contadora" countries—to negotiate a settlement with the Sandinistas.

During 1982 and 1983 it had become increasingly obvious to U.S. intelligence agencies that the flow of Nicaraguan arms to El Salvador had virtually stopped. But instead of moving to resuscitate the Enders proposals of 1981, Reagan signed another presidential finding in September 1983 that authorized support for the FDN in order to induce the Sandinistas to negotiate with its neighbors and to "pressure" them to cease assisting the FMLN. This open-ended goal paved the way for a greatly increased U.S. naval and military presence in Honduras and off the Nicaraguan coast, as well as a contingency plan for an invasion, if provoked. Yet, despite the heady atmosphere that prevailed at the White House in the aftermath of the Grenada "rescue mission," the administration refused to consider seriously directly intervening in Nicaragua, and it even discouraged the FDN from capturing Nicaraguan territory in order to proclaim a "Free Nicaragua" government. And it did so, at least in part, because of the vehement objections of Weinberger and the JCS. The secretary of defense repeatedly raised the specter of Vietnam in high-level policy discussions and "worried over the possibility that the president would be drawn into 'involuntary escalation.'"[117]

In October 1984 Weinberger took the extraordinary step of publicly laying down six "tests" that any proposed U.S. military action must meet prior to presidential approval. If followed, these tests would have effectively removed "limited war" as a foreign policy option. Yet the effectiveness of the Department of Defense's (DOD) preferred tactic—conducting provocative maneuvers in Honduras and along Nicaragua's coastlines—was seriously damaged by the White House decision to announce these operations in advance and to issue assurances that they did not presage an invasion. This practice, of course, stemmed from the perceived need to avoid provoking a hostile domestic reaction.

During 1984 the House, partly in response to credible reports that the CIA had participated in mining Nicaraguan harbors and had helped the *contras* compile an "assassination manual," repeatedly voted to end funding of the "covert" war. It had first done so in September 1983 (H.R. 2760). Yet the Senate, controlled by the Republicans, refused to go along until late 1984. Finally, in March 1985 the House rejected Reagan's request for $14 million in military aid as well as two requests for "humanitarian assistance."[118] Soon thereafter Daniel Ortega visited Moscow, and the administration embarked on a fierce rhetorical campaign. Democrats, their ranks split and on the defensive, sought political cover in the form of "nonlethal, humanitarian" assistance. Reagan, for his part, sent a letter to Congress promising to "pursue political, not military solutions, in Central America." In June 1985 both houses voted to provide $27 million in humanitarian aid to the FDN so long as the *contras* stayed in their Honduran camps and observed a cease-fire. With this action Reagan had established the principle that the *contras* were a legitimate organization worthy of U.S. support, though it remained unclear exactly how humanitarian aid could do much more than feed them.

In February 1986 Reagan went back to Congress to ask for another $100 million, three-quarters of which was military. Once again the administration combined harsh rhetoric and symbolic concessions—the widely respected Philip Habib was appointed as special ambassador to Central America—to wear down congressional resistance. The administration, despite Reagan's pledge to seek a diplomatic resolution, tried its best to frustrate Contadora efforts while blaming Nicaragua for the failure to produce an acceptable treaty. In fact, neither nation wished to compromise, and Habib eventually resigned. And when the World Court decided in June 1986 that the United States had violated international law by helping the *contras* mine Nicaraguan harbors and destroy transportation facilities, the Reagan administration rejected the judgment and reiterated its commitment to the FDN.

But the administration found it much more difficult to sustain its Nicaraguan policy in the wake of the sensational Iran-*contra* revelations. In its zeal to provide Nicaragua with a "democratic" alternative, Reagan officials had solicited *contra* funds from the Saudi royal family, the Sultan of Brunei, and Taiwan. Moreover, in order to evade earlier congressional prohibitions against aiding the FDN, the NSC had helped to organize an "Enterprise" to train and fund the *contras*. Thus Reagan's call for volunteerism and private sector takeovers of previously public responsibilities reached their ultimate conclusion—a private foreign policy!

Nevertheless, Reagan survived and in the autumn of 1987 asked Congress to refund the FDN for yet another year. The administration skillfully exploited the public's infatuation with Lt. Colonel Oliver North and the testimony of a Sandinista defector, which, among other things, claimed that some of the "commandantes" maintained secret Swiss bank accounts. In late December Congress voted to keep the *contras* alive with $8 million in humanitarian aid and promised to vote again in February 1988.

By then Costa Rican president Oscar Arias had developed a regional peace plan that seemed to meet almost all of the administration's professed goals, including internal democratization processes and verification procedures to insure an end to arms trafficking. Reagan officials, however, while awkwardly welcoming the proposals in public, undertook a campaign to damage Arias' credibility and privately urged the FDN to harden its negotiating position. On March 23, 1988, the Sandinistas and the *contras* signed an agreement that Reagan officials feared would lead to the surrender of the FDN. One week later House Speaker Jim Wright (D-TX) succeeded in putting together $47 million in aid that included humanitarian assistance channeled through "neutral organizations," a fund to help children victimized by the war, and money for a verification commission. Both chambers overwhelmingly approved this package.

Yet many in the administration remained convinced that the Sandinistas would never allow "democracy" in Nicaragua and would interpret congressional action as an invitation to destroy the FDN. When, early in March, Congress refused to refund the *contras*, Reagan pounded his desk and exploded: "This is the same old thing by Congress. Look at all the countries that went down the tubes right after Vietnam because of congressional interference in foreign policy."[119]

Reagan's frustration should be measured against the administration's stubborn seven-year effort to publicly legitimate its Nicaraguan policy. From the very beginning its Central American initiatives had provoked controversy. Public hostility had greeted early efforts to shore up the Salvadoran junta with military aid and a few dozen U.S. advisers, because it triggered widespread fears about another Vietnam in the making. Death squad atrocities, apparently carried out with the connivance of the Salvadoran government, outraged many members of Congress, as did Jeane Kirkpatrick's suggestion that the four murdered American nuns were partly responsible for their own deaths. But when the administration began to shift toward a policy of reform in El Salvador, primarily by encouraging legislative and presidential elections, congressional and public support notably increased. While a substantial number of congressional Democrats continued to question the Duarte government's commitment to land reform and human rights, by 1984 Reagan's Salvadoran policy had been substantially legitimated.

But Nicaragua soon replaced El Salvador as an object of domestic controversy, and remained so despite the administration's unending verbal offensive designed to mobilize public support. Reagan literally tried everything to persuade Congress and the public of the wisdom of his Nicaraguan policy. At the core of this effort lay the multifaceted contention, coordinated by the Office of Public Diplomacy, that America's vital interests were at stake in Central America, and that Nicaragua threatened U.S. security. In contrast to Vietnam, where Haig claimed national security had not been directly at issue after all, "in Central America we're talking about the strategic vulnerability of the Canal. . . . We are . . . at the core of United States hemispheric interests."[120] Unlike Southeast Asia, which was half a world away, Central America, the administration argued, was in "our backyard," and, with the Caribbean, formed "our fourth border," a "strategic basin" containing "vital" shipping lanes. Reagan recalled how Nazi submarines in 1942 had threatened these routes and had sunk several allied ships. Other administration officials occasionally claimed that the Caribbean Basin possessed critical strategic materials. They even contended that the United States needed to preserve access to regional air and naval facilities in Puerto Rico, Cuba, and Honduras. More significant was the assertion that Nicaragua as a Soviet-Cuban outpost would pose a genuine threat to Central American stability and ultimately U.S. national security. Like Grenada, a Sovietized Nicaragua could be used as a missile and submarine base to launch attacks against the U.S. mainland. Administration spokespersons more frequently invoked a domino scenario, whereby other Central American states would be subverted, intimidated, or invaded by Nicaragua until Mexico itself crumbled. Moreover, they predicted that the resultant turmoil would unleash floods of refugees that would weaken—in unspecified ways—the social fabric of the United States.

But the administration implied that something more than American physical security was at stake—its credibility as a beacon of freedom and a world leader depended on its willingness to support the FDN. If the United States failed to act in Central America, where would it act? The line had to be drawn, or else our allies would doubt our reliability and our adversaries would be emboldened. Similar arguments had, of course, been used by cold war presidents in a variety of contexts, but they had been rarely heard since Vietnam. After initially denying the validity of the Vietnam analogy to Central America, Reagan officials, as they scrambled for *contra* votes in Congress, began to welcome the comparison. In April 1985 Secretary Shultz noted that during the Vietnam War some Americans had made "an endless and shifting sequence of apologies for the Communists," had condemned "military solutions," and had then turned their attacks on the United States itself. He warned that "we should bear this past experience in mind in our contemporary debates," for "the litany of apology for Communists and condemnation for America and our friends is beginning again." In fact, "our goals in Central America *are* like those we had in Vietnam: democracy, economic progress, and security against aggression."[121] These officials tread very carefully, however, and repeatedly claimed that U.S. support for the FDN constituted an alternative to direct intervention, not the prelude that congressional opponents predicted. Indeed, Reagan argued that to oppose *contra* aid now made direct U.S. involvement in the future more likely.

He also tried to cast the Nicaraguan issue as a moral drama. What had the Sandinistas done to incur Reagan's wrath? After solemnly pledging to liberate Nicaragua from tyranny, they had instead "betrayed" their revolution by refusing to create a genuine democracy. By imprisoning their opponents, persecuting the Catholic Church, forcibly relocating the Mesquito Indians, shutting down a free press, and building an enormous army, the Sandinistas had transformed Nicaragua into a "totalitarian dungeon." Not only had they welcomed Cuban and Soviet military personnel and received vast quantities of offensive weapons, but they had invited "terrorists" to Nicaragua from Libya, Iran, and North Korea and had spearheaded a drive to export illegal drugs to the United States. Facing this unspeakable evil was the "democratic resistance," "our brothers, these freedom fighters of Nicaragua," "the moral equal of our Founding Fathers and the brave men and women of the French Resistance." For Reagan, "the struggle here is not right versus left; it is right versus wrong."[122] Rarely had a president used such words to describe the *U.S.* Army, let alone a five-year-old organization that critics claimed was dominated by Somozistas. Certainly no senior U.S. official had ever lavished such praise on the government of South Vietnam. But that, of course, was the point.

Yet these efforts were damaged by claims that the administration was seeking to overthrow the Nicaraguan government. Reagan and his advisers at times half-heartedly denied these charges, but on other occasions implied that the Sandinistas had to be replaced or at least say "uncle." These congressional concerns compelled Reagan to legitimate his Nicaraguan policy as an effort to find a diplomatic solution. As a result, Reagan appointed a string of special ambassadors to Central America. They and Shultz engaged the Sandinistas in desultory bilateral discussions in Mexico and Nicaragua. But nothing was accomplished, for the Sandinistas demanded that the U.S. withdraw support from the *contras*, while the adminstration would accept nothing less than FDN participation in the Nicaraguan government. Nevertheless, diplomatic initiatives probably convinced twenty to thirty House Democrats to vote for *contra* aid.

Reagan also attempted to portray his policy as bipartisan and consensual, and as part of a larger effort to bring democracy and stability to all of Central America. His Caribbean Basin Initiative, announced in early 1982 and passed by Congress in August 1983, provided economic and military assistance, and investment and trade incentives to the entire region, except, of course, Cuba, Nicaragua, and Grenada. Turning to a favorite device, Reagan appointed the allegedly bipartisan Kissinger Commission, charged with developing additional policy recommendations for Central America. Composed of conservative to moderate Republicans and Democrats, it contended that the "roots of the crisis are both indigenous and foreign," but also claimed that "in the Central American-Caribbean region, our credibility world wide is engaged. The triumph of hostile forces in what the Soviets call the 'strategic rear' of the United States would be read as a sign of U.S. impotence."[123] Despite its endorsement of land reform, congressional liberals correctly saw the Commission as a disguised attempt by the administration to create a center-right coalition supportive of aid to the *contras*. Finally, Reagan officials portrayed non-Nicaraguan Central America as a hotbed of democratic vitality. The Sandinistas' totalitarian grip thus became ludicrously anachronistic as states like Honduras and Guatemala became increasingly democratic. Yet Costa Rica, indisputably the region's foremost democracy, seemed equally critical of both Managua and Washington, and by 1988 the administration was even more seriously embarrassed by revelations tying the CIA to the drug trafficking Manuel Noriega of Panama. Reagan's presumably clear moral categories appeared to be blurring.

Until the blossoming of Soviet-American détente in 1987 and 1988 the tiny nation of Nicaragua had become the central preoccupation of American foreign policy and the focal point of presidential rhetoric. It was also partly responsible for creating the paramount crisis of the Reagan presidency. Yet the reasons for the administration's rather extraordinary exertions remain elusive. From the vantage point of the early 1980s this policy seemed designed to implement the "prevailing with pride" strategy. At the very least, it would raise the cost that Moscow would be obliged to pay to retain a peripheral client, and a policy of unremitting pressure might even succeed in toppling the Sandinistas and thus puncture the Brezhnev Doctrine. Moreover, it would provide an opportunity for the United States to atone in part for its mishandling of the Cuban Revolution in the late 1950s and early 1960s. Reagan, after all, had been disappointed when Kennedy had resolved the missile crisis without invading Cuba.[124] But the paltry sums that the administration requested from Congress to support the FDN undermine this explanation. While it is true that by the late 1980s the Nicaraguan economy lay in ruins, the reasons for its collapse had less to do with the *contras* than with governmental mismanagement, decreases in Soviet aid, and the U.S. trade embargo.[125] On the other hand, the administration could plausibly claim that its economic pressure had contributed to this situation. Yet the destruction of the Nicaraguan economy had never been publicly offered as a policy aim.

From the viewpoint of the late 1980s there was a growing suspicion, however, that Reagan's Nicaragua policy had been a sop to pacify the hard

Right, while the administration built bridges to Gorbachev. John Carbaugh, the Helms aide who played an early role in bringing the *contras* to
the administration's attention, suggested that "Haig and Enders realized
they had to throw a bone to the right-wingers. They can't have the Soviet
Union or the Middle East or Western Europe. All are too important."[126] But
this explanation had little to say about Reagan's attitude. Was he part of
this scheme, or had he been persuaded by Kirkpatrick, Casey, and other
zealots to lead the charge against the Sandinistas? Given the fact that Reagan remained committed to the "democratic resistance" even after virtually
all of the original supporters had left the government, Carbaugh's thesis
appears rather dubious. But it does acknowledge the anomaly of a fiercely
anti-Sandinista president strolling arm-in-arm through Red Square with his
"friend," Mikhail Gorbachev, in May 1988.

A third, and somewhat more compelling explanation would interpret
Reagan's Nicaraguan policy as yet another example of the president's uncanny ability to know how far to push a pet project in the face of public
and congressional resistance. Recognizing from the beginning that his would
inevitably be a Vietnam-traumatized administration, Reagan nevertheless
saw in Central America the opportunity to defeat a Soviet proxy with relatively little risk. According to this view, the administration never had the
slightest inclination to send U.S. troops to Nicaragua. At the very least,
Reagan's fierce rhetoric would drive dissenting Democrats into a political
corner by questioning their commitment to freedom and democracy. The
Democratic party could then be charged with "losing Nicaragua," and the
Republicans could even more thoroughly monopolize the national security
issue.

But unlike Grenada, where Congress and the public applauded the
success of the "rescue mission," the administration never obtained majority
public backing for its Nicaraguan policy. By March 1986 those who believed that Nicaragua posed a threat to the security of the United States had
risen to 56 percent, though only 29 percent deemed it a "major" threat. Yet
at no time between 1983 and 1987 did more than 28 percent believe that
the United States should try to secretly overthrow the Sandinistas (March
1986), and by January 1987, immediately after Iran-*contra*, that figure had
fallen to 16 percent. Opposition to a U.S. invasion of Nicaragua was comparably high. Most of the public (57–59 percent) blamed the trouble in
Central America on poverty and the lack of human rights, though about the
same number opposed the spread of Communism there. A large part of the
public favored nonmilitary approaches to Nicaragua. For example, a May
1984 Harris Poll revealed that 81 percent supported the Contadora process.

And while public fears that the United States was headed for another Vietnam in Central America fell from 68 percent in the early 1980s to 30 percent by 1986, support for the *contras* rarely rose above one-third. Most telling, perhaps, was that Reagan's overall approval rating consistently ran from 15 to 28 percent ahead of his Nicaraguan policy.[127]

Just before leaving office in January 1989, Lt. General Colin Powell, Reagan's sixth NSC adviser, admitted that the administration had failed to educate the public about the seriousness of the Nicaraguan problem and blamed it on insufficient effort. Interviews that we conducted with NSC staffers confirmed that view.[128] It is certainly true that the public's understanding of the Central American situation remained very low. For example, an April 1986 CBS/*New York Times* poll showed that 50 percent of the public did not know anything about the Nicaraguan government, and that among those who did, half believed it to be a right-wing dictatorship.[129] Nor did Reagan's rhetorical warfare change many people's minds. From mid-1983 to 1985 those who supported the overthrow of the Sandinistas rose from 23 to 32 percent, and from March 1985 to July 1986 approval of Reagan's handling of Nicaragua increased nine points to 35 percent.[130] Yet even this modest shift was erased by Iran-*contra*. What more could Reagan have done to "educate" the public? Neither Powell nor his aides had any suggestions.

But the Nicaragua issue did have significant differential impact on the major political parties. A May 1986 *National Journal* poll indicated that 16 percent of the Democrats and 36 percent of the Republicans favored aid to the *contras*, while 75 percent of the Democrats and 51 percent of the GOP opposed it. A 1985 poll showed that of the 38 percent of the pubic who knew of U.S. support for the *contras*, 67 percent of the Republicans approved and 64 percent of the Democrats opposed this policy.[131] In short, this issue seemed to divide the attentive public along party lines.

A NEW FOREIGN POLICY CONSENSUS?

President Reagan's rhetoric left little doubt about the answer to this question. As he put it in December 1988,

> In the decade of the eighties the cause of freedom and human rights has prospered and the spectre of nuclear war has been pushed back because the democracies have recovered their strength, their compass. Here at home a national consensus on the importance of strong national leadership is emerg-

ing. No legacy would make me more proud than leaving in place such a consensus for the cause of world freedom, a consensus that prevents a paralysis of American power from ever occurring again.[132]

Nor was he shy about discovering the reasons:

And as I walk off into the city streets, a final word to the men and women of the Reagan revolution. . . . My friends: We did it. We weren't just marking time. We made a difference. We made the city stronger. We made the city freer, and we left her in good hands. All in all, not bad, not bad at all.[133]

And, in fact, a persuasive case could be made to support Reagan's claims. The United States did seem "more prosperous, more secure and happier"[134] than it had eight years before. An unprecedented period of recession-free, low-inflation economic growth had replaced the stagflationary rut of the 1970s. A resurgence of national self-confidence and pride, predicted by Reagan in 1981, had apparently swept away the guilt, doubt, and introspection of the previous decade. An ambitious program of military expansion and modernization, coupled with the administration's determination to deploy Pershing II and cruise missiles, had frightened the Soviets into signing an asymmetrical arms control agreement and had paved the way for deep strategic cuts as well. The Reagan Doctrine, by deftly exploiting Soviet vulnerabilities on the periphery of its empire, had compelled a withdrawal from Afghanistan and had facilitated a settlement in Angola. The result was a new, and infinitely better détente, based not on Soviet promises of domestic reform and international restraint but on deeds. And in contrast to the 1970s, when superpower détente had been haunted by the spectre of American decline and Russian ascendancy, the 1980s version featured a reenergized United States and an enervated, bankrupt Soviet Union. Finally, the Reagan foreign policy had evidently been instrumental in once again making America relevant to the rest of the world, for its message of freedom and democracy had found eager audiences everywhere. Now a democratic revolution was sweeping the globe from the Philippines and Latin America to Eastern Europe, China, and even the Soviet Union. Indeed, it was difficult to avoid the conclusion that the cold war had ended (or nearly so), that the West had won, and that the old American dream of a world of liberal democratic states would soon be realized.

In light of these achievements and prospects, was not Reagan also correct in claiming as his legacy the reemergence of a domestic foreign policy consensus? After all, signs of consensus abounded. At the elite level, scholars, pundits, and participants in the 1970s had emphasized the seemingly intractable divisions that hindered efforts to achieve a coherent, supportable foreign policy. The notion of consensus was rarely discussed. James Chace, in a 1978 *Foreign Affairs* essay did so, but only to dismiss it as a remote possibility, and, as we have seen, neoconservatives waged a four-year war against the Carter foreign policy.[135] Yet by the mid-1980s this situation had begun to change. During the 1984 presidential campaign the Center for Security and International Studies sponsored a symposium on bipartisanship and consensus and in early 1985 Richard Lugar (R-IN), the new chairman of the Senate Foreign Relations Committee, conducted hearings on "Commitments, Consensus, and U.S. Foreign Policy." And while it may be correctly objected that neither exercise showed much interest in exposing a broad spectrum of opinion, more difficult to ignore was a 1988 *Foreign Affairs* article by Henry Kissinger and Cyrus Vance who buried old hatchets in order to formulate the outlines of a consensual foreign policy.[136] More pessimistically, the Foreign Policy Institute of Johns Hopkins University, acknowledged that "during the past dozen years, the number and intensity of contentious issues in U.S. foreign and defense policy, already severe since the mid-1960s, have risen markedly and now threaten a serious breakdown in the policy process." But in early 1988 it launched a program designed to identify a "middle ground" where a bipartisan consensus could be built on significant issues of immediate relevance.[137] In short, on the eve of the 1988 presidential election, consensus, if not yet achieved, had once again become a prominent feature of elite discourse.

Moreover, by 1988 public attitudes about foreign policy, carefully measured in two extraordinarily detailed surveys—Americans Talk Security (ATS) and the Public Agenda Foundation (PAF)[138] project—appeared to vindicate Reagan's claim of an emergent national consensus. Democratic pollster John Marttila, one of the principal ATS researchers, announced that "the president's success in negotiating with Mr. Gorbachev has . . . reestablished a national bipartisan consensus on U.S.-Soviet relations."[139] The twelve ATS reports demonstrated that about two-thirds of the public believed that the Reagan military buildup had been necessary, that about the same percentage counselled cautious negotiation with the Soviets from a position of U.S. strength, and that a strong majority thought that real opportunities existed for important breakthroughs in the superpower relationship.[140] The PAF project characterized these attitudes as a "rational, hard-headed stance on which a new national consensus, can be firmly built."[141] Though voters remained suspicious of Soviet intentions, 57 percent believed that relations with the Soviets would continue to improve and lead to fundamental change.[142] In a May 1988 ATS survey 75 percent of the respondents gave excellent or good marks to Reagan for "standing up to the Soviets," 73 percent for "keeping America out of war," 73 percent for his arms control record, 71 percent for "developing a sound national defense," and 61 percent for using U.S. military power appropriately.[143] That same poll indicated that clear majorities credited Reagan with "promoting the spread of democracy," "preventing the spread of communism," and "winning respect for America." According to Mitchell E. Daniels, former chief political adviser to Reagan, "Right now, in at least its general outlines, Reagan's view of the world seems to be vindicated in the eyes of most people."[144] And these public perceptions provided the Republican party with an important political edge, for most Americans had come to view it as the party of both strength *and* peace.

George Bush and Michael Dukakis conducted their fall 1988 campaigns as if convinced of an emergent foreign policy consensus. Bush skillfully portrayed himself as Reagan's rightful heir, willing and able to combine negotiations with national power, while dismissing the inexperienced governor of Massachusetts as a warmed-over Jimmy Carter who would bargain away American strength in order to cut imprudent deals with the Soviet Union. Dukakis, though suggesting that Gorbachev deserved much of the credit for improved Superpower relations, pledged to pursue Reagan's Soviet policy, and applauded the window of opportunity opened by the president with an enthusiasm that even Bush found difficult to match.[145] Stung by Bush's charges of weakness on national security issues, Dukakis softened his earlier stand against "modernizing" the U.S. land-based nuclear deterrent, promised to continue SDI research, and took an unfortunate ride in a tank to demonstrate his toughness. Indeed, he did his best to avoid foreign policy issues except to implicate Bush in Iran-*contra* and sleazy dealings with General Noriega.

Had Ronald Reagan left America with its first genuine foreign policy consensus in twenty-five years? Had he, in the conceptual vocabulary of our study, legitimated his grand design, strategy, and tactics?

Certainly Reagan's grand design possessed enormous appeal, largely because it deftly employed powerful symbols to tap into important dimensions of America's civil religion. Reagan's articulation of a shining city on the hill—compassionate, moral, strong, and exceptional—constituted the secular equivalent of a stern yet loving Providence so ingrained in traditional American Protestantism. This city, dedicated to individual freedom and democratic government, had long served as a beacon of hope for all humanity. Reagan's "dream" was for the rest of the world to experience the exhilaration of a democratic revolution, and now that America was once again prosperous and strong, it could help others achieve freedom.

What gave this grand design significance was not its originality. Woodrow Wilson and his cold war successors had shared comparable visions. But Reagan was the first president in a generation to invoke unabashedly these things without fueling firestorms of protests and derision. This "dream" resonated positively through much of the population in part because it captured the essence of the new patriotism and in part because, with the decline of Communism and the retreat of the Soviet Union, it seemed both more plausible and less dangerous.

Furthermore, in contrast to the disguised and fuzzy designs of Nixon and Carter which seemed retreatist and, in Nixon's case, amoral as well, Reagan's vision combined an unshakable faith in the future with moral fervor. In Reagan's America it became politically impermissible to even hint at national decline or to doubt the universal validity of the American dream. Not surprisingly, the president and other administration officials repeatedly scored points by portraying the Democratic party as "doomsayers" and the "Blame-America-First crowd." The Democrats, including Dukakis, responded by protesting the profundity of their optimism and patriotism. George Bush's pledge of allegiance ploy in the 1988 campaign should be viewed as a heavy-handed (and effective) effort to exploit this component of the Reagan legacy.

Reagan's resuscitation of a Wilsonian internationalist grand design—a world of free, democratic, and thus peaceful states—achieved both normative and cognitive legitimacy. But he proved less successful in legitimating his strategy, especially in regard to the critical issue of the use of U.S. military power abroad—the primary cause, after all, of the breakdown of the cold war consensus.

As we have seen, the Regan administration, upon taking office, believed that a reconstituted domestic base—a revived economy, a vast rearmament program, and a renewed vision of and confidence in America and its role in the world—took priority over anything else. This strengthened domestic base could then be used to stop and gradually reverse the decline in America's international standing, to restore a willingness to employ national power, and to halt the expansion of Soviet influence as a prelude perhaps to putting Moscow on the defensive. In retrospect, as Robert W. Tucker has correctly noted, President Reagan possessed an even grander strategic goal: the alteration of the essential conditions that had defined American security for most of the postwar era—nuclear deterrence and the Soviet threat.[146]

Reagan, to the utter disbelief of many observers, harbored deeply antinuclear sentiments. Though many of his advisers wished to transcend deterrence by achieving strategic superiority and war-fighting capabilities, Reagan embraced SDI primarily because he viewed nuclear weapons as intrinsically evil and threatening and secondarily as an insurance policy against the possibility that an agreement eliminating all nuclear weapons might eventually be violated.[147] Moreover, while these advisers offered arms control proposals and verification demands that they knew the Soviet Union would reject, Reagan took these initiatives seriously. When Gorbachev surprisingly accepted many of them, Reagan, to the horror of Weinberger, Richard Perle, and others, moved to conclude agreements that eliminated intermediate range nuclear forces and anticipated deep strategic reductions. A clear majority of the public supported SDI as a population shield and START as a way to reduce nuclear arms.[148] Though most experts continued to dismiss SDI as either technologically infeasible—at least its "leakproof" version—or strategically destabilizing (or both), Reagan nevertheless played a major role in forging a nascent antinuclear national consensus. But if Reagan helped to erode the public's faith in nuclear deterrence, it remained to be seen what, if anything, would replace it. Thus far attempts to redefine the conditions of American security—for example, conventional deterrence and common security—have yet to become part of the political mainstream.

On the other hand, Reagan's antipathy toward containment had been more widely recognized—and feared. These long-standing moral and strategic doubts, which he shared with many American conservatives, dated at least from the 1950s. For Reagan, the United States failure in Vietnam demonstrated the moral and strategic bankruptcy of containment, not because it had produced indiscriminate intervention as liberal critics had claimed, but because it was insufficiently ambitious. Hence the Johnson administration, in its fastidious attempt to implement containment in Vietnam, refused to win the war by destroying the external sources of Vietcong support. That decision had produced a military stalemate which, in turn, unleashed the antiwar movement at home. It and Congress then proceeded to prevent U.S. forces from winning in Vietnam. Moreover, the war's legacy left a deep national skepticism about the overall utility and legitimacy of American military power.

The Soviet Union, meanwhile, had allegedly taken advantage of this post-Vietnam paralysis to vastly expand its global influence. The United States, Reagan and many of his advisers believed, might take advantage of the resulting imperial overstretch if it could move beyond containment to chip away at these new outposts and perhaps trigger a chain reaction throughout the Soviet empire. By 1985 this vague aspiration had been codified in the Reagan Doctrine which proclaimed for the United States the right to intervene against Marxist-Leninist governments on the grounds that they had come to power through illegitimate means.

Yet in the absence of a new public consensus about the proper use of U.S. military power which in turn implied a drastically revised memory of the Vietnam War, the grand objectives of the Reagan Doctrine could not be fulfilled. Nevertheless, as we have seen, the administration in its otherwise assertive declaratory history of recent American foreign policy, tried to avoid even mentioning Vietnam. It certainly did not undertake a systematic revision of the prevailing understanding of the war. The very nature of the Reagan Doctrine—the support of "freedom fighters" as an alternative to direct intervention—implicitly acknowledged the administration's refusal to challenge the "Vietnam syndrome" despite occasional rhetoric about the "noble cause." It might disparage the "Solarz Doctrine" as the willingness to aid anti-Soviet guerrillas so long as they stayed "eight time zones away," but the eagerness of anti-*contra* Democrats to support Afghan and Angolan rebels went to the heart of the matter. There was, after all, absolutely no possibility that U.S. troops would be sent to rescue the *mujahadeen* or UNITA (National Union for the Total Independence of Angola), but both Congress and the nation fretted that Reagan would indeed directly intervene to save the FDN or facilitate their overthrow of the Sandinistas. And, as we have seen, the administration itself remained ambivalent about whether the *contras* would suck America into another Vietnam-type quagmire. The Grenada "rescue mission" and the April 1986 bombing of Libya demonstrated that the public would support low-risk, ends-specific, limited-cost military operations, but it would doubtless have also supported a successful "Desert One" outcome in the Carter years. After eight years of Reagan rhetoric about a fully democratic world the nation remained deeply divided about the external conditions of American security. A January 1989 ATS poll indicated that a 45 to 49 percent plurality agreed that the failure in Vietnam showed that the United States should only fight a war to repel an invasion of the nation itself.[149] If, however, the cold war had all but ended and the world was on the verge of universal democracy, then the continuing dissensus about U.S. military power would presumably be irrelevant, for there would no longer be any need to intervene anywhere.

Reagan's détente indeed attained a domestic legitimacy that far exceeded Nixon's. Unlike the early 1970s when the so-called global correlation of forces appeared to tilt away from the West toward Moscow (and the Third World as well), Détente II crystallized at a time of perceived U.S. resurgence and growing Soviet weakness. On that basis alone it became much more difficult for American skeptics to dismiss Reagan's détente as disguised appeasement. Those who tried did so largely from *within* the administration, but by late 1987 most of them had resigned. Second, whereas a politically insecure Nixon had promised much and delivered relatively little, Détente II's evident accomplishments came as a pleasant surprise in part because Reagan had not raised public expectations. When, with relatively little forewarning, the Soviets withdrew from Afghanistan, showed new interest in an Angolan compromise, signed an asymmetrical INF treaty with an intrusive inspection regime, and announced *glasnost* and *perestroika* at home, the American public grew increasingly optimistic about the prospects for superpower amity. Moreover, much of the public remembered the disillusionment produced by the disappointments of Détente I and was more inclined to proceed cautiously this time.[150] Finally, and perhaps most importantly, in contrast to the Nixon-Kissinger strategy, which had insisted that Soviet domestic institutions be insulated from the issue of superpower relations, from the start Reagan had emphasized the moral shortcomings of the Soviet system. And while he never explicitly made internal reform a precondition for improved relations, the administration did put human rights on the agenda of every Reagan-Gorbachev summit and publicly applauded Soviet progress. Given this record the public seemed understandably puzzled when Reagan during the Moscow summit blamed remaining Soviet domestic repression not on Communism, but on "bureaucracy." The Soviet Union had apparently become just another over-centralized state.

But if Nixon's détente lacked domestic legitimacy because it tried to ignore Moscow's moral turpitude, Détente II risked becoming hostage to ever-expanding Soviet political reforms. During 1988 these reforms, as well as greatly moderated external behavior, were largely responsible for lowering by fifteen points—to forty-five—the percentage of Americans who believed the Soviet Union constituted a serious threat to the United States. Nevertheless 66 percent still believed that Communism threatened American moral and religious values.[151] If Gorbachev's political reforms were halted or reversed, Détente II would be difficult to sustain in the United States even if Soviet foreign policy failed to grow more provocative. In this sense Reagan's domestically appealing dream of a democratic world inevitably endangered any détente that did not demand continued Soviet democratization.

At the same time, the rather drastic diminution of the perceived Soviet threat thrust to the surface a variety of less conventional security issues that hounded the Reagan administration during its final months in office. Thus, in the 1988 ATS surveys the public consistently indicated that international drug trafficking, terrorism, nuclear proliferation, and economic competition from Japan and West Germany would pose greater threats to the United States in the 1990s than Soviet expansionism.[152] Moreover, less than 50 percent believed that the administration had handled these issues well, while a mere 26 percent approved of its policy toward General Manuel Noriega.[153] Yet in light of the experience of the last forty-five years, it seems likely that if Détente II began to unravel, public concerns about the Soviet Union would push these newer issues to the background. Nevertheless these polls suggested that if the cold war were to end, potentially divisive issues—particularly those related to drugs and economic security—might prevent a new national consensus from soon emerging.

In sum, while Ronald Reagan did achieve more domestic legitimacy for his foreign policy strategy than the other post-Vietnam presidents, his accomplishments should not be exaggerated. He helped to shake the public's faith in nuclear deterrence without necessarily providing a workable alternative. He argued that U.S. support for anti-Soviet "freedom fighters" constituted self-defense, but most of the public remained unmoved by the primary focus of the Reagan Doctrine. And although his Soviet policies were overwhelmingly popular with the American public, Reagan's détente—built on the public expectation of continuing Soviet democratization—could yet prove to be evanescent.

On the other hand, there can be little doubt that Reagan's rhetoric—central to his foreign policy tactics—captivated the American public like no president since Franklin D. Roosevelt or perhaps John F. Kennedy. Whether employed to send hostile or friendly signals to Moscow or to mobilize domestic support, Reagan's words were paramount. And when his simple moral messages became uncharacteristically garbled, as during the Iran-*contra* affair, Reagan's public standing plummeted. More often, however, Reagan (and his speechwriters) used words to spectacular effect to make his policies appear not only prudent but ethically superior. And that, ironically, was achieved by a president who presided over an administration marked by more scandal than any since Warren G. Harding.

Did Reagan reconstruct the cultural components of a domestic foreign policy consensus? At the conclusion of his first Inaugural Address the new president told a story about Martin Treptow, a doughboy killed in France. On his body was found a diary containing an entry entitled "My Pledge." It read: "America must win this war. Therefore I will work, I will save, I will sacrifice, I will endure, I will fight cheerfully and do my utmost, as if the issue of the whole struggle depended on me alone." But this tale did not foreshadow a "bear any burden, pay any price" message, for Reagan quickly assured the nation that the present crisis did not demand the sort of sacrifice made by Martin Treptow. Rather it would only require "our best effort and our willingness to believe in ourselves and to believe in our capacity to perform great deeds. . . . "[154] Three years later George Shultz, in a surprisingly frank statement, admitted that "We cannot pay *any* price or bear *any* burden. We must discriminate. We must be prudent and careful. . . . " Yet while praising Kennedy's inspiring vision Shultz parodied Jimmy Carter's emphasis on global complexity as "a counsel of helplessness," unworthy of an American president.[155] Notwithstanding the secretary's reproof, however, Carter, as we have seen, did search for ways to reinstill an ethic of sacrifice in the American public and delivered sobering sermons about limits and constraints. The same cannot be said for President Reagan. Just as his invocation of the traditional domestic symbols of family and God disguised a message of national self-indulgence (except, of course, for the poor) so too did his rhetoric about a world democratic revolution ask very little of the American people. That was the meaning of his Martin Treptow homily, and it set the tone for the ensuing eight years: pride and confidence without sacrifice. According to Reagan, false limits had been imposed on Americans by an obtrusive federal government, which constrained individual freedom, and naysaying experts, who had lost faith in the American dream. The nation had, of course, for most of the post-1945 era demonstrated a disturbing reluctance to pay for what it wanted. Harry Truman, for example, faced a public who simultaneously demanded military demobilization and a vigorous assault on international Communism. NSC–68 had squared this circle by reassuring him that economic growth rather than increased taxation could finance much higher defense spending. But what had previously been done sporadically, Ronald Reagan institutionalized by tolerating enormous budget deficits that eventually became a structural feature of the U.S. economy. Moreover, by banishing words like *decline*, *limits*, and even *solvency* from contemporary political discourse Reagan repeatedly refused to confront the public with an honest appraisal of America's true global position.[156] Reagan sated the public's understandable desire to "feel good" and thus facilitated a cultural consensus that involved a large dose of illusion.

But not even the irrepressibly optimistic Ronald Reagan could claim to have reconstructed a procedural foreign policy consensus. Most observers agreed that he left executive-legislative relations in at least as much disarray as he had found them in 1981. In one of his valedictory addresses he blamed Congress for "on-again, off-again indecisiveness on resisting Sandinista tyranny and aggression" that "left Central America a region of continuing danger." Moreover, Reagan suggested that some congressional actions in foreign affairs—for example, the War Powers Resolution and attempts to restrict the president's power to implement treaties (that is, ABM)—had institutionalized an "adversarial relationship." These and other legislative intrusions had weakened the "strength and resiliency of the presidency."[157] His words echoed those of Oliver North who eighteen months before had indicted Congress for its "fickle, vacillating, unpredictable, on-again, off-again policy toward the Nicaraguan democratic resistance."[158] At least some members of Congress agreed with Reagan's diagnosis. Two prominent senators, David L. Boren (D-OK) and John C. Danforth (R-MO), after surveying two decades of congressional activism in foreign affairs, deemed much of it "incessant and irrelevant meddling."[159] Thus, members of Congress "take almost limitless opportunities to specify everything from the maximum allowable height above sea level of embassies to the precise manner of deployment of U.S. forces in the Persian Gulf."[160] Or to cite another example, a task force appointed by the House Foreign Affairs Committee to review Congress's role in foreign aid programs and cochaired by Lee Hamilton (D-IN) and Benjamin Gilman (R-NY) concluded that "Foreign assistance is vital to promoting U.S. foreign policy and domestic interests, but the program is hamstrung by too many conflicting objectives, legislative conditions, earmarks, and bureaucratic red tape."[161] One scholar, after interviewing substantial numbers of congressional members and staffers, found that most of the Republicans and perhaps half of the Democrats believed that Congress intervened too directly in the conduct of foreign policy, was too involved in policy formulation, and that its deliberative function had consequently suffered.[162] But some of Reagan's most exuberant admirers blamed the president for allowing Congress to gain an allegedly disproportionate influence over foreign policy. According to this reasoning Reagan had erred in failing to force an up or down vote by Congress that would have established clear responsibility if the *contras* were defeated. Moreover, instead of permitting Attorney General Edwin Meese to treat Iran-*contra* as a possible crime, the president should have told the American people immediately that while the diversion of profits had not been authorized, it was consistent with his policy of using the White House to support the FDN. But rather than claim executive supremacy he invoked the ignorance defense and thus nearly paralyzed the presidency for his remaining two years in office.[163] As George Bush prepared to enter the White House op-ed pages and policy journals brimmed with urgent advice about the need to restore "bipartisanship."[164]

No doubt pervasive congressional intrusions into the technical minutiae of foreign policy had frequently degenerated into absurdity, and some of these proposals for procedural reform would have helped eliminate these sorts of roadblocks and detours. Yet the causes of presidential-congressional frustrations went deeper. Many of these disputes, as we have previously noted in our discussion of the Nixon and Carter years, reflected genuine policy disagreements about the requirements of U.S. security and America's role in the world, and they continued to characterize executive-legislative conflicts during the Reagan administration. Nor can this turmoil be attributed primarily to "mere" partisanship, though with the House under Democratic control for Reagan's entire tenure and the Senate as well after 1986, this factor surely played a role. But the Democratic party itself continued to suffer from the ideological tensions that had marked its foreign policy outlook since the mid-1960s. During the Reagan administration the Democratic party contained at least three identifiable foreign policy factions that, although all subscribing to a vague vision of internationalism, differed sharply on several important issues involving, for example, aid to the *contras*, funding for SDI, foreign trade, and South African sanctions. Indeed, Dukakis's virtual silence on foreign policy during the 1988 campaign stemmed form his need to keep the Sam Nunn–Chuck Robb wing and the Jesse Jackson wing tied to the center of the Democratic party. And while many observers believed that Bush was politically vulnerable on the *contra* issue, Dukakis could not raise it because he and his chosen running mate, Lloyd Bentsen (D-TX), took opposing sides on the funding question.

But if some congressional Democrats relied on procedural devices to obstruct administration policies, Ronald Reagan's reluctance to reassert boldly claims of presidential supremacy in foreign affairs demonstrated the continuing relevance of the Vietnam legacy. To be sure, he grumbled about the Boland amendments, challenged the constitutionality of the War Powers Resolution, argued against stronger South African sanctions, and denounced Senate efforts to compel a strict interpretation of the ABM Treaty. Yet in the end he compromised or surrendered on all of these issues. And he did so because—his rhetoric notwithstanding—he appreciated the limits imposed on presidential prerogatives by the public's collective memory of Vietnam.

NOTES

1. See Jeffrey B. Abramson, F. Christopher Atherton, and Garry R. Orren, *The Electronic Commonwealth: The Impact of New Media Technologies on Democratic Politics* (New York: Basic Books, 1988).

2. Alonzo M. Hamby, *Liberalism and Its Challengers: F.D.R. to Reagan* (New York: Oxford University Press, 1985), 350.

3. Hugh Heclo, "Reaganism and the Search for a Public Philosophy," in John L. Palmer, ed., *Perspectives on the Reagan Years (Washington,* DC: The Urban Institute, 1986); 39.

4. Craig Allen Smith, "MisteReagan's Neighborhood: Rhetoric and National Unity," *Southern Speech Communication Journal* 52 (1987): 220–1.

5. Ronald Reagan, "Address before a Joint Session of the Congress on the State of the Union," January 25, 1983, *Public Papers of the Presidents: Ronald Reagan, 1983, I* (Washington, DC: Government Printing Office, 1984): 110.

6. Ronald Reagan, "Inaugural Address," January 20, 1981, *Public Papers of the Presidents: Ronald Reagan, 1981* (Washington, DC: Government Printing Office, 1982): 2.

7. William K. Muir, Jr., "Ronald Reagan: The Primacy of Rhetoric," in Greenstein ed., *Leadership in the Modern Presidency*, 271.

8. Ronald Reagan, "Address to the Nation on the Economy," February 5, 1981, *Public Papers, 1981*: 80.

9. Ronald Reagan, "Address to the Nation on the Economy," October 13, 1982, *Public Papers of the Presidents: Ronald Reagan, 1982, II* (Washington, DC: Government Printing Office, 1984): 1310.

10. Reagan, "Economy Address, February 5, 1981" 80; Reagan, "Address on Economy," October 13, 1982: 1308.

11. Ronald Reagan, "Address before a Joint Session of the Congress on the State of the Union," January 25, 1984, *Public Papers of the Presidents: Ronald Reagan, 1984, I* (Washington, DC: Government Printing Office, 1985): 88.

12. Heclo, 39–40.

13. Quoted in Heclo, 43.

14. Heclo, 43.

15. Heclo, 46.

16. Ronald Reagan, "Remarks at the Annual Convention of the American Bar Association," July 8, 1985, *Public Papers of the Presidents: Ronald Reagan, 1985, II* (Washington, DC: Government Printing Office, 1986): 898.

17. William Greider, *Atlantic Monthly*, October 1982.

18. Ronald Reagan, "Address to Members of the British Parliament," June 8, 1982. *Public Papers of the Presidents: Ronald Reagan, 1982, I* (Washington, DC: Government Printing Office, 1983): 745, 744, 746.

19. Samuel P. Huntington, "The Defense Policy of the Reagan Administration, 1981–1982," in Fred I. Greenstein, ed., *The Reagan Presidency: An Early Assessment* (Baltimore: Johns Hopkins University Press, 1983): 92.

20. Huntington, 94.

21. William P. Clark, "National Security Strategy," Address Center for Strategic and International Studies, Georgetown University, May 21, 1982: 2.

22. Clark, 3.

23. Huntington, 98.

24. Huntington, 101.

25. *New York Times*, June 26, 1981: 11 and May 30, 1982: 1, 12; Caspar W. Weinberger, *Annual Report to the Congress Fiscal Year 1983* (Washington, DC: Government Printing Office, 1982): 1–16.

26. Jeane J. Kirkpatrick, "Dictatorships and Double Standards," *Commentary*, November 1979: 34–45. In this article Kirkpatrick castigated the Carter administration for its harsh public criticism of friendly dictators like Anastazio Somoza for human rights violations, while largely ignoring the much more serious transgressions of totalitarian regimes. This strategy had played into Moscow's hands by destabilizing these dictatorships and bringing to power unreformable totalitarians.

27. *New York Times*, June 1, 1986: 6.

28. Gaddis, *Strategies of Containment*, 227–8.

29. Barry Blechman with Ethan Gutmann, "A $100 Billion Understanding," *SAIS Review* 9.2 (1989): 74.

30. Terry L. Deibel, "Reagan's Mixed Legacy," *Foreign Policy* 75 (1989): 55.

31. Coral Bell, "From Carter to Reagan," *Foreign Affairs, America and the World, 1984* 63 (1985): 496.

32. Peter M. Benda and Charles H. Levine, "Reagan and the Bureaucracy: the Bequest, the Promise, and the Legacy," in Jones, ed., *The Reagan Legacy*, 136.

33. Muir, 289, 291, 290.

34. Alexander M. Haig, Jr., "Relationship of Foreign and Defense Policies," July 30, 1981 (Washington, DC: U.S. Department of State, *Current Policy*, No. 308).

35. Alexander M. Haig, Jr., "American Power and American Purpose," April 27, 1982 (Washington, DC: U.S. Department of State, *Current Policy*, No. 279).

36. Ronald Reagan, "Remarks at the Annual Washington Conference of the American Legion," February 22, 1983, *Public Papers 1983, I*: 265.

37. Ronald Reagan, "Question-and-Answer Session with High School Students on Domestic and Foreign Policy Issues," January 21, 1983, *Public Papers, 1983, I*: 86.

38. Ronald Reagan, "Excerpts from an Interview with Walter Cronkite of CBS News," March 3, 1981, *Public Papers, 1981, I*: 192–3.

39. Ronald Reagan, "Address to the National Republican Convention in Dallas, Texas," August 23, 1984, *Public Papers of the Presidents: Ronald Reagan, 1984, II* (Washington, DC: Government Printing Office, 1985): 1176.

40. Ronald Reagan, "Address to the Nation on National Defense and National Security," March 23, 1983, *Public Papers, 1983, I*: 442.

41. Ronald Reagan, "Question-and-Answer with Reporters on Domestic and Foreign Policy Issues," May 4, 1983, *Public Papers, 1983, I*: 639.

42. Ronald Reagan, "Address Before a Joint Session of the Congress on Central America," April 27, 1983, *Public Papers, 1983, I*: 604–5.

43. Cf. Ronald Reagan, "Interview with Representatives of NHK Television in Tokyo, Japan," November 11, 1983, *Public Papers of the Presidents: Ronald Reagan, 1983, II* (Washington, DC: Government Printing Office, 1984): 1582.

44. Haig, "Relationship of Policies."

45. Ronald Reagan, "Address to Members of the British Parliament," June 8, 1982, *Public Papers, 1982, I*: 743.

46. Ronald Reagan, "Paths Toward Peace: Deterrence and Arms Control," November 22, 1982 (Washington, DC: U.S. Department of State, *Current Policy*, No. 435).

47. Jeane J. Kirkpatrick, "The Atlantic Alliance and the American National Interest," April 30, 1984 (Washington, DC: U.S. Department of State, *Current Policy*, No. 581). Emphasis added.

48. *New York Times*, August 19, 1980, D17.

49. *New York Times*, February 21, 1982, IV, 2.

50. Ronald Reagan, "Remarks on Presenting the Medal of Honor to Master Sergeant Roy P. Benavidez, February 24, 1981, *Public Papers, 1981*: 155.

51. Ronald Reagan, "The President's News Conference," March 6, 1981, *Public Papers, 1981, I*: 215.

52. Ronald Reagan, "The President's News Conference," April 18, 1985, *Public Papers, 1985, I*: 454.

53. Ronald Reagan, "Remarks to the Corps of Cadets at the U.S. Military Academy," October 28, 1987, *Weekly Compilation of Presidential Documents* 23.43: 1234.

54. Ronald Reagan, "Remarks to the World Affairs Council of Western Massachusetts in Springfield, Massachusetts," April 21, 1988, *Weekly Compilation of Presidential Documents*, 24.16: 504.

55. Ronald Reagan, "Remarks and a Question-and-Answer Session with Students and Guests at the University of Virginia in Charlottesville, Virginia," December 16, 1988, *Weekly Compilation of Presidential Documents*, 24:50: 1633.

56. Ronald Reagan, "Farewell Address to the Nation," January 11, 1989, *Weekly Compilation of Presidential Documents*, 25.2: 53.

57. I. M. Destler, "The Evolution of Reagan Foreign Policy," in Greenstein, ed., *The Reagan Presidency*, 130–1.

58. Bell, 492.

59. Ronald Reagan, "Address at Commencement Exercises at the United States Military Academy," May 21, 1981, *Public Papers, 1981*: 464.

60. John Lewis Gaddis, "Remarks at Panel on the Reagan Foreign Policy Legacy," Midwest meeting of the International Studies Association, Columbus, Ohio, November 11, 1988.

61. See, for example, Michael Krepon, *Strategic Stalemate: Nuclear Weapons and Arms Control in American Politics* (New York: St. Martin's Press, 1984).

62. Ronald Reagan, "Address to the Nation on the Iran Arms and *Contra* Aid Controversy," November 13, 1986, *Public Papers of the Presidents: Ronald Reagan, 1986, II* (Washington, DC: Government Printing Office, 1989): 1546.

63. CBS/*New York Times* Poll, September 10, 1986 and November 13, 1986.

64. Background interviews, May 1988.

65. Ronald Reagan, "Address before a Joint Session of the Congress on the State of the Union," February 6, 1985, *Public Papers, 1985, I*: 135.

66. Reagan, "1985 State of the Union," 134.

67. Reagan, "1985 State of the Union," 135.

68. Ronald Reagan, "Remarks on the Caribbean Basin Initiative to the Permanent Council of the Organization of American States," February 24, 1982. *Public Papers, 1982, I*: 215.

69. Ronald Reagan, "Radio Address to the Nation on Central America," February 14, 1985. *Public Papers, 1985, I*: 173.

70. The Committee of Santa Fe, "A New Inter-American Policy for the Eighties," ed. Lewis Tambs (Washington, DC: Council for Inter-American Security, 1980), 52.

71. "A New Policy," 52.

72. "A New Policy," 52.

73. "A New Policy," 26.

74. Sally A. Shelton at Hearing before the Subcommittee on Inter-American Affairs of the Committee on Foreign Affairs, House of Representatives, 97th Congress, Second Session, June 15, 1982, "United States Policy Toward Grenada" (Washington, DC: Government Printing Office, 1982): 56.

75. *Washington Post*, 6 July 1979: A1.

76. Caleb Rossiter, "The Financial Hit List," *International Policy Report*, February 1984: 4.

77. Rossiter, 4.

78. Rossiter, 4.

79. *Washington Post*, February 27, 1983: A1.

80. *Transafrica Forum* 2 (November–December 1983): 7.

81. *Washington Post*, February 27, 1983: A1.

82. *Transafrica Forum*, November–December, 1983: 7.

83. "House Hearing on Grenada, 1982," 31.

84. Ronald Reagan, "Remarks at Bridgetown, Barbados," April 8, 1982, *Public Papers, 1982, I*: 448.

85. Ronald Reagan, "Central America and El Salvador at the Annual Meeting of the National Association of Manufacturers," March 10, 1983, *Public Papers, 1983, I*: 373.

86. Ronald Reagan, "Address to the Nation on Defense and National Security," March 23, 1983, *Public Papers, 1983, I*: 440.

87. *Washington Post*, February 27, 1983: A1.

88. *Congressional Record*, October 28, 1983, S14884.

89. *Washington Post*, June 8, 1983: A10; *New York Times*, June 10, 1983: 8.

90. Ronald Reagan, "Remarks of the President and Prime Minister Eugenia Charles of Dominica Announcing the Deployment of United States Forces in Grenada," October 25, 1983, *Public Papers, 1983, II*: 1506.

91. For a fuller analysis see Kai P. Schoenhals and Richard A. Melanson, *Revolution and Intervention in Grenada: The New Jewel Movement, the United States, and the Caribbean* (Boulder: Westview Press, 1985), 139–47.

92. Background interviews, Washington, D.C., Summer 1984.

93. *New York Times*, November 7, 1983: 12.

94. "Ambassador Kirkpatrick's Statement, UN Security Council, October 27, 1983," *Department of State Bulletin*, December 1983: 74–6.

95. Ronald Reagan, "Address to the Nation on Events in Lebanon and Grenada," October 27, 1983, *Public Papers, 1983, II*: 1520, 1521, 1518.

96. *Congressional Record*, 25 October 1983, H8580.

97. *Congressional Record*, October 25, 1983, H8582.

98. *Congressional Record*, October 26, 1983, S14694.

99. *Congressional Record*, October 26, 1983, S14695.

100. *Congressional Record*, October 26, 1983, H8639.

101. *Congressional Record*, October 26, 1983, H8640.

102. *Congressional Record*, October 26, 1983, H8644.

103. *Congressional Record*, October 26, 1983, H8646.

104. *Congressional Record*, October 26, 1983, H8691.

105. *Congressional Record*, October 27, 1983, H8703.

106. *Congressional Record*, October 27, 1983, H8706.

107. *Congressional Record*, October 28, 1983, H8846.

108. *Congressional Record*, October 28, 1983, S14870.

109. *New York Times*, June 21, 1989, C22.

110. Until the very eve of the Sandinista takeover, the administration pursued its search for a "moderate" alternative to Somoza and the *Frente Sandinista de Liberación National* (FSLN).

111. Robert A. Pastor, *Condemned to Repetition: The United States and Nicaragua* (Princeton: Princeton University Press, 1980), 236.

112. Pastor, 234.

113. Roy Gutman, *Banana Diplomacy: The Making of American Policy in Nicaragua, 1981–1987* (New York: Simon & Schuster, 1988), 78.

114. Gutman, 78.

115. Pastor, 237.

116. Testimony of Alexander M. Haig, Jr., Hearings before the Committee on Foreign Relations, United States Senate, 99th Congress, First Session, February 7, 1985, "Commitments, Consensus, and U.S. Foreign Policy" (Washington, DC: Government Printing Office): 233–4, 242–3.

117. Alexander M. Haig, Jr., *Caveat: Realism, Reagan, and Foreign Policy* (New York: Macmillan, 1984), 127–8.

118. Cynthia Arnson, "The Reagan Administration, Congress, and Central America: The Search for Consensus," in Nora Hamilton, Jeffry A. Frieden, Linda Fuller, and Manuel Pastor, Jr., *Crisis in Central America: Regional Dynamics and U.S. Policy in the 1980s* (Boulder, CO: Westview Press, 1988), 46.

119. Fred Barnes, "Reagan's Last Stand," *New Republic*, April 11, 1988: 10.

120. *Economist*, February 13, 1982: 26.

121. George Shultz, "The Meaning of Vietnam," *Current Policy, no. 269* (Washington, DC: U.S. Department of State): April 25, 1985.

122. Ronald Reagan, "Remarks at the Annual Dinner of the Conservative Political Action Conference," March 1, 1985, *Public Papers, 1985, I*: 228–9.

123. U.S. National Bipartisan Commission on Central America, "Report of the National Bipartisan Commission on Central America," (Washington, DC: U.S. Department of State, 1984): 4, 93.

124. Ronnie Dugger, *On Reagan: The Man and His Presidency* (New York: McGraw-Hill, 1983), 360.

125. *New York Times*, June 24, 1989: A9.

126. Gutman, 59.

127. Richard Sobel, "Public Opinion toward U.S. Involvement in Central America." Paper presented to the annual meeting of the American Political Science Association, Chicago, IL, September 2–5, 1987: 2–11.

128. Background interviews, Spring 1989.

129. Sobel, 2.

130. Sobel, 13–4.

131. Pastor, 260.

132. Reagan, "University of Virginia Address," 1631.

133. Reagan, "Farewell Address," 57.

134. Reagan, "Farewell Address," 57.

135. James Chace, "Is a Foreign Policy Consensus Possible?," *Foreign Affairs* 57 (Fall 1978): 1–16.

136. Henry Kissinger and Cyrus Vance, "Bipartisan Objectives for Foreign Policy," *Foreign Affairs 66* (Summer 1988): 899–921.

137. Harold Brown, "Building a New Consensus," *SAIS Review* 9.1 (1989): 1.

138. The ATS project conducted twelve sets of interviews between October 1987 and December 1988 with the assistance of Market Opinion Research, Marttila & Kiley, Inc., and The Daniel Yankelovich Group, Inc. The PAC/Brown study involved exposing nearly one thousand eligible voters to some three hours of discussion focused on four alternative futures of U.S.-Soviet relations.

139. Ronald Brownstein, "The New Politics of National Security," *Public Opinion* 11.3 (1988): 18.

140. John Marttila, "American Public Opinion: Evolving Definitions of American Security," in Edward K. Hamilton, ed. *America's Global Interests: A New Agenda* (New York: W. W. Norton, 1989), 280, 270, 291.

141. Daniel Yankelovich and Richard Smoke, "America's 'New Thinking'," *Foreign Affairs* 67 (Fall 1988): 2.

142. Brownstein, 19.

143. Martilla, 313.

144. Brownstein, 19.

145. Simon Serfaty, *After Reagan: False Starts, Missed Opportunities and New Beginnings*, Foreign Policy Institute Papers in International Affairs (Lanham, MD: University Press of America, 1988), 4.

146. Robert W. Tucker, "Reagan's Foreign Policy," *Foreign Affairs, America and the World, 1988/89* 68.1 (1989): 10.

147. Tucker, 24.

148. ATS surveys.

149. ATS #12: 33.

150. Yankelovich and Smoke, 1.

151. ATS, #12: 11; Marttila, 272.

152. Marttila, 265–6.

153. Marttila, 315.

154. Ronald Reagan, "Inaugural Address," January 20, 1981, *Public Papers, 1981, I:* 4.

155. George Shultz, "Power and Diplomacy in the 1980s," *Current Policy, no. 561* (Washington, DC: U.S. Department of State): April 3, 1984.

156. Tucker, 27.

157. Quoted in L. Gordon Crovitz, "How Ronald Reagan Weakened the Presidency," *Commentary*, September 1988: 28.

158. Reagan, "University of Virginia Address," 1633, 1634.

159. Quoted in Jay Winik, "Restoring Bipartisanship," *Washington Quarterly* 12.1 (1989): 111.

160. Winik, 111.

161. Quoted in Bernard E. Brown, "The Structural Weaknesses of United States Foreign Policy," *American Foreign Policy Newsletter* 12.2 (1989): 8.

162. Brown, 8.

163. Crovitz, 27, 28.

164. For example, the symposium, "Building a New Consensus: Congress and Foreign Policy," *SAIS Review* 9.2 (1989): 61–72 and David L. Boren, "Speaking with a Single Voice: Bipartisanship in Foreign Policy," *SAIS Review* 9.1 (1989): 51–64.

CHAPTER 5

The Bush Administration: A Postscript

Ronald Reagan's victory in 1980 owed more to the alarming state of the economy than to the appeal of his ideological agenda, but Reagan's firm convictions gave to his new administration clear priorities and a sense of purpose. That George Bush apparently lacked deeply held views encouraged Democrats to believe—despite reasonably healthy economic conditions and a widely applauded improvement in superpower relations—that they would recapture the White House in 1988. Bush appeared as little more than a sycophant, willing to walk in Reagan's shadow as vice president, ever hopeful that he would emerge as the annointed successor. But after spotting Michael Dukakis a seventeen point lead in the public opinion polls in mid-July, Bush roared into the lead in early September and won the general election in a minor landslide.

Dukakis's feeble and belated efforts to respond to Bush's scalding attacks in a largely issueless campaign doubtlessly contributed to his defeat, but at a deeper level Bush kept his opponent on the defensive by his ability to manipulate important symbols of conservative populism. Thus, like Clint Eastwood, he invited free-spending congressional liberal Democrats to read his lips—"no new taxes." He relentlessly castigated Governor Dukakis for having vetoed as unconstitutional a bill requiring that teachers lead their students in the Pledge of Allegiance, and in time his campaign unveiled a devastating television ad that deftly exploited the feelings aroused by Bush about convict Willie Horton's crime spree and the Massachusetts prison furlough system. And whereas Dukakis—fearing a hostile response—sent the more conservative Lloyd Bentsen to address veterans organizations—the vice president eagerly sought these groups' endorsements and portrayed his opponent as dangerously weak on defense.

Having co-opted cultural and fiscal conservatives Bush was free to move toward the center, and he did so by acknowledging the need for a cleaner environment, better education, a workable child-care system, and continuing improvements in U.S.-Soviet relations. His goal, as he told the Republican convention in August, was "a kinder, gentler America."

In light of these conflicting campaign signals, as well as his evident willingness to do just about anything to win the election, George Bush entered the White House as something of an enigma. Nevertheless, by late 1989 the outlines of his approach to governance had become increasingly clear. First, unlike Reagan who had characterized the federal government as the enemy of "we the people," Bush's understanding of its proper role more closely resembled Carter's: as a useful instrument that within limits could solve a variety of problems. Though Bush avoided Carter's mistake of immediately confronting Congress with an overwhelming number of "comprehensive" proposals, he did, in fact, gradually launch a substantive number of initiatives that preempted much of the Democrats' agenda. For example, after less than a year in office President Bush had proposed legislation to curb air pollution, solve the savings and loan crisis, provide child care, expand Medicaid, reform the campaign finance system, fight crime, and most dramatically, wage war on drugs. Furthermore, for only the third time in history, the nation's governors were convened by a president to discuss a single issue—in this case, education. And, in marking the twentieth anniversary of the Apollo moon landing, Bush announced the new goal of sending people to Mars. At the same time, however, his self-proclaimed "unbreakable" pledge not to raise taxes—indeed he wanted to cut the capital gains tax—meant that these initiatives could only be funded at the expense of other budgetary items, and Bush, as well as his Office of Management and Budget Director Richard Darman, implied that Congress bore the responsibility for those decisions. Thus, even if all of these proposals came to naught, President Bush had still succeeded in "seizing the high ground."[1] In contrast to Carter, who had acknowledged that his policy solutions would impose pain and sacrifice, Bush preferred to let Congress wrestle with costs and burdens and take the credit for courageously offering solutions to very difficult challenges.

But while acting as a problem-solving centrist, Bush hardly abandoned the conservative populist symbols of his presidential campaign. Notwithstanding his declaration of war on drugs the president steadfastly refused to support a ban on semi-automatic firearms—weapons used by urban gangs to fight for control of drug territory. Even after William Bennett, the administration's drug czar and resident neoconservative, implored Bush to soften his opposition to outlawing these guns, he would only agree to stop the importation of such weapons. When in June 1989 the Supreme Court voted five to four to overturn a Texas law that prohibited the desecration of the American flag, Bush exploited the issue by loudly demanding a constitutional amendment to "protect" it against disrespectful acts. And with Lee Atwater, an architect of the 1988 campaign now chair of the National Republican Committee, some commentators discerned a "good cop, bad cop" political strategy, wherein George Bush walked the high road of conciliation and kindness, while Atwater orchestrated smear campaigns against congressional Democrats and liberal interest groups.[2] In these and other ways Bush attempted to hold the cultural Right, satisfy the policy Center, and blame liberals for clinging to the discredited "tax and spend" approaches of the past.

Finally, George Bush, like other modern presidents, understood the importance of political theater in governing. Though lacking the acting and rhetorical abilities of Reagan and unable to rely on the staging talents of Michael Deaver, his predecessor's impresario, Bush employed to good advantage media coverage of the presidency. He proved especially adept at finding powerfully symbolic venues to unveil or press for policy initiatives. Thus he proposed the flag amendment before the Iwo Jima monument, visited the Grand Tetons after offering his clean air legislation, presented his ethics reforms to an audience that included young congressional interns, appeared with Lech Walesa at the Lenin shipyards in Gdansk, and went to a hospital ward filled with babies with AIDS the day after his war on drugs speech. The reliance on potent environments to mobilize public support represented an extension of a successful campaign tactic that Bush demonstrated most dramatically by a cruise through the filthy waters of Boston harbor.[3]

Throughout the 1988 election campaign and during the early months of his presidency, journalists and scholars routinely castigated George Bush for his alleged lack of "vision." According to this widely shared view Bush, despite an impressive foreign policy "resumé"—CIA Director, ambassador to China and the UN, head of Reagan's crisis team—possessed no grand design about America's role in the world. In contrast to Reagan, whose settled convictions had provided his administration with a useful foreign policy road map, Bush was accused of resurrecting Jimmy Carter's practice of list-making and tinkering with details.[4] Moreover, many observers believed that his senior foreign policy appointments merely reinforced these worrisome tendencies. Neither Secretary of State James Baker, a political crony with limited foreign affairs experience, nor NSC chief Brent Scowcroft, a defense policy "mechanic," were geostrategists on the order of Kissinger and Brzezinski. And Deputy Secretary of State Lawrence S. Eagleburger, a Kissinger protegé, who could look at the "big picture," would allegedly be constrained by the Republican Right.

Such criticisms may have been well founded, but they accounted for only part of the story. Bush and his senior advisers took considerable pride in their prudence and pragmatism, and several of them, particularly Scowcroft, perceived some of Reagan's superpower overtures as reckless and short-sighted. Firm advocates of deterrence, they rejected Reagan's nuclear abolitionism—most evident at the 1986 Iceland summit—and worried that the momentum of START could, if not slowed, produce a treaty that denuclearized U.S. defenses. Furthermore, Scowcroft and others wished to shorten the wild pendulum swings that had characterized the American public's approach to U.S.-Soviet relations since the early 1970s. Reagan had supposedly exacerbated this problem by first helping to fuel a second cold war and then by exaggerating the potential of a second détente. The Bush administration desired instead a superpower nexus immune to apocalyptic fears and unfulfilled hopes.

Yet such a foreign policy, difficult to produce in even the most settled conditions, was made even more elusive by the ongoing drama in the Soviet Union and Eastern Europe. Not since Harry Truman entered the White House at the very beginning of the cold war in 1945 had anyone assumed the presidency at a time of comparable international flux. Whereas Truman's domestic task had been to mobilize public support for an active U.S. world role in the context of deteriorating relations with Moscow, Bush's challenge was to make policy sense out of these seemingly historic global upheavals. By 1947 containment had begun to fill the policy vacuum in Washington created by the breakup of the Grand Alliance. In late 1989 momentous changes in the Soviet Union and its erstwhile satellites had produced many more questions than answers. To cite but a few of the more intriguing ones: What kind of a Soviet Union would Gorbachev's reforms produce? Should the U.S. want him to succeed? How attainable (and reversible) were his goals? What would be the new status of Eastern Europe? Could (should) NATO survive if the Soviet threat were removed or dramatically diminished? How should the United States exploit its "victory" (if that was what it was) in the cold war? Could a domestic foreign policy consensus be fashioned in this "post-cold war" environment?

In light of these circumstances a certain amount of initial confusion in the Bush administration was understandable. Senior officials were hard-pressed to discern Gorbachev's motives, predict the outcome of his domestic program, or evaluate their implications for Soviet-American relations.

Concerned that "Gorby fever" would threaten NATO as well as domestic support for defense spending, the administration at first attempted to score public relations points by, for example, announcing a thirty thousand U.S. troop reduction in Western Europe. But its rather odd initial annoyance with the Soviet leader occasionally boiled over in public, as when White House Press Secretary Marlin Fitzwater dismissed Gorbachev as a "drugstore cowboy" presumably dispensing phony elixirs to a gullible public. In fact, the administration expressed general irritation that the media was "responding to Gorbachev the way people responded to Dr. Johnson's famous dancing dog. It isn't how he dances, it is the fact that he dances at all."[5] But senior advisers were themselves divided by this changing landscape. When in April 1989 Secretary of Defense Richard Cheney "guessed" that Gorbachev would fail in his efforts to reform the Soviet Union and be replaced by someone much more hostile to the West, Bush publicly disagreed.

In part to develop a grand design and strategic objectives and in part to buy time, President-elect Bush had ordered a top-level, systematic strategic policy review. Urged by Scowcroft to do so, this review had by early April 1989 yielded a thirty-page document designed to "insure compatibility among . . . commitments, capabilities, and resources." Somewhat reminiscent of Eisenhower's "Operation Solarium," the study of Soviet policy, known as National Security Review 3, produced a recommended approach called "status quo plus," provisionally concluding that the process of change in the Soviet Union was likely to continue throughout the Bush administration even if Gorbachev were replaced.[6] It counseled the president to carefully broaden the superpower dialogue to include regional issues like eastern Africa, as well as combatting terrorism and the spread of chemical weapons. Yet according to one official, while the analysis might prove to be a valuable tool, "the vision . . . is not articulated very strongly, and there are plenty of caveats and what-ifs in there."[7]

Indeed, the administration spent much of its first year attempting to delineate a vision and a strategy appropriate to a world that appeared, temporarily at least, turned upside down. This imminent end of the postwar era proved unsettling to some policy makers who had grown almost fond of its verities. In September 1989 Lawrence Eagleburger gave voice to these sentiments in a Georgetown University address that suggested that "the process of reform in the Soviet bloc and the relaxation of Soviet control over Eastern Europe" were "bringing long-suppressed ethnic antagonisms and national rivalries to the surface, and putting the German question back on the international agenda." The waning of unchallenged superpower domination had produced an emergent multipolar world which would not necessarily be "a safer place than the cold war era . . . given the existence and proliferation of weapons of mass destruction."[8]

George Bush, however, in a series of springtime speeches devoted to foreign policy, tried to interpret these changes optimistically by suggesting that they were helping fulfill America's eternal dream: a world of freedom and democracy purged of the bane of war. While Bush may have harbored misgivings about Reagan's foreign policy strategy, he eagerly embraced his predecessor's domestically appealing (rhetorical) grand design. Thus in a commencement address at the Coast Guard Academy in May, he echoed Reagan by asserting that

> the eclipse of communism is only one-half of the story of our time. The other is the ascendancy of the democratic idea. Never before has the idea of freedom so captured the imagination of men and women the world over. . . . What is it we want to see? It is a growing community of democracies anchoring international peace and stability, and a dynamic free–market system generating prosperity and progress.[9]

Bush reiterated these themes during a June trip to Hungary and Poland and in a speech to the UN General Assembly in September. Responding to Gorbachev's call for a single European house from the Atlantic to the Urals, the president insisted that all Europeans should have the right to move freely from room to room in such a dwelling.

Yet George Bush found it much easier to present this essentially Wilsonian vision than to articulate a strategy designed to implement it. Rhetorically, at least, he argued that his strategy involved moving "beyond containment." In May he told a commencement audience at Texas A & M University that containment had worked, the Soviet Union had been forced to "turn inward and address the contradictions of its inefficient repressive, inhumane system" just as Truman, Eisenhower, Vandenberg, Rayburn, Marshall, Acheson, and Kennan had predicted. Now, Bush claimed,

> It is time to move beyond containment to a new policy for the 1990s, one that recognizes the full scope of change taking place around the world and in the Soviet Union itself. In sum, the United States now has as its goal much more than simply containing Soviet expansionism. We seek the integration of the Soviet Union into the community of nations.[10]

Bush might have added that "integration" had been the strategic goal of Franklin Roosevelt "before containment," but in fact, the president had little idea about the meaning of his own message. By the fall senior officials had conceded that there existed no overarching strategy that guided the administration, and that Bush's goal of moving "beyond containment" was little more than a public relations tool.[11]

This lack of a strategy reflected the administration's fundamental uncertainty about the implications of dramatic change in the Soviet Union and Eastern Europe. Would the Soviet Union allow its "domestic" empire to dissolve as it had allowed its Warsaw Pact allies to break free? Could it even prevent it if it so desired? Would Gorbachev, like other Russian reformers, be overthrown by anti-Western reactionaries? The Truman administration had confronted a situation in which the Soviet grip on Eastern Europe was tightening. The Bush administration faced the opposite reality and found it equally confounding.[12] In light of this understandable confusion it relied primarily on tactics designed to improve Soviet-American relations, while not succumbing to "Gorbomania": Bush's call for an "Open Skies" regime to monitor troop strengths and cruise missiles, conventional and chemical arms proposals, a long series of confidence-building measures, and the granting of IMF observer status to Moscow were but a few of the tactical initiatives unveiled during 1989.

The American people, however, had (at least momentarily) moved far beyond containment and concluded that drugs now constituted the single most pressing issue and the primary threat to national security. And, in time, Bush responded to this concern with a televised national address—his first—which mapped a "national strategy" for waging "war" on drugs. Due largely to heightened media coverage of the crack "epidemic," as well as Colombia's vow to eliminate its drug cartels, the proportion of Americans who cited drugs as the most important problem soared to a phenomenal 64 percent by September 1989.[13] While many drug enforcement and treatment officials saw little new in Bush's program—one former Senate special counsel termed it "modestly reworked Richard Nixon"—69 percent of the public approved of his proposals. The president's drug czar, William Bennett, even claimed that there was "consensus like we have not seen in recent history about being tough and firm on this issue."[14]

Yet the administration was notably coy about whether combat troops would be sent to Latin America to wipe out drugs at the source. During much of the summer senior officials like Chief of Staff John Sununu and Attorney General Richard Thornburgh floated (and punctured) trial balloons about this extremely sensitive issue. Secretary of Defense Richard Cheney, while warily vowing to make the antidrug campaign a top Pentagon priority by training local forces and protecting U.S. borders against smuggling, rejected some congressional proposals to allow military aircraft to shoot down planes suspected of carrying narcotics. Moreover, both he and Bush claimed they did not contemplate sending combat troops to Colombia, although White House officials said they would consider such a request if Colombia's president made one.[15] Not only did the Colombian government refuse to offer such an invitation, but on the eve of the February 1990 drug "summit" held among Bolivia, Colombia, Peru, and the United States, President Barco embarrassed Bush by rejecting Bush's plan to place American warships off the Colombia coast. But in April 1990 the White House announced that U.S. Army Special Forces would be sent to Peru to build a training base in the cocoa-growing area, to train and equip six Peruvian battalions, to provide river patrol boats, and to refurbish twenty ground-attack jets.

Public support for the Bush administration's drug plan foundered on this question. A CBS/*New York Times* Survey conducted shortly after the president's national speech showed that 42 percent favored and 47 percent opposed the dispatch of U.S. troops in response to a Colombian request, and only 34 percent would allow the forces to remain there for more than a year. While support for such an operation was somewhat higher than that given to military intervention in Nicaragua during the Reagan years, it nevertheless seemed surprisingly tepid in light of the widely held perception about the national security threat posed by narcotics. Yet only 39 percent expressed a willingness to pay $100 a year more in taxes to increase spending for antidrug programs.[16]

How, then, did the Bush administration initially attempt to legitimate bureaucratically and publicly its grand design, strategic objectives, and tactics? Certainly Bush's appointment of close, personal friends and "centrists" who had served Gerald Ford in the mid-1970s facilitated the task of bureaucratic legitimation. In contrast to the chronic squabbling that had characterized the foreign policy upper echelons of the Carter and Reagan administrations, the Bush team, while slow to articulate a vision and a strategy, appeared to function reasonably smoothly. The most widely reported problem concerned James Baker's management of the State Department. The secretary, a Bush confidant and political strategist with limited foreign policy experience, who surrounded himself with a handful of loyalists and seemed to prefer the company of the press to that of the department's professionals, let it be known that he perceived himself as the president's man in "the building" and not State's representative at the Oval Office. Unlike Reagan who relied on "the speech" to animate ideological brethren and provide overall direction, George Bush adopted a much more hands-on, problem-solving approach that emphasized an involved, knowl-edgeable, pragmatic president. Bureaucratic compliance was to be gained by projecting an image of competence at the most senior levels.

The administration's early public legitimation efforts involved three main elements: (1) a declaratory history that hailed the achievements of the architects of containment; (2) the reassurance that its global vision, like Reagan's, anticipated an increasingly free and democratic world; and (3) the occasional claim that domestic critics of its foreign policy were moti-vated by mere "politics."

More than any other post-Vietnam president, Bush's declaratory his-tory of American foreign relations emphasized the centrality of contain-ment. This focus began during the 1988 campaign in one of the Republican candidate's first attacks on Michael Dukakis. Charging that the Massa-chusetts governor's foreign policy views amounted "to a repudiation of the Truman Doctrine and the vision of John Kennedy," Bush claimed that there had been a bipartisan consensus since World War II based on an "effective deterrent, unsurpassed military force and the demonstrated will to use it." In praising Truman's boldness in the Berlin blockade and Ken-nedy's firmness during the Cuban missile crisis, Bush asked, "Do today's liberals understand what it means to stand up to a challenge and meet our commitments? I guarantee I will."[17] Similarly, his early presidential speeches, in anticipating the end of the cold war era, characterized containment as a policy that had served America well for over forty years. This declaratory history had nothing to say about the Vietnam War and its aftermath. More surprisingly, it largely ignored the Reagan Doctrine and instead portrayed his predecessor as a faithful servant of containment. This account did sub-stantial violence to the actual historical record, yet it seemed somehow appropriate that George Bush, whose background and credentials would in an earlier day have made him a leader of the old establishment, chose to extol that group's major contribution to postwar foreign policy. Then, too, in order to move "beyond containment" (if only rhetorically) it was first necessary to pay homage to its original architects and to argue for the essential continuity of American foreign relations.

President Bush's grand design borrowed more explicitly from Rea-gan's domestically appealing vision of a world on the road to freedom and democracy. Like his predecessor, Bush repeatedly noted the bankruptcy and failure of Communism and the widespread trend toward market econ-omies, personal freedom, and democratic government. In late May 1989, for example, he announced that "never before has the hope of freedom beckoned so many—trade unionists in Warsaw, the people of Panama, rulers consulting the ruled in the Soviet Union, . . . the dramatic events in Tiananmen Square." And Bush promised that

> everywhere those voices are speaking the language of democracy and freedom, and we hear them and the world hears them, . . . America will do all it can do to encourage them.[18]

But the Bush administration found it fully as difficult to make its publicly articulated grand design mesh with its strategic objectives as had Reagan and his advisers. Thus when Chinese troops brutally crushed the Tiananmen Square pro-democracy students in early June, Bush, citing the importance of the Sino-American "relationship," demonstrated great reluctance to do more than "deplore" the savage attack. And his secret dispatch of Scowcroft and Eagleburger to Beijing in December provoked an angry congressional response. Yet the president persisted, vetoing a bill designed to grant permanent residency to Chinese students studying in the United States, and in May 1990 extending for one year China's Most Favored Nation trading status. In a similar effort to avoid provoking the Soviet Union, the president, while fulsome in his praise for Solidarity during a visit to Poland, initially offered it a mere $119 million in assistance. Nor would anti-Noriega rebels receive any U.S. help in their unsuccessful effort to oust the Panamanian dictator in early October. The vision remained upliftingly Wilsonian, but the strategic instruments seemed more "Hooverian" until Bush, at the end of 1989, militarily intervened in El Salvador, the Philippines, and, most dramatically, Panama. Bush's commitment to the principle of national self-determination came under renewed scrutiny after Lithuania's declaration of independence in March 1990. Despite the president's oblique threats to punish Moscow for its imposition of harsh economic sanctions against the Baltic republic, Bush stunned many in Congress by concluding a trade agreement with Gorbachev during the Washington summit in June while the Lithuanian situation remained unresolved.

Throughout 1989 domestic critics complained that the Bush administration had repeatedly missed opportunities to achieve dramatic breakthroughs in East-West relations. House Majority Leader Richard Gephardt (D-MO) wryly termed it the "year of living timidly." Arthur M. Schlesinger, Jr., implored the president to "stop trivializing these historic transformations by running on about 'public relations' battles and by calling every Soviet initiative 'an obvious ploy . . . designed principally to create problems within the alliance,' as . . . Scowcroft called the unilateral reduction of its short-range nuclear arms."[19] Others termed U.S. foreign policy "procrastinating" rather than "prudent."[20] The administration found it more difficult to ignore this charge by Senate Majority Leader George J. Mitchell (D-ME):

> Instead of encouragement and engagement [of changes in Eastern Europe], the Administration has adopted an almost passive stance. "Show me," the President says. His officials warn of the unpredictability of change. The Bush Administration seems almost nostalgic about the cold war and the rigid superpower relationship that divided the world into two hostile and isolated camps.[21]

Secretary Baker tried to deflect such criticism and to legitimate Bush's "prudential" approach by dismissively noting that "When the President . . . is rocking along with a 70 percent approval rating on his handling of foreign policy, if I were the leader of the opposition, I might have something similar to say."[22] Mitchell responded by reminding Baker "that this is not a political campaign. This is an effort, in good faith, to deal with serious questions of public policy."[23] Yet, like so much of post-Vietnam U.S. foreign relations it *was* to a large extent a political campaign as presidents and their advisors tried to frame policies that would win the instant approval of the American public. Baker's remark merely acknowledged this reality.

Did this extraordinarily high level of public support for the Bush foreign policy signify the successful reconstruction of a domestic consensus? Let us look, in turn, at the policy, cultural, and procedural dimensions.

Public satisfaction with the administration's foreign policy record stood in contrast to political elites who showed much less enthusiasm for Bush's "wait-and-see," "prove it" approach. Indeed, elites arrayed themselves along a policy spectrum that included at least a half dozen identifiable positions.[24] At one end were "old faithfuls" like Arnold Beichman and Richard Pipes who maintained that Gorbachev's "reforms" could yet prove an elaborate ruse to deceive and divide the West. They claimed therefore that the cold war bipolar paradigm remained valid and sought to continue to serve as the basis for U.S. policy. At the other extreme were those systemic optimists such as Francis Fukuyama and Richard Rosecrance who anticipated an increasingly harmonious, interdependent world, "with the efficacy of force declining, competitiveness among states losing its vicious edge, barriers between people lowering, democracy and the market economy spreading, and prosperity rising."[25] Close to this group, but more self-satisfied, were "triumphalists" like Gregory Fossedal who urged the Bush administration to exploit America's cold war victory by actively leading

the world into a twenty first century of universal democracy.[26] Then there
were neo-Kennanites who sought to prepare U.S. foreign policy for a multipolar, fluid, less manageable international system which would reward
adroitness and adaptability, characteristics notably lacking in the American
diplomatic tradition.[27] "Grand designers" like Henry Kissinger represented
a fifth position, one that argued that a post-Yalta, European settlement
should be actively pursued in order to prevent a retreating Soviet Union
from fracturing NATO, driving the United States from Western Europe,
and reopening the volatile question of German reunification.[28] Finally,
there were, to be sure, elites who applauded Bush's prudentialism as the
proper course in a changing situation, but they faced articulate advocates
of at least five other positions.[29] Yet by mid-1990 this elite debate had been
rendered largely moot by Chancellor Helmut Kohl's audacious diplomacy
that culminated in a July agreement with Gorbachev to keep a unified
Germany in NATO in exchange for substantial economic assistance from
Bonn.

The public, on the other hand, in its consensus levels of foreign policy
support, seemed untouched by these elite quarrels. So long as the Soviets
continued to liberalize domestically and moderate externally the public
could afford to focus on new national security "threats" such as illegal
drugs. And the low-cost invasion of Panama won wide support. Yet the
longer-term consequences of Soviet reform and retreat could easily destroy
this nascent public consensus, for at some point, the diminution of the
Soviet threat will create powerful domestic cross-pressures about the nature
and extent of U.S. international interests and commitments. Foreign policy
retrenchment of a dramatic kind could emerge as an appealing, though
hardly uncontested, option for an American public weary of budget deficits
and decaying public services.[30] In such circumstances the apparent eupho-
ria of the late Reagan and early Bush years would be overwhelmed by a
new national debate about the purposes of American power in a post–cold
war era.

George Bush seemed less than wholly comfortable with Ronald Reagan's attempts to build a cultural consensus on the shoulders of a "national
greatness without sacrifice" rhetoric. He did, to be sure, embrace some of
the conservative populist symbols that his predecessor had so adeptly exploited. Both, for example, relied on Clint Eastwood—a complex of alien-
ation, *machismo*, and fair play—for their most memorable lines as Reagan's "make my day" resonated in Bush's "read my lips." Similarly, Bush
rather suddenly emerged, as both candidate and president, as a self-proclaimed defender of the American flag against verbal and physical desecra-

tion. At the same time, however, his vision of a "kinder, gentler" America implied, among other things, a more compassionate, active federal government or, at the very least, the general recognition that some people need assistance in coping with social and economic distress. And, indeed, Bush's acknowledgment that certain things required urgent national attention—education, the environment, illegal drugs, day care—indicated that his administration would do more than merely celebrate patriotic pride. Yet the budgetary circumstances (and politics) of the late 1980s, by ruling out the means to pay for new programs, made it more likely that Bush, like Reagan, would rely ever more heavily on an empty rhetoric of national renewal, in order to stimulate both the domestic and foreign-policy realms. Greatness without sacrifice became the implicit and politically popular message of both presidents.

In contrast to Ronald Reagan, a self-described "outsider" who seemingly relished combat with Congress, George Bush, a former House member, tried hard to adjust the cosmetics, at least, of executive-legislative relations and foreign affairs. In matters of style, Bush broke with his predecessor in his ability to discuss issues with members of Congress without the need for note cards and in his eagerness to establish friendly, personal ties by, for example, entertaining legislators in the White House living quarters. More substantively, James Baker, in his Senate confirmation hearings, vowed to help end the procedural bickering that had frequently stalemated American foreign policy, and Bush echoed these sentiments in his Inaugural Address. In late March 1989 the administration, due largely to Baker's tenacious efforts, announced a bipartisan accord on Central America that aimed to remove Nicaragua as a source of presidential-congressional conflict. Under the terms of the accord the United States promised to provide $4.5 million a month to the *contras* for food, clothing, shelter, and medical supplies until the Nicaraguan elections scheduled for February 1990. But these funds would cease after November 1989 unless Bush received letters of approval from four (Democratically controlled) congressional committees.[31] The bitterest criticism of this unusual arrangement came not from diehard congressional supporters of the *contras* but from the White House legal counsel C. Boyden Gray, who condemned it as an unconstitutional abrogation of executive power in foreign relations. Gray, in turn, received an equally surprising public rebuke from presidential press secretary Marlin Fitzwater who claimed the agreement did not abrogate Bush's authority but did "bring to a conclusion years of dissension between the executive and legislative branch."[32] Yet as the February 1990 Nicaraguan elections approached new disputes developed. Vice President Dan Quayle repeatedly charged that the Sandinistas would never allow free elections, and the administration, in order to guarantee fair balloting, asked Congress for money to supervise them and to aid the opposition. Congressional liberals argued that neither the CIA or the National Endowment for Democracy—the administration's nominees—should be allowed to interfere in the process, while some conservatives objected that such aid would legitimate inevitably unfair elections and enable the Sandinistas to claim an untainted victory. Violeta Charmorro's upset victory over Daniel Ortega surprised the White House and many in Congress. Yet Bush's effort to provide emergency aid to Nicaragua and Panama was repeatedly thwarted by members of Congress who wished to make that assistance conditional on a drastic cut in aid to El Salvador as punishment for that government's reluctance to prosecute those responsible for the 1989 murders of several leading university clerics.

Moreover, the aftermath of the failed Panamanian coup of October 1989 demonstrated that a procedural consensus in foreign policy remained elusive. Bush, Baker, and other senior officials had frequently called on Panama to overthrow Noriega and establish democracy. But when mid-level offices in the Panamanian Defense Force (PDF) attempted to oust the general, the administration, though apparently informed in advance of its imminence, did very little to assist the rebels. Some congressional leaders, House Speaker Thomas Foley (D-WA) and George Mitchell, for example, declined to attack Bush at a time of acute embarrassment, but not all key members rallied around the president. Jesse Helms, perhaps predictably, provided an alternative and highly critical chronology of events that blamed administration hesitation for the coup's collapse—charges that Defense Secretary Cheney termed "ridiculous." More extraordinary in this supposed new "era of good feeling" was the public squabble between David Boren, Chairman of the Senate Select Committee on Intelligence, and Brent Scowcroft. When Boren ridiculed the administration's lack of coordination and planning with the PDF rebels, the NSC adviser bitterly complained that Boren's own committee had previously made that sort of activity impossible. And other Bush officials berated Congress for placing crippling restrictions on potential U.S. involvement in coups.[33] President Bush moved quickly to mend fences with Boren and other Intelligence Committee members, but this episode showed that administration promises to build a new procedural consensus had not yet borne fruit. On the other hand, congressional support for the invasion of Panama and overthrow of Noriega in December recalled reactions to the Grenada "rescue mission." In March 1990 President Bush offered this mixed assessment of executive-legislative relations in foreign affairs:

I am proud of the successful examples of bipartisan cooperation in the past year—on Central America, on aid to Eastern Europe, on Panama, to name a few. Yet other issues remain contentious, such as various attempts to constrict Presidential discretion and authority in fields ranging from covert actions to the excessive earmarking of assistance funds.[34]

David B. Rivkin, Jr., legal adviser to the counsel to the president, showed considerably less restraint in a May 1990 public exchange with Theodore Draper, a leading critic of the Panamanian invasion, in noting a "legislative usurpation of executive power . . . particularly blatant in foreign affairs" and "a virtual constitutional *coup d'état*" since the early 1970s. This "antifederalist counterrevolution," Rivkin concluded, had resulted in "imperial and highly partisan congressional foreign policy micromangement."[35] Rivkin's rhetoric appeared to reflect the continuing absence of a procedural consensus.

NOTES

1. Elizabeth Drew, "Letter from Washington," *New Yorker*, August 28, 1989: 75. By July 1990, however, Bush had reneged on his "no new taxes" pledge as the deficit soared.

2. Hendrik Hertzberg, "At Watergate," *New Republic*, July 3, 1989: 4.

3. Drew, August 28, 1989: 76.

4. Kevin Philips, "Did We Elect Another Carter?" *New York Times*, February 9, 1989: 25.

5. *New York Times*, May 18, 1989: 6.

6. *New York Times*, April 9, 1989: 1.

7. *New York Times*, April 9, 1989: 1.

8. *New York Times*, September 16, 1989: 1.

9. George Bush, "Security Strategy for the 1990s," *Current Policy 1178* (Washington, DC: U.S. Department of State): May 24, 1989.

10. George Bush, "Remarks at the Texas A & M University Commencement Ceremony in College Station, Texas," May 12, 1989, *Weekly Compilation of Presidential Documents*, 25.20: 702.

11. *New York Times*, September 10, 1989: 16.

12. By the autumn of 1989 some observers detected a tacit, though perhaps only temporary, understanding between the United States and the Soviet Union in regard to Eastern Europe. According to this view both nations were attempting to pursue their interests in a rapidly changing regional environment without antagonizing the other. President Bush announced, for example, that the administration would aid Poland and Hungary without "poking a stick" in Moscow's eye, which presumably meant that Washington would not entice these countries into NATO (*New York Times*, September 28, 1989, p. 6).

13. CBS/*New York Times* Poll, September 6–8, 1989, *New York Times*, September 12, 1989: 8.

14. *New York Times*, September 12, 1989: 8.

15. *New York Times*, September 19, 1989: 7.

16. *New York Times*, September 12, 1989: 8.

17. *New York Times*, August 5, 1988: A12, A1.

18. Bush, "Security Strategy."

19. *Wall Street Journal*, May 17, 1989: A18.

20. Charles W. Kegley, Jr., "The Bush Administration and the Future of American Foreign Policy: Pragmatism or Procrastination?," *Presidential Studies Quarterly* 19 (1989): 717–32.

21. *New York Times*, September 19, 1989: A14.

22. *New York Times*, September 20, 1989: A1.

23. *New York Times*, September 21, 1989: A1.

24. Owen Harries, "Between Paradigms," *The National Interest* 17 (1989): 101–7.

25. Harries, 105.

26. Gregory Fossedal, *The Democratic Imperative: Exporting the American Revolution* (New York: A *New Republic* Book, Basic Books, 1989).

27. See, for example, Charles Krauthammer, a "neo–Kennanite," at least, in "Beyond the Cold War," *New Republic*, December 19, 1988: 14–15.

28. Harries, 103–04.

29. Harries, 102–03.

30. In the summer of 1989, for example, many House Democrats (and some Republicans) "revolted" against defense spending proposals presented by Secretary Cheney and endorsed by Les Aspin (D-WI), chairman of the Armed Services Committee. The House, temporarily, at least, voted to cut MX production in half, to freeze production of the B–2, to kill the Midgetman missile, and to drastically reduce spending on SDI. According to Senator John McCain (R-AZ), "The White House worked hard, but it's obvious that Congress is not as cowed by Bush as they were by Reagan. They were always afraid that Reagan would go to the people" (*New York Times*, July 29, 1989: 9).

31. "U.S. Support for Democracy and Peace in Central America," *Selected Documents No. 36* (Washington, DC: U.S. Department of State): n.d.

32. *New York Times*, March 28, 1989: 8.

33. *New York Times*, October 12, 1989: 1, 8.

34. *National Security Strategy of the United States* (Washington, DC: Government Printing Office, March 1990): 32.

35. "'The Constitution in Danger': An Exchange," *New York Review of Books*, May 17, 1990: 50, 52.

CHAPTER 6

Conclusions

Very early in this study it was suggested that the last twenty years of American foreign policy could be treated as a "lump," wherein unifying themes, recurrent patterns, and overarching generalizations imposed intellectual order on these decades. Conversely, a chronicler of these years who objected to such a search for unity, might look for evidence of discontinuity, idiosyncracy, and happenstance in order to explain that diplomatic and national security record. By employing the method of structured, focused comparison, *Reconstructing Consensus* has attempted to identify those concepts, approaches, behaviors, and goals that have united *and* distinguished the foreign policies and domestic legitimation efforts of presidents Nixon, Ford, Carter, and Reagan. To this end we posed an identical set of questions to each of these administrations:

1. What were their domestic priorities?
2. How did these presidents perceive the problem of governance?
3. What were the relationships of (1) and (2) to their foreign policies?
4. What were the grand designs, strategic objectives, and tactics of the Nixon (Ford), Carter, and Reagan foreign policies?
5. How did these presidents attempt to legitimate their foreign policies to the bureaucracy and the public?
6. Did any of them succeed in reconstructing the substantive, cultural, and procedural components of a domestic foreign policy consensus?

Detailed answers to these questions were offered in earlier chapters. Tables 6–1 through 6–6 briefly summarize these findings and will help to assess the accomplishments and failures of these presidents as well as the roles that domestic consensus and legitimacy have played in American foreign policy since Vietnam.

Table 6–1. Domestic Priorities

Nixon	Carter	Reagan
Molding a post–New Deal "new majority" that tapped the resentments of those opposed to Great Society "excesses," federal social engineering, the youthful "counterculture," and anti-Vietnam protesters	Restoring the trust of the American people in government after Watergate and Vietnam by personally embodying the values of the public, offering comprehensive, "fair" policies to complex, long-standing national problems such as energy, health care, tax structure, and welfare	Restoring the American economy through tax and federal social spending cuts. Returning effective political and economic power to "we the people" from federal social engineers
Replacing the "failed" leadership of the liberal establishment—enemies —with Main Street loyalists	Emphasizing the limits of the federal government's capacity to solve problems	Undertaking a massive defense buildup to make up for the "decade of neglect"
Returning to the states such services as education, job training, and public health, while enlarging the federal role in areas like welfare, energy, and the environment		

Table 6–2. Approaches to Governance

Nixon	Carter	Reagan
Government as the legitimate expression of the "new majority's" values and aspirations	Problem-solving competence	Presidential rhetoric as national motivator
"Hard-ball" politics employed to expose and dislodge liberal elites from power and influence	Presidential responsibility to transcend "politics" in the name of the national interest	Government as the "problem" to be tamed by decentralization, voluntarism, and the market
President as fearless leader determined to do the "right," not the "easy," thing	President as a flawed, average citizen drawing strength from the people	President as but another "extraordinary, ordinary American"

Table 6–3. Relationship of Foreign Policy to Domestic Priorities and Approaches to Governance

Nixon	Carter	Reagan
Little direct relationship: Nixon hoped that "silent majority" would tolerate phased withdrawal from Vietnam and that "new majority" would allow the pursuit of a largely amoral foreign policy	Very close relationship: Human rights, the management of détente, and the resolution of regional and transnational disputes would support Carter's domestic themes of competence and moralism	Very close relationship: Emphasis on free markets, individual liberty, and democratic community at home to be reflected in the rising tide of democratic revolution and the defeat of "big" governments abroad

Table 6–4. Grand Designs, Strategic Objectives, and Tactics

Nixon	Carter	Reagan
Grand Design Stable, multipolar equilibrium guided primarily by the United States, misleadingly described by Nixon as a stable structure of peace	*Grand Design* (*1977–78*): A stable, just world featuring an increasingly cooperative superpower relationship, a mutually beneficial North-South "dialogue," and a "mature" United States adapting to change and leading through example (*1979–80*): The same essential vision, but the realization that its achievement would be indefinitely delayed because of the "shocks" of 1979	*Grand Design* A gradually articulated vision of a fully democratic world reflective of U.S. (i.e., universally shared) values
Strategic Objectives Superpower détente designed to (self-) contain the Soviet Union through the deft management of incentives, threats, and proscriptions and the conclusion of nuclear arms control agreements.	*Strategic Objectives* (*1977–78*): Effective U.S. management of "complex interdependence" through adroit manipulation of shifting, global coalitions	*Strategic Objectives* An initial "prevailing with pride" strategy involving economic warfare against the Soviet Union, avoidance of superpower arms control agreements,

Table 6–4. (*Continued*)

Nixon	Carter	Reagan

Strategic Objectives

Gradual withdrawal from Vietnam intended to preserve U.S. credibility and thus contribute to the emerging international equilibrium

A "peripheral" policy expressed in the Nixon Doctrine that would avoid future Vietnams by relying on local resistance to aggression and subversion and/or collaborating with Moscow to resolve regional disputes. Normalization of relations with the PRC designed to complicate Moscow's security dilemma, facilitate an honorable U.S. withdrawal from Vietnam, and encourage the growth of a multipolar balance

Strategic Objectives

Emphasis on human rights to restore domestic confidence and end international "philosophical isolation"

Restoration of a balance between U.S. commitments and resources by reducing commitments, shifting burdens to allies, and accommodating rivals

Achievement of Brzezinski's ten goals

(*1979–80*): A new strategy of containment designed to punish Soviet aggression in Afghanistan and to deter it from further expansion

The determination— expressed in the Carter Doctrine—to defend the Persian Gulf as a vital U.S. interest

Strategic Objectives

nuclear and conventional force modernization facilitating "horizontal escalation," an information offensive, and support for "freedom fighters" struggling to unseat Third World communist governments

A personal presidential commitment to nuclear abolition through SDI and arms reduction agreements

Tactics

Radical centralization of power in White House to formulate and implement foreign policy

Emphasis on speed, dexterity, manipulation and geopolitical ruthlessness

Tactics

(*1977–78*): Explicit rejection of Nixon-Kissinger approach in favor of openness, honesty, and public participation in foreign policy making

(*1979–80*): Renewed emphasis on strong presidential leadership at a time of "crisis"

Tactics

Declaratory signaling aimed initially at intimidating the Soviet Union and later focused on lending rhetorical support to "democratic revolutions"

Reliance on presidential character to reflect the values of "ordinary, extraordinary Americans"

Table 6–5. Legitimation Strategies

Nixon	Carter	Reagan
A laudatory declaratory history of post–war American foreign policy	*(1977–78)* A rather critical historical account of American foreign policy since World War II	A declaratory history that condemned the U.S. foreign policy of the 1930s and 1970s and extolled the record of the 1940s, 1950s, and, in time, the 1980s
An explanation of the ways in which the world had changed since 1947 and how his policies appropriately addressed those changes	The claim that the world had changed decisively since 1945	The reassurance that recent foreign policy setbacks could easily be reversed
An effort to castigate domestic isolationists who would abandon U.S. world leadership	The claim that his foreign policy reflected the character, values, experiences, and aspirations of the American people	A description of the contemporary world that stressed continuity rather than change
Surprises and televised spectaculars designed to demonstrate Nixon's indispensability	The description of his foreign policy as one that dealt courageously and comprehensively with complexity	The assertion that his foreign policy was well equipped to fight evil in the world
A Wilsonian promise of a "full generation of peace"	The assurance that America could afford to be generous and cooperative	The claim that both the United States and the world constituted very similar political "neighborhoods"
The warning that "peace with honor" in Vietnam would produce a world to challenge the character, will, and spiritual strength of the American people	The promise of an emergent, cooperative global community	The increasingly confident promise of a fully democratic world as a result of his foreign policy
	(1979–80) A laudatory declaratory history of U.S. foreign policy stressing its wisdom and continuity	
	A predominately negative portrayal of international change	
	A description of a complex, turbulent world requiring a strong U.S. economic and military foundation	

Table 6–5. (*Continued*)

Nixon	Carter	Reagan
	(1979–80) The reassurance of U.S. military superiority after a period of neglect	
	A plea for national unity at a time of unparalleled "crisis"	
	Theatrical exercises designed to demonstrate his determination to confront a world in "crisis"	

Table 6–6. Success in Reconstructing Consensus

Nixon	Carter	Reagan
Policy Consensus Short-lived consensus about the *promise* of détente	*Policy Consensus* Largely unsuccessful in achieving consensus for either world order initiatives or neocontainment	*Policy Consensus* Substantial success except for Central America
Cultural Consensus Goal was *Kulturkampf*, not consensus, and was largely successful in that regard	*Cultural Consensus* Unsuccessful in reinstilling an ethic of sacrifice	*Cultural Consensus* Substantially successful in instilling an ethic of "national greatness through self-indulgence"
Procedural Consensus Heightened dissensus	*Procedural Consensus* Largely unsuccessful in working out new co-determination arrangements	*Procedural Consensus* Largely unsuccessful in either reasserting the primacy of the president or reaching agreement about proper congressional role

THE NIXON ADMINISTRATION

If Richard Nixon had been elected in 1960 instead of 1968 he probably would have pursued a policy of anti-Communist global containment largely indistinguishable from that of Truman and Eisenhower. Furthermore, his efforts would have been sustained by a broad domestic consensus regarding the goals, instruments, and interests of American foreign policy. But by 1968 deep, angry cleavages among elites and the wider public produced mostly, though not solely, by the Vietnam War, had shattered the consensus and all but paralyzed U.S. foreign policy. Many observers feared that the country lay on the edge of civil war.

The Nixon-Kissinger foreign policy reformulation and their attempts to achieve "peace with honor" in Vietnam should be viewed as improvised responses to both domestic dissensus and a series of unwelcome international changes that had begun to erode America's preeminent global position. Because the American people, in the aftermath of Tet, opposed further increases in U.S. ground troop strength, Nixon reluctantly decided to rely primarily on American air power and Vietnamization to preserve a non-Communist South Vietnam. Nixon did little to mobilize a domestic consensus for this policy of phased withdrawal. Instead, he tried to build majority support by unleashing a vicious *Kulturkampf* against "effete snobs, isolationists, bums," "nattering nabobs of negativism" (an Agnew contribution), and other "easy roaders" who allegedly sought defeat and disgrace in Vietnam. Against these liberal, elite appeasers Nixon juxtaposed the "silent" or "new" majority—patriotic, Main Street Americans who resented the excesses of the Great Society fully as much as they desired "peace with honor" in Southeast Asia. In this way Nixon attempted to build a post–New Deal conservative *social* coalition that, among other things, would provide majority support for his Vietnam policy.

On the other hand, Nixon's pursuit of superpower détente at a time of growing Soviet strength risked condemnation by the "new majority" as dangerously retreatist. Moreover, Nixon and Kissinger made détente even more vulnerable to conservative criticism by professing to be unconcerned with Soviet domestic practices so long as its foreign policy demonstrated prudence and responsibility. Aware of these potential domestic difficulties Nixon tried to disguise the "European" character of his détente behind a Wilsonian promise of a "full generation of peace," a promise that could only be fulfilled, he asserted, if "peace with honor" were achieved in Vietnam. And, for a brief moment in 1972 and 1973, Nixon did enjoy something approaching consensual support for his strategy of détente.

Yet even in the absence of Watergate it appears unlikely that Nixon could have constructed a lasting consensus upon this version of détente. First, the promises Nixon made on behalf of détente—arms control, regional stability, Soviet adherence to a superpower code of conduct—were perceived by many Americans (led by neoconservative elites) as greater than the concrete results of détente. According to this view, SALT had granted numerical superiority to Soviet strategic weapons, the 1973 Middle East war had demonstrated Moscow's determination to expand recklessly its influence in a volatile region, and its massive arms buildup proved its commitment to military superiority, not stable parity. Second, Nixon's (and Ford's) subsequent efforts to emphasize the "tough" side of détente by threatening to intervene militarily in regional disputes to maintain U.S. "credibility" were defeated by a public and a Congress that wanted no part of another Vietnam. Indeed, the Nixon Doctrine had obscured rather than defined those interests in defense of which the United States would employ military force. Nixon and Kissinger had hoped to avoid the dilemma of peripheral intervention by improving superpower relations, but renewed Soviet activity in the Third World exposed the continuing cleavage in U.S. public opinion over the issue of military power. Furthermore, it seems doubtful that Nixon—even without Watergate—could have persuaded Congress to authorize a reintervention in Vietnam, in part because of the deep animosities previously planted by Nixon in his war against the liberal establishment.

Still, despite these significant failures, Nixon and Kissinger were responsible for some solid foreign policy accomplishments. First, by implicitly acknowledging that American power had finite limits, they sought ways to accommodate a new world no longer wholly susceptible to U.S. fiat. Though, as for example in Chile, they found it difficult to live with the consequences of their insights, the overall impact of their reformulation resulted in a modest "deideologization" of American foreign policy. "Stability" now vied with "mission" as a U.S. priority. Second, by recognizing that simple anti-Communism could no longer serve as the sole basis of U.S. foreign policy, Nixon and Kissinger searched for alternative definitions of the national interest, notions that included the necessity of working with the Soviet Union. Third, by placing nuclear arms control on the superpower agenda, Nixon and Kissinger at least raised the possibility that an uncontrolled arms race could be regulated in mutually beneficial ways. Fourth, in moving to normalize relations with China, Nixon and Kissinger signaled a willingness to use the international status quo in order to encourage the growth of a stable equilibrium.

Yet notwithstanding these admirable efforts to achieve a "philosophical deepening" of American foreign policy, the Nixon-Kissinger reformulation ultimately failed the test of domestic politics, for both liberals and conservatives condemned the search for a "stable equilibrium" as the abandonment of America's values and principles.

THE CARTER ADMINISTRATION

Members of the Carter administration shared the perception that the American people, traumatized by Vietnam, Watergate, inflation, and the energy crisis, had lost faith in themselves and their institutions. Fearing that this widespread disillusionment could result in overwhelming pressure for an isolationist foreign policy, Carter attempted to reestablish the global relevance of the United States by "getting on the right side of change" and by emphasizing his dedication to human rights. America's new task would be the adroit management of complex interdependence in an era of increasingly diffused power. Carter hoped that the competence and courage that he displayed in pursuit of a moral, humane, and mature foreign policy would help to restore national self-confidence.

On occasion this approach bore fruit as, for example, in the Panama Canal treaties and the Camp David Accords. And if Jimmy Carter had faced the reform-minded Mikhail Gorbachev, instead of the intransigent Leonid Brezhnev, in the late 1970s, Nixon's détente might have been strengthened and expanded. But his early efforts to portray the Soviet Union as a largely satisfied power that could positively contribute to world order appeared increasingly at odds with Moscow's actual behavior. Furthermore, Carter's inability to tame domestic inflation or to manage Third World crises in Iran and Nicaragua raised disturbing questions about his competence. Neoconservative and conservative commentators and politicians eagerly attacked Carter as both incompetent and *ideologically* mistaken. They argued persuasively that at the core of Carter's "mature" foreign policy lay retreatism, appeasement, and hypocrisy.

Confronted with this acute domestic challenge as the 1980 election drew closer, Carter tried to placate these critics by embracing a more traditional, Soviet-centered, foreign policy approach. Now he claimed—at Brezezinski's urging—that the American people had so "overlearned" the lessons of Vietnam that the use of U.S. military power in *any* circumstance had wrongly been proscribed. In place of his earlier efforts at retrenchment and burden sharing, President Carter enunciated a Persian Gulf doctrine that significantly expanded the vital interests of the United States. Yet opinion polls indicated that although the public wanted America to reassert its "global leadership," there remained widespread resistance to the employment of military power abroad. In sum, the ambiguous and divisive legacy of Vietnam haunted U.S. foreign policy at the end of the 1970s just as the reality of that war had deepened domestic dissensus at the beginning of the decade.

THE REAGAN ADMINISTRATION

Ronald Reagan shared Jimmy Carter's conviction about the necessity for restoring national self-confidence. But whereas his predecessor had initially offered a complex program of unfocused moralism, managerial competence, and world order initiatives to achieve this goal, Reagan resurrected the priorities of cold war presidents: a high-growth, low-inflation economy, a powerful national defense, and a strident, anti-Communist rhetoric. Reagan and his advisers may have harbored the vague hope that the patient pursuit of these goals might eventually result in the moderation or capitulation of the Soviet Union, but in the early 1980s they anticipated a long, "twilight struggle" comparable in intensity to the cold war. The administration's early "prevailing with pride" strategy neatly captured this outlook.

Yet Reagan faced a public that, while eager to reassert American global leadership after the national embarrassments of the late 1970s, simultaneously feared superpower nuclear war and another Vietnam quagmire. These public concerns severely constrained Reagan's foreign policy options by forcing him to enunciate an arms control program and to renounce any intention of direct intervention in Central America. The result was that Reagan—the "Great Communicator"—unveiled a foreign policy distinguished by heavy declaratory signaling to overseas adversaries and the American public. By ridiculing rival governments and by lavishing praise on the American people, Reagan was able to pursue an essentially cautious foreign policy that largely replaced deeds with words. At the same time, however, the partial restoration of the U.S. economy enabled Reagan's rhetoric to find a receptive domestic audience.

Indeed, it was rhetoric that united the otherwise disparate foreign policies of Reagan's first and second terms, for if the early years witnessed a heavily stylized new cold war that featured evil empires and similar monsters, the late 1980s were alleged by Reagan to be a new era of "democratic revolutions" sweeping away the last vestiges of authoritarian rule. If nothing else, Reagan had succeeded in persuading the American people of the revitalized global relevance of the American dream.

BUSH AND BEYOND

Has the post-Vietnam era of U.S. foreign policy finally ended? Have the deep disagreements about the purposes and limits of American power that shaped and constrained U.S. foreign policy for twenty years disappeared? Will George Bush and future presidents enjoy a reliable base of public and elite support for their grand designs and strategies?

The extraordinary withdrawal of Soviet power from Central and Eastern Europe and the reform of its domestic economy and political institutions have transformed the structure of international relations. These events, as well as the imminent economic union of Western Europe, the reunification of Germany, the incredible growth of Japan and its Asian progeny, and the continued decline in the competitiveness of the United States, threaten (or promise) to spawn a genuinely multipolar international system freed from the likelihood of armed conflict among its members.

In these circumstances the domestic legacy of Vietnam may simply lose its remaining relevance, for, with the removal of the Soviet threat, presidents would have little need to deploy combat troops to counter Moscow's Third World "clients." Rather, they could be confidently used to dispose of "local" problems like Noriega. In this sense, the primary organizing principle of post-1945 U.S. foreign policy—opposition to Soviet expansion—could be safely exorcised.

On the other hand, there lay on the horizon of the 1990s at least three potentially formidable barriers that could block the emergence of a solid, sustained domestic foreign policy consensus. First, in order to preserve the fruits of the "era of democratic revolutions," it might be necessary to provide substantial military assistance to democratic governments threatened by domestic turmoil. In December 1989 for example, Philippine President Aquino, facing a military coup, received crucial air cover from Washington. If United States support for democratic revolutions constitutes something more than domestically appealing rhetoric, then Bush or a successor could be called on to send combat troops to save more than one threatened democratic ally. Would the American public tolerate such action, or would the residue of the Vietnam "syndrome" be revived? Second, in order to resurrect a cold war–like "negative consensus" there might be significant political temptations to "bash" Japan (or, more remotely, a reunified Germany), especially if the international competitive position of the United States continues to deteriorate. This sort of effort could intensify domestic disagreements about trade policy, foreign investment in the United States, and the advisability of an industrial policy. Third, and most immediately, the dramatic changes in East-West relations are likely to create a "peace dividend," as U.S. defense spending decreased by perhaps 50 percent by the mid-90s. According to James Sasser (D-TN), Chair of the Senate Budget Committee, "this moment in history," represents "the dawn of the primacy of domestic economics."[1] Finding ways to spend the peace dividend threaten to trigger a serious political debate about domestic priorities. The outcome of that debate will doubtless have an indirect, though important, impact on U.S. foreign policy.

In sum, the disturbing and divisive issues raised by the Vietnam War have been transcended rather than resolved, and it remains unclear whether in the 1990s American foreign policy will be animated by a coherent sense of purpose and a clear understanding of interests or by the continuing tyranny of presidential rhetoric largely disconnected from international and domestic realities.

NOTE

1. *New York Times*, December 14, 1989, p. 1.

Bibliography

BOOKS

Abramson, Jeffrey B., F. Christopher Atherton, and Garry R. Orren. *The Electronic Commonwealth: The Impact of New Media Technologies on Democratic Politics*. New York: Basic Books, 1988.

Almond, Gabriel A. *The American People and Foreign Policy*. New York: Harcourt Brace, 1950.

Ambrose, Stephen E. *Nixon: The Triumph of a Politician, 1962–1972*. New York: Simon & Schuster, 1989.

Americans Talk Security: A Series of Surveys of American Voters: Attitudes Concerning National Security Issues. Winchester, MA, 1988–90.

Anderson, Martin. *Revolution*. New York: Harcourt Brace Jovanovich, 1988.

Arnson, Cynthia J. *Crossroads: Congress, the Reagan Administration, and Central America*. New York: Pantheon, 1989.

Bell, Coral. *The Reagan Paradox: U.S. Foreign Policy in the 1980's*. New Brunswick: Rutgers University Press, 1990.

Bill, James A. *The Eagle and the Lion: The Tragedy of American-Iranian Relations*. New Haven: Yale University Press, 1988.

Brandon, Henry. *The Retreat of American Power*. Garden City, NY: Doubleday, 1973.

Brown, Harold. *Thinking about National Security: Defense and Foreign Policy in a Dangerous World*. Boulder, CO.: Westview Press, 1983.

Brzezinski, Zbigniew. *Power and Principle: Memoirs of the National Security Advisor, 1977–1981*. New York: Farrar, Straus & Giroux, 1983.

Cannon, Lou. *Reagan*. New York: Putnam, 1982.

Carter, Jimmy. *Keeping Faith: Memoirs of a President*. New York: Bantam, 1982.

———. *Why Not the Best*? Nashville: Broadman Press, 1975.

Christopher, Warren, Harold H. Saunders, Gary Sick, et al. *American Hostages in Iran: The Conduct of a Crisis*. New Haven: Yale University Press, 1985.

Crabb, Cecil, Jr., and Pat Holt. *Invitation to Struggle: Congress, the President, and Foreign Policy*. 3rd ed. Washington: Congressional Quarterly Press, 1989.

Dallek, Robert A. *Ronald Reagan: The Politics of Symbolism*. Cambridge: Harvard University Press, 1984.

Destler, I. M., Leslie H. Gelb, and Anthony Lake. *Our Own Worst Enemy: The Unmaking of American Foreign Policy*. New York: Simon & Schuster, 1984.

Dugger, Ronnie. *On Reagan: The Man and His Presidency*. New York: McGraw-Hill, 1983.

Edsall, Thomas, and Sidney Blumenthal, eds. *The Reagan Legacy*. New York: Pantheon Books, 1988.

Feinberg, Richard E. *The Intemperate Zone: The Third World Challenge to U.S. Foreign Policy*. New York: W. W. Norton, 1983.

Ford, Gerald R. *A Time to Heal: The Autobiography of Gerald R. Ford*. New

York: Harper & Row, 1979.

Fossedal, Gregory. *The Democratic Imperative: Exporting the American Revolution*. New York: A *New Republic* Book, Basic Books, 1989.

Franck, Thomas M., and Edward Weisband. *Foreign Policy by Congress*. New York: Oxford University Press, 1979.

Fraser, Steve and Gary Berstle, eds. *The Rise and Fall of the New Deal Order, 1930–1980*. Princeton, NJ: Princeton University Press, 1989.

Gaddis, John Lewis. *The Long Peace: Inquiries into the History of the Cold War*. New York: Oxford University Press, 1987.

———. *Strategies of Containment: A Critical Appraisal of Postwar American National Security Policy*. New York: Oxford University Press, 1982.

Gallup Opinion Index 92 (February 1973).

Gallup Opinion Index (June 1974).

Gallup Opinion Index 71 (September 1980).

The Gallup Poll, Public Opinion 1935–1971. Vols 1–3. New York: Random House, 1972.

Gardner, Lloyd. *The Great Nixon Turnaround*. New York: New Viewpoints, 1973.

Garthoff, Raymond L. *Détente and Confrontation: American-Soviet Relations from Nixon to Reagan*. Washington: The Brookings Institution, 1985.

Gelb, Leslie H., with Richard K. Betts. *The Irony of Vietnam: The System Worked*. Washington: The Brookings Institution, 1978.

Gibbons, William Conrad. *The U.S. Government and the Vietnam War: Executive and Legislative Roles and Relationships*, Parts I–III. Princeton: Princeton University Press, 1986 and 1989.

Glad, Betty. *Jimmy Carter: In Search of the Great White House*. New York: W. W. Norton, 1980.

Greenstein, Fred I., ed. *Leadership in the Modern Presidency*. Cambridge, MA: Harvard University Press, 1988.

———. *The Reagan Presidency: An Early Assessment*. Baltimore: Johns Hopkins University Press, 1982.

Gutman, Roy. *Banana Diplomacy: The Making of American Policy in Nicaragua, 1981–1987*. New York: Simon & Schuster, 1988.

Hagstrom, Jerry. *Beyond Reagan: The New Landscape of American Politics*. New York: W. W. Norton, 1988.

Haig, Alexander M., Jr. *Caveat: Realism, Reagan, and Foreign Policy*. New York: Macmillan, 1984.

Hamby, Alonzo L. *Liberalism and Its Challengers: F.D.R. to Reagan*. New York: Oxford University Press, 1985.

Hamilton, Edward K., ed. *America's Global Interests: A New Agenda*. New York: W. W. Norton, 1989.

Hamilton, Nora, Jeffry A. Frieden, Linda Fuller, and Manuel Pastor, Jr. *Crisis in Central America: Regional Dynamics and U.S. Policy in the 1980s*. Boulder, CO: Westview Press, 1988.

Hargrove, Erwin C. *Jimmy Carter as President: Leadership and the Politics of the Public Good*. Baton Rouge: Louisiana State University Press, 1988.

Hart, Roderick P. *The Sound Leadership: Presidential Communication in the Modern Age.* Chicago: University of Chicago Press, 1987.

Hersh, Seymour. *The Price of Power: Kissinger in the White House.* New York: Summit Books, 1983.

Hoffmann, Stanley. *Primacy or World Order: American Foreign Policy since the Cold War.* New York: McGraw-Hill, 1978.

Hogan, J. Michael. *The Panama Canal in American Politics: Domestic Advocacy and the Evolution of Policy.* Carbondale, IL: Southern Illinois University Press, 1986.

Holsti, Ole R., Randolph M. Siverson, and Alexander M. George, eds. *Change in the International System.* Boulder, CO: Westview Press, 1980.

Holsti, Ole R., and James N. Rosenau. *American Leadership in World Affairs: Vietnam and the Breakdown of Consensus.* Boston: Allen & Unwin, 1984.

Hyland, William G. *Mortal Rivals: Understanding the Pattern of Soviet-American Conflict.* New York: Random House, 1987.

Isaacson, Walter, and Evan Thomas. *The Wise Men: Six Friends and the World They Made.* New York: Simon & Schuster, 1986.

Johnson, Haynes. *In the Absence of Power: Governing America.* New York: Viking Press, 1980.

Jones, Charles O. *The Trusteeship Presidency: Jimmy Carter and the United States Congress.* Baton Rouge: Louisiana State University Press, 1988.

———. ed. *The Reagan Legacy: Promise and Performance.* Chatham, NJ: Chatham House, 1988.

Jordan, Hamilton. *Crisis: The Last Year of the Carter Presidency.* New York: Putnam, 1982.

Kissinger, Henry A. *American Foreign Policy.* Expanded edition. New York: W. W. Norton, 1974.

———. *White House Years.* Boston: Little, Brown, 1979.

———. *A World Restored: The Politics of Conservatism in a Revolutionary Era.* London: Victor Gollancz, 1977.

Krepon, Michael. *Strategic Stalemate: Nuclear Weapons and Arms Control in American Politics.* New York: St. Martin's Press, 1984.

Krieger, Joel. *Reagan, Thatcher, and the Politics of Decline.* New York: Oxford University Press, 1986.

Kymlicka, B. B., and Jean Matthews, eds. *The Reagan Revolution?* Chicago: Dorsey Press, 1988.

Lake, W. Anthony, ed. *The Legacy of Vietnam.* New York: New York University Press, 1976.

Larson, Deborah Welch. *Origins of Containment: A Psychological Explanation.* Princeton: Princeton University Press, 1985.

Leigh, Michael. *Mobilizing Consent: Public Opinion and American Foreign Policy.* Westport, CT: Greenwood Press, 1976.

Lippmann, Walter. *Public Opinion.* New York: Macmillan, 1922.

Litwak, Robert. *Détente and the Nixon Doctrine: American Foreign Policy and the Pursuit of Stability, 1969–1976.* New York: Cambridge University, 1984.

Lowi, Theodore J. *The Personal President: Power Invested, Promise Unfulfilled.* Ithaca: Cornell University Press, 1985.

May, Ernest R. *Lessons of the Past: The Use and Misuse of History in American Foreign Policy.* New York: Oxford University Press, 1973.

Mayers, David. *Cracking the Monolith: U.S. Policy against the Sino-Soviet Alliance, 1949–1955.* Baton Rouge: Louisiana State University Press, 1986.

———. *George Kennan and the Dilemmas of American Foreign Policy.* New York: Oxford University Press, 1988.

McLellan, David S. *Cyrus Vance.* Totowa, NJ: Rowman and Allenheld, 1985.

Melanson, Richard A., and Kenneth W. Thompson eds. *Foreign Policy and Domestic Consensus.* Lanham, MD: University Press of America, 1985.

Morris, Roger. *Richard Milhouse Nixon: The Rise of an American Politician.* New York: Henry Holt, 1989.

———. *Uncertain Greatness: Henry Kissinger and American Foreign Policy.* New York: Harper & Row, 1977.

Mower, A. Glenn, Jr. *Human Rights and American Foreign Policy: The Carter and Reagan Experiences.* Westport, CT: Greenwood, 1987.

Muravchik, Joshua. *The Uncertain Crusade: Jimmy Carter and the Dilemmas of Human Rights.* Lanham, MD: University Press of America, 1986.

Nathan, Richard P. *The Plot That Failed: Nixon and the Administrative Presidency.* New York: John Wiley & Sons, 1975.

Newhouse, John. *Cold Dawn: The Story of SALT.* New York: Holt, Rinehart, and Winston, 1973.

Newsome, David D. *The Soviet Combat Brigade in Cuba: A Study in Political Diplomacy.* Bloomington: Indiana University Press, 1987.

Nixon, Richard M. *RN: The Memoirs of Richard Nixon.* New York: Grosset and Dunlop, 1978.

Noonan, Peggy. *What I Saw at the Reagan Revolution: A Political Life in the Reagan Era.* New York: Random House, 1990.

Nye, Joseph S., Jr., ed. *The Making of America's Soviet Policy.* New Haven: Yale University Press, 1984.

Oye, Kenneth A., Donald Rothchild, and Robert J. Lieber, eds. *Eagle Defiant: United States Foreign Policy in the 1980s.* Boston: Little, Brown, 1983.

———. *Eagle Entangled: U.S. Foreign Policy in a Complex World.* New York: Longman, 1979.

———. *Eagle Resurgent? The Reagan Era in American Foreign Policy in the 1980s.* Boston: Little, Brown, 1987.

Palmer, John L., ed. *Perspectives on the Reagan Years.* Washington: The Urban Institute, 1986.

Pastor, Robert A. *Condemned to Repetition: The United States and Nicaragua.* Princeton: Princeton University Press, 1987.

Phillips, Kevin. *The Emerging Republican Majority.* New Rochelle: Arlington House, 1969.

Powell, Jody. *The Other Side of the Story.* New York: William Morrow, 1984.

Quandt, William B. *Camp David: Politics and Peacemaking.* Washington, DC:

The Brookings Institution, 1986.

Ranney, Austin, ed. *The American Elections of 1980*. Washington: The American Enterprise Institute, 1980.

Regan, Donald T. *For the Record: From Wall Street to Washington*. New York: Harcourt Brace Jovanovich, 1988.

Reichley, A. James. *Conservatives in an Age of Change: The Nixon and Ford Administrations*. Washington, DC: The Brookings Institution, 1981.

Rielly, John E. ed. *American Public Opinion and U.S. Foreign Policy 1975*. Chicago: Chicago Council on Foreign Relations, 1975.

———. *American Public Opinion and U.S. Foreign Policy 1979*. Chicago: Chicago Council on Foreign Relations, 1979.

———. *American Public Opinion and U.S. Foreign Policy 1983*. Chicago: Chicago Council on Foreign Relations, 1983.

———. *American Public Opinion and U.S. Foreign Policy 1987*. Chicago: Chicago Council on Foreign Relations, 1987.

Rosati, Jerel A. *The Carter Administration's Quest for World Community: Beliefs and Their Impact on Behavior*. Columbia: University of South Carolina Press, 1987.

Rosecrance, Richard, ed. *America as an Ordinary Country: US Foreign Policy and the Future*. London: Cornell University Press, 1976.

Rubin, Barry. *Paved with Good Intentions: The American Experience and Iran*. New York: Oxford University Press, 1980.

Safire, William. *Before the Fall: An Inside View of the Pre-Watergate White House*. Garden City, NY: Doubleday, 1975.

Sanders, Jerry W. *Peddlers of Crisis: The Committee on the Present Danger and the Politics of Containment*. Boston: South End Press, 1983.

Scammon, Richard M., and Ben J. Wattenberg. *The Real Majority*. New York: Coward-McCann, 1970.

Schoenhals, Kai P., and Richard A. Melanson. *Revolution and Intervention in Grenada: The New Jewel Movement, the United States, and the Caribbean*. Boulder, CO: Westview Press, 1985.

Schoultz, Lars. *National Security and United States Policy toward Latin America*. Princeton: Princeton University Press, 1987.

Schram, Martin. *Running for President: A Journal of the Carter Campaign*. New York: Simon & Schuster, 1977

Schulzinger, Robert D. *The Wise Men of Foreign Affairs: The History of the Council on Foreign Relations*. New York: Columbia University Press, 1984.

Serfaty, Simon. *After Reagan: False Starts, Missed Opportunities and New Beginnings*, Foreign Policy Institute Papers in International Affairs. Lanham, MD: University Press of America, 1988.

Sick, Gary. *All Fall Down: America's Tragic Encounter with Iran*. New York: Random House, 1985.

Sills, David L., ed. *International Encyclopedia of the Social Sciences*. New York: Crowell, Collier, and Macmillan, 1968.

Smith, Gaddis. *Morality, Reason, and Power: American Diplomacy in the Carter*

Years. New York: Hill and Wang, 1986.

Smith, Hedrick. *The Power Game: How Washington Works*. New York: Random House, 1988.

Spanier, John and Joseph Nogee, eds. *Congress, the Presidency, and Foreign Policy*. New York: Pergamon Press, 1981.

Szulz, Tad. *The Illusion of Peace*. New York: Viking Press, 1978.

Talbott, Strobe. *Endgame: The Inside Story of SALT II*. New York: Harper & Row, 1979.

————. *The Master of the Game: Paul Nitze and the Nuclear Peace*. New York: Alfred A. Knopf, 1988.

Tucker, Robert W. *Nation or Empire? The Debate over American Foreign Policy*. Baltimore: Johns Hopkins University Press, 1968.

Tulis, Jeffrey K. *The Rhetorical Presidency*. Princeton: Princeton University Press, 1987.

Vance, Cyrus. *Hard Choices: Critical Years in America's Foreign Policy*. New York: Simon & Schuster, 1983.

Warburg, Gerald F. *Conflict and Consensus: The Struggle between Congress and the President over Foreign Policymaking*. New York: Harper & Row, 1989.

White, John Kenneth. *The New Politics of Old Values*. Hanover, NH: University Press of New England, 1988.

Wills, Garry. *Reagan's America: Innocents at Home*. Garden City, NY: Doubleday, 1987.

Witcover, Jules. *Marathon: The Pursuit of the Presidency, 1972–1976*. New York: New American Library, 1977.

Wittkopf, Eugene R. *Faces of Internationalism: American Public Opinion and Foreign Policy*. Durham: Duke University Press, 1990.

Woodward, Bob. *Veil: The Secret Wars of the CIA 1981–1987*. New York: Simon & Schuster, 1987.

Wooten, James. *Dasher*. New York: Summit, 1978.

Yankelovich, Daniel, and Sidney Harmon. *Starting with the People*. Boston: Houghton Mifflin, 1988.

ARTICLES

Allison, Graham, Ernest May, and Adam Yarmolinsky. "U.S. Military Policy: Limits to Intervention." *Foreign Affairs* 48 (January 1970).

Barnes, Fred. "Reagan's Last Stand." *New Republic*, April 11, 1988.

Bell, Coral. "From Carter to Reagan." *Foreign Affairs, America and the World, 1984* 63.3 (1985).

Bell, Daniel. "The End of American Exceptionalism." *Public Interest* 41 (1975).

Blechman, Barry with Ethan Gutmann. "A $100 Billion Understanding." *SAIS Review* 9.2 (1989).

Boren, David L. "Speaking with a Single Voice: Bipartisanship in Foreign Policy." *SAIS Review* 9.1 (1989).

Brown, Bernard E. "The Structural Weaknesses of United States Foreign Policy." *American Foreign Policy Newsletter* 12.2 (1989).

Brown, Harold. "Building a New Consensus." *SAIS Review* 9.1 (1989).

Brownstein, Ronald. "The New Politics of National Security." *Public Opinion* 11.3 (1988).

Carlson, Allan C. "Foreign Policy and 'the American Way': The Rise and Fall of the Post-World War II Consensus." *This World* 5 (1983).

Chace, James. "Is a Foreign Policy Consensus Possible?" *Foreign Affairs* 57 (Fall 1978).

Crovitz, L. Gordon. "How Ronald Reagan Weakened the Presidency." *Commentary* 86 (September 1988).

Deibel, Terry L. "Reagan's Mixed Legacy." *Foreign Policy* 75 (1989).

Drew, Elizabeth. "Letter from Washington." *New Yorker*, August 28, 1989.

Falk, Richard A. "Lifting the Curse of Bipartisanship." *World Policy Journal* 1 (1983).

Fallows, James. "The Passionless Presidency." *Atlantic Monthly*, May 1979.

Gershman, Carl. "The Rise and Fall of the New Foreign-Policy Establishment." *Commentary* 24 (July 1980).

Greider, William. "The Education of David Stockman." *Atlantic Monthly*, December 1981.

Griffith, E. S., John Plamenatz, and J. Roland Pennock. "Cultural Prerequisites to a Successfully Functioning Democracy: Symposium." *American Political Science Review* 50 (1956).

Harries, Owen. "Between Paradigms." *The National Interest* 17 (1989).

Hassner, Pierre. "The State of Nixon's World (3): Pragmatic Conservatism in the White House." *Foreign Policy* 3 (Summer 1971).

Hertzberg, Hendrik. "At Watergate." *New Republic*, July 3, 1989.

Hodgson, Godfrey. "The Establishment." *Foreign Policy* 10 (1973).

Hoffmann, Stanley. "Will the Balance Balance at Home?" *Foreign Policy* 7 (1972).

Holsti, Ole R. "Public Opinion and Containment," in Terry L. Deibel and John Lewis Gaddis, eds. *Containment: Concept and Policy*. Washington: National Defense University Press, 1986.

Hughes, Thomas R. "The Crack Up," *Foreign Policy* 40 (1980): 52, 53.

Kegley, Charles W., Jr. "The Bush Administration and the Future of American Foreign Policy: Pragmatism or Procrastination?" *Presidential Studies Quarterly* 19 (1989).

Kennan, George F. "The Sources of Soviet Conduct," in Walter Lippmann, *The Cold War*. New York: Harper & Row, 1972.

Kirkpatrick, Jeane J. "Dictatorships and Double Standards." *Commentary*, November 1979.

Kissinger, Henry. "Domestic Structure and Foreign Policy." *Daedalus* 95: 2 (Spring 1966).

Kissinger, Henry and Cyrus Vance. "Bipartisan Objectives for Foreign Policy." *Foreign Affairs* 66 (Summer 1988).

Krauthammer, Charles. "Beyond the Cold War." *New Republic*, December 19, 1988.

Lipset, Seymour Martin. "Some Further Comments on 'The End of Ideology'." *American Political Science Review* 60 (1966).

Lipsitz, Lewis. "The Study of Consensus," in Sills, ed. *International Encyclopedia,* 266.

Melanson, Richard A. "Action History, Declaratory History, and the Reagan Years." *SAIS Review* 9.2 (1989).

———. "The Social and Political Thought of William Appleman Williams." *Western Political Quarterly* 31 (1978).

Miller, Warren E. "Misreading the Public Pulse," *Public Opinion* II (1979).

———. "Opinion Roundup," *Public Opinion* II (1979).

Nixon, Richard M. "Asia after Vietnam." *Foreign Affairs* 46 (October 1967).

Phillips, Kevin. "Did We Elect Another Carter?" *New York Times*, February 9, 1989.

"Of Rifts and Drifts: A Symposium on Beliefs, Opinions, and American Foreign Policy." *International Studies Quarterly* 30 (1986).

Roskin, Michael. "From Pearl Harbor to Vietnam: Shifting Generational Paradigms and Foreign Policy." *Political Science Quarterly* 89 (1974).

Rossiter, Caleb. "The Financial Hit List." *International Policy Report* (Feb. 1984).

Sanders, Jerry W. "Empire at Bay: Containment Strategies and American Politics at the Crossroads." *World Policy Paper No. 25.* New York: World Policy Institute, 1983.

Schneider, William. "The Public and Foreign Policy." *Wall Street Journal*, November 7, 1979.

Smith, Craig Allen. "MisterReagan's Neighborhood: Rhetoric and National Unity." *Southern Speech Communication Journal* 52 (1987).

Tannanbaum, Duane L. "The Bricker Amendment Controversy: Its Origins and Eisenhower's Role." *Diplomatic History* 9.1 (1985).

Trout, Thomas B. "Rhetoric Revisited: Political Legitimation and the Cold War." *International Studies Quarterly* 19 (1975).

Tucker, Robert W. "Reagan's Foreign Policy." *Foreign Affairs, America and the World, 1988/89* 68.1 (1989).

Winik, Jay. "Restoring Bipartisanship." *Washington Quarterly* 12.1 (1989).

Wittkopf, Eugene R. "On the Foreign Policy Beliefs of the American People: A Critique and Some Evidence." *International Studies Quarterly* 30 (1986).

Yankelovich, Daniel, and Richard Smoke. "America's 'New Thinking'." *Foreign Affairs* 67 (Fall 1988).

UNPUBLISHED WORKS

Balzano, Michael P., Jr. "The Silent Majority: Support for the President." *Richard Nixon: A Retrospective on His Presidency*, Hofstra University, Hempstead, New York, November 20, 1987.

Clark, William P. "National Security Strategy." Address. Center for Strategic and International Studies, Georgetown University, May 21, 1982.

Colson, Charles W. "The Silent Majority: Support for the President." *Richard Nixon: A Retrospective on His Presidency*, Hofstra University, Hempstead, New York, November 20, 1987.

Gaddis, John Lewis. "Remarks at Panel on the Reagan Foreign Policy Legacy."

Midwest meeting of the International Studies Association, Columbus, Ohio, November 11, 1988.

Grayden, Margaret M.. "Foreign Policy Legitimation: A Preliminary 'Framework for Analysis.'" Paper presented to the annual meeting of the American Political Science Association, Chicago, IL, September 2–5, 1987.

Hult, Karen M., and Charles Walcott. "Writing for the President: Evolution of an Organizational Function." Paper presented at the annual meeting of the American Political Science Association, Washington, DC, September 1–4, 1988.

Katz, Andrew Z. "Public Opinion, Congress, President Nixon and the Termination of the Vietnam War." Ph.D. diss., Johns Hopkins University 1987.

Levering, Ralph B. "Public Opinion, Foreign Policy, and American Politics Since the 1960s." Paper presented at the annual Baker Peace Conference, Ohio University, Athens, Ohio, April 1988.

Morris, Roger. "The Foreign Policy Process." *Richard Nixon: A Retrospective on His Presidency*, Hofstra University, Hempstead, NY, November 1987.

Rodgers, Donald F. "The Silent Majority: Support for the President." *Richard Nixon: A Retrospective on His Presidency*, Hofstra University, Hempstead, NY, November 20, 1987.

Rosati, Jerel A., and John Creed. "Clarifying Concepts of Consensus and Dissensus: Evolution of Public Beliefs in U.S. Foreign Policy." Paper presented at the annual meeting of the International Studies Association, St. Louis, March 29–April 2, 1988.

Skidmore, David G. "The Politics of Decline: International Adjustment versus Domestic Legitimacy during the Carter Administration." Unpublished essay. 1989.

Sobel, Richard. "Public Opinion toward U.S. Involvement in Central America." Paper presented to the annual meeting of the American Political Science Association, Chicago, IL, September 2–5, 1987.

Wittkopf, Eugene R. and James M. McCormick. "Was There Ever a Foreign Policy Consensus?" Paper presented at the annual meeting of the American Political Science Association, Washington, DC, September 1–4, 1988.

GOVERNMENT DOCUMENTS

Congressional Record. Washington, DC, October 1983.

Haig, Alexander M., Jr. "Relationship of Foreign and Defense Policies." *Current Policy no. 308*. Washington, DC: U.S. Department of State, July 30, 1981.

———. "American Power and American Purpose," *Current Policy no. 279*. Washington, DC: U.S. Department of State, April 27, 1982.

Haig, Alexander M., Jr. Testimony. U.S. Congress. Senate. *Hearings before the Committee on Foreign Relations* 99th Cong., 1st sess., February 7, 1985, "Commitments, Consensus, and U.S. Foreign Policy." Washington, DC: Government Printing Office, 1985.

Kirkpatrick, Jeane J. "The Atlantic Alliance and the American National Interest." *Current Policy, No. 581*. Washington, DC: U.S. Department of State, April 30, 1984.

"Ambassador Kirkpatrick's Statement, UN Security Council, October 27, 1983." *Department of State Bulletin*. Washington, DC: U.S. Department of State, December 1983.

Lake, W. Anthony. "Pragmatism and Principle in U.S. Foreign Policy." Address to the Boston Council of World Affairs, June 13, 1977. Washington, DC: U.S. Department of State, *Current Policy No. 213*.

National Security Strategy of the United States. Washington, D.C.: Government Printing Office, March 1990.

President's Special Review Board (The Tower Commission Report). Washington, DC: Government Printing Office, 1987.

Public Papers of the Presidents of the United States: Richard Nixon, 1969. Washington, DC: Government Printing Office, 1971.

Public Papers of the Presidents of the United States: Richard Nixon, 1970. Washington, DC: Government Printing Office, 1972.

Public Papers of the Presidents of the United States: Richard Nixon, 1971. Washington, DC: Government Printing Office, 1973.

Public Papers of the Presidents of the United States: Richard Nixon, 1972. Washington, DC: Government Printing Office, 1974.

Public Papers of the Presidents of the United States: Richard Nixon, 1973. Washington, DC: Government Printing Office, 1975.

Public Papers of the Presidents of the United States: Gerald R. Ford, 1974. Washington, DC: Government Printing Office, 1975.

Public Papers of the Presidents of the United States: Jimmy Carter, 1977. Washington, DC: Government Printing Office, 1978.

Public Papers of the Presidents of the United States: Jimmy Carter, 1978. Washington, DC: Government Printing Office, 1979.

Public Papers of the Presidents of the United States: Jimmy Carter, 1979. Washington, DC: Government Printing Office, 1980.

Public Papers of the Presidents of the United States: Jimmy Carter, 1980. Washington, DC: Government Printing Office, 1982.

Public Papers of the Presidents of the United States: Jimmy Carter, 1981. Washington, DC: Government Printing Office, 1983.

Public Papers of the Presidents of the United States: Ronald Reagan, 1981. Washington, DC: Government Printing Office, 1983.

Public Papers of the Presidents of the United States: Ronald Reagan, 1982. Washington, DC: Government Printing Office, 1984.

Public Papers of the Presidents of the United States: Ronald Reagan, 1983. Washington, DC: Government Printing Office, 1985.

Public Papers of the Presidents of the United States: Ronald Reagan, 1984. Washington, DC: Government Printing Office, 1986.

Public Papers of the Presidents of the United States: Ronald Reagan, 1985. Washington, DC: Government Printing Office, 1987.

Public Papers of the Presidents of the United States: Ronald Reagan, 1986. Washington, DC: Government Printing Office, 1988.

Public Papers of the Presidents of the United States: Ronald Reagan, 1987. Washington, DC: Government Printing Office, 1989.

Reagan, Ronald. "Paths toward Peace: Deterrence and Arms Control." *Current Policy, no. 435.* Washington, DC: U.S. Department of State, November 22, 1982.

Report of the Congressional Committees Investigating the Iran-Contra Affair. Washington, DC: Government Printing Office, 1987.

Shelton, Sally A. U.S. Congress. House. *Hearing before the Subcommittee on Inter-American Affairs of the Committee on Foreign Affairs.* 97th Cong., 2nd sess., June 15, 1982, "United States Policy Toward Grenada." Washington, DC: Government Printing Office, 1982.

Shultz, George. "The Meaning of Vietnam." *Current Policy, no. 269.* Washington, DC: U.S. Department of State, April 25, 1985.

———. "Power and Diplomacy in the 1980s," *Current Policy, no. 561.* Washington, DC: U.S. Department of State, April 3, 1984.

U.S. Congress. Senate. Committee on Foreign Relations. *Détente.* 93rd Cong., 2nd sess., 1974.

———. *Nomination of Henry A. Kissinger to be Secretary of State.* 2 parts. 93rd Cong., 1st sess., 1973.

U.S. Department of State, Bureau of Public Affairs. *Current Policy,* 1977–90.

U.S. National Bipartisan Commission on Central America, "Report of the National Bipartisan Commission on Central America." Washington, DC: U.S. Department of State, 1984.

U.S. Congress. Senate. *Hearings Before the Committee on Foreign Relations, Détente.* 93rd Cong., 2nd sess., August 15, 20, and 21, September 10, 12, 18, 19, 24, and 25, and October 1 and 8, 1974.

U.S. President. *US Foreign Policy for the 1970s: A New Strategy for Peace.* A Report to the Congress by Richard M. Nixon, President of the United States, 18 February 1970. Washington, DC: Government Printing Office, 1970.

———. *US Foreign Policy for the 1970s: Building for Peace.* A Report to the Congress by Richard M. Nixon, President of the United States, 25 February 1971. Washington, DC: Government Printing Office, 1971.

———. *US Foreign Policy for the 1970s: The Emerging Structure of Peace.* A Report to the Congress by Richard M. Nixon, President of the United States, 9 February 1972. Washington, DC: Government Printing Office, 1973.

———. *US Foreign Policy for the 1970s: Shaping a Durable Peace.* A Report to the Congress by Richard M. Nixon, President of the United States, 3 May 1973. Washington, DC: Government Printing Office, 1973.

U.S. President. *Weekly Compilation of Presidential Documents,* 1969–76.

U.S. President. *Weekly Compilation of Presidential Documents,* 1986–90.

"U.S. Support for Democracy and Peace in Central America." *Selected Documents No. 36.* Washington, DC: U.S. Department of State, n.d.

Vance, Cyrus. "Meeting the Challenges of a Changing World." Address before the Chicago Council on Foreign Relations, June 1, 1979. Washington, DC: U.S. Department of State, *Current Policy No. 501.*

Weinberger, Caspar W. *Annual Report to the Congress Fiscal Year 1983.* Washington, DC: Government Printing Office, 1982

Index